NAVY SEALs

THE COMBAT HISTORY OF THE DEADLIEST WARRIORS ON THE PLANET

Don Mann and Lance Burton

Skyhorse Publishing

Copyright © 2019 by Don Mann and Lance Burton

Skyhorse Publishing books may be purchased in bulk at special discounts for sales
promotion, corporate gifts, fund-raising, or educational purposes. Special editions
can also be created to specifications. For details, contact the Special Sales
Department, Skyhorse Publishing, 307 West 36th Street, 11th Floor, New York,
NY 10018 or info@skyhorsepublishing.com.

Skyhorse® and Skyhorse Publishing® are registered trademarks of Skyhorse
Publishing, Inc.®, a Delaware corporation.

Visit our website at www.skyhorsepublishing.com.

10 9 8 7 6 5 4 3 2 1

Library of Congress Cataloging-in-Publication Data is available on file.

Cover design by Brian Peterson

ISBN: 978-1-5107-1655-1
Ebook ISBN: 978-1-5107-1656-8

Printed in the United States of America

"It is not the critic who counts; not the man who points out how the strong man stumbles, or where the doer of deeds could have done them better. The credit belongs to the man who is actually in the arena, whose face is marred by dust and sweat and blood; who strives valiantly; who errs, who comes short again and again, because there is no effort without error and shortcoming; but who does actually strive to do the deeds; who knows great enthusiasms, the great devotions; who spends himself in a worthy cause; who at the best knows in the end the triumph of high achievement, and who at the worst, if he fails, at least fails while daring greatly, so that his place shall never be with those cold and timid souls who neither know victory nor defeat."

—Theodore Roosevelt

CONTENTS

ACKNOWLEDGMENTS

I am very grateful to the very talented and professional staff that supported our efforts in writing this book. Thank you Jay Cassell, our publisher and my good friend at Skyhorse Publishing, James O'Shea Wade, our exceptional editor and military historian, and Joseph Craig, our editorial director, for your hard work, expertise, and advice.

My sincere appreciation goes out to Lance Burton for the countless hours he devoted to research and writing this book and to Joan Stobbs, who conducted extensive research in selecting the photos and obtaining photo permissions and provided her professional and caring guidance throughout the process.

Finally, I salute all of the courageous men and woman in the SEAL community, past and present who inspired me to write this book.

—Don D. Mann

PREFACE

When tasked with the formidable challenge of writing about the history of a unit as decorated as the Navy SEALs, of whom story after story of countless acts of heroism and valor are now etched into the minds of people all over the world, it becomes a matter of not just telling the story but also of something much more important: honoring the legacy of the men who have given their last full measure of devotion to the cause of freedom.

However, we also felt it necessary to attempt a slightly different style of book while still achieving our objective. Libraries are stacked full of history and textbooks that provide endless streams of facts, all of which are important, but do not always provide the full *story* of those facts. Moreover, it has been said that the victors of war write the histories, and therefore are perpetually written with an agenda of glamorizing their own side. With this book we have one agenda and one agenda only—to honor the men of the U.S. Navy SEALs by telling some of their stories in order to ensure that they will never be forgotten.

This is a narrative history; stories based on either direct experiences or exhaustive research. In order to make the narrative as readable as possible, as specified in the book's notes, a few operations and action scenes were created to show how and why certain types of operations and actions played out. The men (and one woman) in those scenarios are not actual people but are representative of the types of SEALs or personnel who would be playing their parts in a particular situation. The symbol of a trident will be inserted at the start and end of these passages.

Each chapter gives an overview of the events during a particular era of the SEALs followed by narratives based upon direct experience or exhaustive research of historical accounts. In almost all cases we have changed the names of the men to preserve the SEAL tradition of selfless anonymity, but also have taken a small amount of literary license in the retelling. Our hope is that this mixture of styles will not only cover the genesis of the Teams, but also provide some inspiring stories that highlight the kind of missions the men have undertaken over the years.

This book is not encyclopedic in scope or intent but focuses on memorable events in SEAL history—and the men who made them memorable by their courage, skill, and discipline, which have become the hallmark of the SEAL Teams.

In writing this history we particularly had in mind the families of these brave warriors as well as those who aspire to become one of America's best. This has been written for the families so that they may pass on the tales of what their loved ones have sacrificed and for Americans considering becoming SEALs so that they may begin to grasp the reality of what they are facing should they be successful. Also for the potential student, we have chosen to include a section on the current training pipeline along with a brief narrative highlighting some of the experiences faced going through Basic Underwater Demolition/SEAL Training (BUD/S). There is no special secret to becoming a Navy SEAL beyond this: you must have a burning desire to earn the title beyond anything else in your life and be willing to die before you would quit.

Train hard to prepare, harder than you ever have in your life, but never forget that it is the inner fire and desire to become a SEAL that will push you past all boundaries and allow you to persevere during those moments when you are beyond cold, beyond tired, and have been wet and sandy hour after hour with no end in sight. Remember that in order for our citizens to remain able to live free there must be those brave souls who answer the call and be willing to fight to preserve it. You could be part of that next generation.

We would also like to honor and thank the families of these men who hold down the fort and provide the support for the men who live much of their life away from those they love, both in training and in war, which allows them to maintain the absolute focus and razor edge required to do the work they are called upon to do every day.

—Hooya,
Don Mann and Lance Burton

INTRODUCTION

A book about the combat history of the Navy SEALs is essentially one about the evolution of warfare. Since the dawn of civilization there has existed a special class of individual who is called upon to defend those with whom he loves and lives. As society has developed, each era of history has seen peoples and nations take a divergent path, often leading to conflict. At the core of such conflict are very fundamental elements of what it means to be human—we all have basic needs and desires, some as foundational as the need for food and water, and others as complicated as what bloodlines make up our ancestors or what religious or philosophical premises we hold dear. However, in each case, when conflict arises someone must take on the role of defender. In this way, the U.S. Navy SEALs are the result of thousands of years of lessons learned on the bloody battlefields of history.

In order to truly understand what makes a Navy SEAL what he is now, we must go back and take a closer look at the warriors from ages past who inspired them to do the things they have done in the pursuit of honor and skill on the battlefield. First and foremost, a Navy SEAL is a professional—he is neither conscript nor slave—and at the root of his being is a steadfast belief that the ultimate dishonor would be to fail to stand up with his brothers in the face of the enemy. To not fight when he is needed and called upon is tantamount to the one thing that is anathema to a SEAL: to quit.

Simply put, quitting is not an option.

The bond forged in training and on the field of battle has been an essential ingredient of the glue that holds men together when their lives are at stake. It has been said that there exists no greater bond than the one formed in battle as one willingly risks his life for the sake of something greater than himself. But, what is the true lineage of the Navy SEAL?

In recorded history, the lineage can be traced all the way from the first human beings on the planet through various major points along the way. In fact, the Assyrians are many times noted as bearing the title, "the first superpower of the world." Although which ancient culture has a right to that title is debatable, the Assyrian army set the standard for warrior cultures that came after them in one important way: discipline.

Membership in the Assyrian military was an extremely disciplined affair. Regulations involving uniformity, order, and conduct were encoded in texts of which every solider was to be familiar. Refusal to follow "good order and discipline" was met with harsh punishment, offering strong motivation to toe the line. In this way, the Assyrian soldiers were one of the first to be held to such a uniform standard. From the tenth century B.C. until the seventh century B.C., the Assyrian culture dominated the far reaches of Mesopotamia and held the mantle as the most powerful army of its day, in part due to their harshly imposed discipline.

Following the Assyrians, from approximately the seventh century B.C. until the third century B.C. were the warriors of the steppes—the Scythians. If the Assyrians brought the notion of discipline and order to warfare, the Scythians instituted the concept of extreme skill. The horsemen of the Scythian tribes were masters of the bow, specifically the use of the bow from horseback. According to legends, a highly skilled Scythian rider could make incredible shots such as taking down a bird in flight while riding at full gallop, even if their prey was behind them.

During this time, the elite Spartans were also known as the dominant land power in their region and their exploits during the Peloponnesian War are legendary. Brutally hard and relentless training in the Agoge, the official training program of the Spartan warrior, began in the crucial early years of life and hardened the Spartans, imbuing them with a fanatical sense of duty to Sparta. Dying in service to their beloved land was considered the highest honor a man could achieve. The extreme regimentation of their training program along with the personal honor achievable only through combat is yet another thread tying together warrior cultures through the ages.

Next, the Roman Legions become the masters of the known world by imposing the Assyrian notion of extreme discipline, combined with a well-developed and strict code of laws, as well as the Spartan ideal of societal-driven honor. This unique combination made it appealing to become a soldier even if one hadn't been destined and trained to be one as a young man. For example, a Roman soldier had to enlist for a full term of twenty-five years; however, at the end of his enlistment he could retire with a lifelong stipend and a plot of land granted to him by the emperor.

"For the glory of the Empire" was a common rallying cry for the Roman Legionnaire.

Moving forward, the Viking raiders brought the concept of amphibious assault to the battlefield. Launching raids from the sea became a primary method of conquest throughout their era in history. Along with this innovative approach, they perfected what was essentially an early version of shock combat. The idea was to attack with such ferocity that each individual raider would allow himself to enter into a deadly frenzy. When in this state of mind, the Vikings, and later, the Franks and other tribes of Northern Europe, were nearly unstoppable in combat. This barbaric approach was highly feared due to its unpredictable nature.

Centuries later, English knights and organizations such as the Knights Templar brought a religious element to warfare. Aside from the Jewish people, the gods of most other cultures were considered only vaguely and intermittently interested in human affairs and many (especially the Greek and Roman) gods had many "human" attributes such as a lust for power or prestige and envy of his or her fellows in the heavens. The Christian faith now weaved together the concept of fighting for a cause directly attributed to and based upon direction from the divine Creator. While previous cultures, again the Jewish peoples notwithstanding, might invoke the name of a particular god they would fancy, the Christians now also believed their Holy Scriptures revealed a singular God (a Trinity, in which God is made up of three distinct parts) who was holy and deeply involved in the direction of humanity.

Meanwhile, Japan experienced the development of a feudal society and the concept of a military professional was further implemented. A strict code of honor combined with training from birth in the art of warfare, in particular the "Way of the Sword," became the dominant element of society and of political maneuvering. In a way, the Samurai devotion to the art of swordplay has been adopted by the Navy SEALs—the art or "Way of the Gun" being the new weapon of choice. Many other groups over the years could be identified, such as Roger's Rangers or American Indian trackers, but even this cursory glance at the lineage has shown a direct chain of development—the discipline and order of the Assyrians, the extreme skill of the Scythians, the brutal training and sense of duty of the Spartans, the advanced code of law enacted by the Romans, the use of amphibious warfare by the Vikings, the religious element of the Knights, a total devotion to the art of war and the "Way of the Sword" from the Samurai, and the skills of tracking and of the hunt from the American Indian and early Rangers have all combined through accretion to help create those who have now become known as some of the deadliest warriors in history: the U.S. Navy SEALs.

The pivotal development of various technologies has also obviously contributed to the evolution of the SEALs, with each new major advance expanding the missions they are capable of carrying out. The modern Frogman, while spiritually kin to his many predecessors, has now morphed into something more—something greater—than ever before. The United States Navy along with its counterparts in the U.S. Army, U.S. Air Force, and U.S. Marine Corps, has continuously pushed the limits of how a modern special operations force can integrate high technology in order to make the SEALs even more effective and deadly. Partnerships with companies such as Northrop Grumman, Lockheed Martin, and many others have further pushed the envelope of what can be accomplished with equipment created through advanced technology.

In many ways, such technology does enhance the deadliness of any modern combat unit and also allows them to operate in ways inconceivable to those warriors from previous generations. Advances in aircraft, weaponry, optics, sensors, explosives, and other such fields give the modern Navy SEAL and his special operations counterparts the ability to engage targets and prosecute America's wartime missions with precision and effectiveness.

Even so, we must not forget that no matter how much technology we may have access to in our current culture, it will always be the individual discipline and fighting spirit of the men who use it that will always make all the difference. Without that spirit the military professional is merely a shell of what he could become and of what missions he is capable.

Only time can tell us what the SEALs could eventually become. Nearly anything is possible, and it only takes a small amount of imagination to consider how this now legendary unit could develop. Perhaps the next step will be Navy SEAL assault Teams conducting raids on an enemy space station or assisting the Human Space Flight program by sending men like the SEALs to Mars and beyond.

Either way, it will be exciting to watch.

And so, now we will begin our quest to understand the modern evolution of the Teams, from the early Scouts and Raiders to the beaches of Normandy in World War II to the present Global War on Terror. This is ultimately an incredible story of men who have gone before and answered the call—men possessing the highest levels of honor, courage, and sacrifice. Please bear in mind that the goal of this book is to offer an extensive overview of the evolution of the Teams and detailed examples of many of the major milestones along the way.

For those brave souls—past, present, and future—and those who wish to honor them—their story is in the pages that follow.

FORGED IN FIRE—
BECOMING A NAVY SEAL

Men don't get assigned to a SEAL Team; they volunteer for this extreme and arduous duty. From World War II to the present, very exceptional men have volunteered for some very tough assignments, and many have made the ultimate sacrifice. But who are these men? What is their heritage? And what is it that separates them from all others?

A deep-seated desire to become one of the best warriors alive matched with the discipline to carry on through any adversity . . . the man who would rather die than quit. Intangible traits like these separate these men from the pack.

So then, what does it take to become an elite U.S. Navy SEAL commando? You might think the answer is simple; however the Naval Special Warfare Center (NSWC), the Navy SEAL training center located in Coronado, California, does not have a specific answer.

The fact is that there simply doesn't exist a quick-and-easy answer to the question, "What makes a person a great SEAL candidate?"

This remains true despite the continual efforts of scores of social and biological scientists to identify those qualities most desirable in a candidate for SEAL training. For years, SEALs have striven to discover what some call the mysterious "golden key" to becoming a SEAL, but to no avail. There was simply no way to predict who had the guts to go through the six months of hell called BUD/S (Basic Underwater Demolition/SEAL training).

However, while many SEALs are convinced that such a golden key does not exist, there was one characteristic common to every BUD/S graduate: the trait SEAL instructors call "fire in the gut."

While this attribute cannot be precisely defined, in the aggregate it includes courage, the ability to ignore pain, obedience, intelligence, and respect of fellow teammates.

You might have noticed that physical endowments are not listed as characteristic of the "fire in the gut." While it's obvious that a potential SEAL must be able to measure up in a physical sense, BUD/S doesn't require superhuman strength or endurance. As a matter of fact, many times it is the most physically capable members of a particular class are first ones to "ring the bell," or quit.

One might say those who quit simply had other priorities, while a successful trainee had only one—becoming a Navy SEAL.

One former Commanding Officer (CO) of the Naval Special Warfare Command (NSWC) was often asked during interviews what he looked for in a SEAL candidate. Typically, he would answer by telling the interviewer what he *did not* like to see in a trainee: being too self-centered, overly concerned with physical appearance, or excessively individualistic.

Still, knowing nothing else about a trainee, in many SEALs experience, they would prefer the kid of average build and physical ability who simply wants to be a SEAL most in life rather than the athletic superstar who has spent half his life in the gym, on the track, or in the pool. The harsh reality is that beyond the required minimum level of athletic ability and stamina, there is little or no relationship between physical prowess and success in BUD/S training.

As a somewhat fascinating side-light to the business of predicting BUD/S success, there is the work of

⊼ BUD/S Students struggling through "Log PT"

Dr. Rob Carlson, chairman of the Department of Physical Education at San Diego State University. Asked to be part of an effort by Naval Special Warfare to optimize the selection process for potential SEALs, Dr. Carlson was contracted to develop a testing instrument to predict failure for BUD/S training. At the end of his study, not only was Dr. Carlson able to do this with 95 percent accuracy, but he was also able to identify with 80 percent accuracy the 10 percent of class members most likely to graduate.

Interestingly, the key indicators in the latter assessment also included a strong sense of patriotism, deeply held religious beliefs, and a solid sense of traditional values. Conversely, a lack of these elements

⌃ **Surf Passage: BUD/S students learning how to work as a team in adverse conditions**

was a very important factor in predicting failure during his study of each man's motivations.

Today, the graduation rate hovers at around 33 percent and most instructors are convinced this rate or higher is sustainable only by a Herculean effort on the part of the BUD/S staff to keep good trainees in the program.

The key element in keeping graduation rates higher while retaining the training program's integrity is what was initially informally referred to as the "Fourth Phase." The original idea was conceived by Master Chief Boatswain's Mate Rick Knepper. Fourth Phase is an "Intense Prep Phase" for those trainees who have either reported aboard in less-than-satisfactory physical condition or who have been injured during BUD/S training.

In years past, any trainee who could not pass the BUD/S physical training (PT) test shortly after reporting aboard got sent back to the fleet. Such also was the fate of a trainee who experienced an injury requiring treatment of more than a few days. Fourth Phase, now called BUD/S Orientation, was designed to salvage trainees who would otherwise leave the program without having had a chance to prove their mettle. This also allowed them to recoup and either start BUD/S at the proper level of physical conditioning, or reenter upon recovery from illness or injury.

While some of the old-line instructors objected to incorporating Fourth Phase into BUD/S, it is now viewed as a vital part of the constant effort to ensure that every qualified trainee has an opportunity to graduate. And for those trainees who enjoy life on Coronado's "Silver Strand," Fourth Phase gives them the opportunity to get to know that place intimately, with some of them being assigned to it for up to a year before reentering training.

In some ways, it took a special kind of guts to work through Fourth Phase's tedium of physical therapy and conditioning exercise, only so a student can yet again subject himself to the rigors of BUD/S. It is sort of like practicing for the proverbial kick in the butt. Nevertheless, now all students go through Fourth Phase. And, it is not surprising that the winner of the "Fire in the Gut" trophy awarded to a deserving graduate of each BUD/S class was consistently an alumnus of Fourth Phase before the phase became mandatory—such a student would have had to show even more tenacity and desire than his compatriots, who have merely spent six months in the hell of BUD/S.

≋ **BUD/S Students with their logs racing over the sand berm—it pays to be a winner**

An important note is that the last fifteen to twenty years, the path to become a Navy SEAL was only hinted at by a small amount of published material and numerous rumors, most of which were patently false. It was kept mysterious, and only those few who had endured the training knew what to expect. But popular media has begun to change all of that, and now books, movies, articles, podcasts, and almost all other means of communication and information have reported to varying degrees about the process and the training pipeline. In fact, you can get a pretty good overview straight from the official U.S. Navy website dedicated to the SEALs.

Still, there is nothing quite like going through it all yourself.

To become a Navy SEAL is to become one of America's most elite warriors. This essential fact can't be over emphasized; you are not preparing to become just an elite athlete—you are preparing to become a warrior forged in the fires of the hardest military training on the planet.

What, then, separates an elite athlete from a Navy SEAL? Isn't becoming an Olympian or top pro in a demanding sport similar to becoming one of America's greatest warriors? Yes and no. Yes, both must constantly push their limits and endure thousands of hours of hard training and conditioning. But one thing in particular stands out above all the rest: the willingness to risk everything to successfully carry out the most dangerous missions our brave warriors must endure. Failure is not an option. You must be prepared to sacrifice your life in the effort to complete your team's mission. Athletes, even the toughest and most gifted of them, are not required to do the same.

This is the essence of a Navy SEAL warrior: *My team and my mission come first—I will never quit and am never out of the fight while I am still breathing.*

The path to becoming one of America's elite warriors is long and each person called to that path may take a slightly different road.

NAVAL SPECIAL WARFARE CENTER

CORONADO, CALIFORNIA

BUD/S CLASS 239

The sun had yet to rise as the members of BUD/S Class 239 stood on the beach, preparing for yet another Monday morning and the first evolution of yet another week: a four-mile timed run in combat boots and camo trousers. It was cold, but we were still dry for the moment. We all knew that wouldn't last long.

"IN-STRUC-TOR Rector!!" I yelled as the Class Leader, followed by the whole class repeating it in unison. As each of the First Phase instructors made their way over the berm, we repeated the drill until they were all present.

"Class Leader, what's the count?" Instructor Burke, the lead First Phase instructor, asked sternly.

"One hundred and fifty-five present and accounted for Instructor Burke," I said as I stepped up in front.

"Very well, line 'em up!"

We had started pre-training, called Fourth Phase, with 212 students. Just because of the timing of being a winter class, we ended up with an extended Fourth Phase, which the lead instructor for the phase, a then young SEAL named Rob, had taken advantage of nicely. He took our preparation for First Phase very seriously and figured the best way to do it was to mimic First Phase as much as possible by keeping us very cold, constantly wet and sandy, and busting our asses in PT every day. Later when training was over, Rob and I became best friends.

The cold already had taken a toll on our numbers early on, but most of the guys actually appreciated it. We wanted to become elite warriors and knew it was going to be hard. Everyone got up near the starting line and waited for the command to go. Every week we were under pressure to continue progressing and getting better at every evolution, whether it was the running, swimming, O-Course, pool skills, or whatever.

Constant pressure and unrelenting expectations to improve were standard.

The instructors said go and started their timers. As the Class Leader, I was the only one allowed to wear a watch, which included wearing it on the runs and swims. We took off at a solid pace.

Going through BUD/S you will find that there is going to be someone in the class better than you at something . . . guaranteed. Someone will have been a track or cross-country star and will smoke you on the runs, or another guy will be a former water polo player and make the water evolutions look easy. But in Naval Special Warfare there are a couple rules of thumb you learn to live by that are absolute and contribute to the nature of the Teams: You are *never* done training, and you must "be the best at something and solid at everything else."

≈ **As a SEAL, much of your work will be done while cold, wet, and sandy**

You need to be *the* go-to guy for something. The best shooter, best tactician, most knowledgeable about explosives, the best swimmer—whatever your best gift is, make it better and be the best. Then, continually shore up any weaknesses and keep learning. I'll say that again—keep learning and always seek to improve.

This was etched into my brain early on, and I'll never forget the day it hit home forever. My now close friend and early mentor, Johnny Heil, was sitting with me hanging out in the Training Department office at SEAL Team [redacted] when a conversation got started about an upcoming evolution to practice IADs (Immediate Action Drills) and somewhere along the way I said something like, "Johnny, you've been with the Teams for nearly fifteen years now—what do you have to prove at this point?"

He looked at me like I had three heads and gave me a stern glare, "I have to prove every single day that I still belong here, man."

Damn. He was absolutely right and I was absolutely wrong. It was one of the best lessons I ever learned.

But, back to the four-mile run on the beach.

The four-mile timed run is a staple event that you will do over and over again almost every single week during training. The passing time for First Phase was Thirty-two minutes. Now, I know you runners out there are thinking, "Thirty-two minutes? That's just a measly eight-minute mile pace!"

Yes, but until you do it on the beach in soft sand, wearing combat boots, camo trousers, and you have water sloshing up around your feet from the surf, you need to hold off on your judgment of how difficult it can be to accomplish.

However, by this point in training, most guys are beating the required time by a couple minutes at least and some by a whole lot more than that. Comparatively speaking, I was a slower runner and swimmer despite an exceptional overall PFT score on the screening test to get into BUD/S. Either way, I was still coming in well under the required time and eventually logged a 26:30 when at my best. One of my good friends, who later ended up [redacted], was also on the slower side and kept asking me how we were doing, since I got to wear a watch as the Class Leader.

As long as you passed, you were technically good to go, but you should *never* expect to just coast. First Phase is all about pushing your limits constantly to test your commitment to become a SEAL and somehow, some way, the Instructor Staff will find a way to increase the suck factor no matter what happens. You just have to take it all in stride and focus on the mission. It's actually a lot of fun in its own twisted kind of way. For me, it was fun knowing that each day was a day closer to your goal, another day further along the warrior path, and every evolution was making you tougher and stronger than you were before. It is truly a special time in your life and although relatively short in the scheme of life, it is something you cannot forget.

During a typical day of First Phase, you'll do your first evolution around 5:00 a.m., run to the chow hall to eat, and be back by 7:00 a.m. for the next evolution. On Monday's, that usually meant PT on the Grinder for a couple hours. For those who don't know, the Grinder is the big center concrete court-yard where you will spend many hours finding out what pain is all about.

Entering the Grinder for PT was somewhat of a formal affair. The squad leaders and I would organize the men and get ready to do our little jog from the holding area near the Fourth Phase barracks and chant the little song as we made our way onto the large concrete slab in the middle of the compound, yellow fins painted in rows to mark where to stand. I'd start the warm-up until the instructors arrived and got ready to take on yet another brutal PT session.

It is hard to convey the absolute volume of physical training you do while at BUD/S. There is nothing else like it, and in some ways I think it is partly what separates it from other special operations training pipelines. It is relentless and never lets up during the entire course. Obviously, the infamous Hellweek is also a separator, but that is another story altogether.

Hundreds of push-ups, pull-ups, dips, flutter kicks, mountain climbers, the dreaded 8-Count bodybuilders, and a myriad of other exercises are always on the menu and served up by the Instructor Staff in great portions. And, that doesn't count the extra for beatdowns that you will undoubtedly earn somehow. Remember, this is a team evolution even if you are being evaluated individually, so if someone in the class does something stupid, expect to pay for it together. In the case of the Class Leader and Leading Petty Officer, expect to pay even more and often.

"Prepare to mount the bar! Mount the bar! Ready, Up . . . Down . . . Up . . . Down!"

You'll hear those words a lot.

Other things you will hear a lot: "Drop!" or "Go get wet and sandy!" or "It pays to be a winner gentlemen!"

The pace is non-stop and brutal. I know I said that already, but for the prospective candidates out there reading this, you must get it through your head that you will do more than you have ever done before. Most students experience a certain amount of shock at the sheer volume of training you will do. After the Grinder, you might end up in the classroom discussing anything from basic SEAL history to understanding tide charts. You may be thinking, "Okay, so I'll get a breather during classroom time." You'd be wrong about that one.

Did I mention that someone inevitably is going to mess something up?

It might be the guy who simply cannot stay awake in the back of the room, or it is the joker of the class (every class and every team has at least one guy who is the team jokester) making a comment which, although funny, is undoubtedly made at the wrong time and it turns the classroom into yet another "smoke session." In military parlance, that just means you get to do even more physical training designed to simply be painful. It isn't uncommon to end up doing a whole academic class wet and sandy because of one of the aforementioned guys and their antics.

But, like I said, you must take it in stride.

Eventually, you'll have a chance to go eat again and will run as a class to the chow hall (although currently that is no longer the case, as the dining facility was moved to the "water side" of Naval Amphibious

Base Coronado). When you get the chance to eat, you better take advantage of it. As one of our instructors kept saying over and over throughout First Phase, "Feed the machine gents!"

After lunch you'll have another evolution around 1:15 p.m. or so. It might be Surf Passage or the O-Course or Log PT (a real fan favorite) or pool skills (Drownproofing, underwater drills, etc.). No matter what, expect it to be cold, expect it to be wet, and expect it to be a competition between boat crews. The motto, "it pays to be a winner" is taken very seriously around the BUD/S compound.

Why? Because we want to instill in the student the absolute desire to win. None of this current cultural nonsense that says "everyone gets a trophy." Fact: if you want to be a Navy SEAL, you should *always* want to win and *always* be trying to win.

If you don't want to win, I don't want you on my team.

That is because the business of a Navy SEAL is war—you win or die trying.

Hours become days and days become weeks, but the punishment continues. Some guys simply come to the realization that it really wasn't for them. Others decide that it is simply too hard. Whatever the reason, a steady stream of men, many of whom you'd never think would do so, line up to ring the infamous bell. If you ring out, that's it, you're done. Your helmet will be placed in the row of other ones just like it in front of the First Phase office, right along the Grinder for everyone to see. It serves as a constant reminder as to the toughness of the training.

And that brings up an interesting phenomenon widely discussed over the years: what makes some guys quit and others stick it out?

When we first "classed up" there were already students taking about how tough this guy or that guy was and how they would never quit. One of the stories that always remains etched in my memory about this is one in which a certain student had grown up in an American Indian tribe with a reputation for making young men endure multiple "tests of manhood" and things like that while they were growing up. This particular guy had stories floating around about him sitting in a pit for days in the cold and stuff like that while he was a teenager. It gave him a reputation as some kind of super tough guy.

He quit in less than two weeks of First Phase.

Another story like that always comes to mind as well, but it's about a particularly good swimmer. He was an NCAA Division I champion swimmer and way better than me and pretty much everyone else in the pool and not by just a little. When that guy was in the water he was amazing to watch—fast and smooth and could tread water seemingly forever without effort.

He quit after our first night swim in the ocean with full gear.

You didn't read that wrong. The best swimmer in the class quit after a swim. It was early on in First Phase and we were about to do a familiarization swim out past the "surf zone" and back. Simple. All you had to do was get with your swim buddy and swim about 1,000 meters out and 1,000 meters back in full wet suit and combat swimmer gear at night with a little bit of surf, like maybe four feet or so.

Well, we got back to the beach and I'll never forget what happened. He came jogging over to me looking white as a ghost, "Lieutenant Burton, that was really dangerous."

Come again?

I wasn't sure I heard him right and took a second to make sure I had registered his comment correctly. "Yeah, man, but what freaking job did you think you were signing up for exactly?" I mean, we were there to become Navy SEALs, some of the deadliest warriors in all of history, not join the Girl Scouts of America.

Less than an hour later the thought of it all overwhelmed him and he was gone.

Now it is important to understand something: he was *much* better in the water than me and everyone else. I had trained my whole life in martial arts, sprinting, PT, and had been through some great training at the U.S. Naval Academy (Class of 1996) before eventually getting to BUD/S, and so was in great shape, but I was still on the slow end of the totem pole in the water. As time went on I got better and faster, but this guy was a beast in the pool.

But, he didn't want to be a SEAL bad enough.

And, that is what it will come down to 99.9 percent of the time. There are occasional anomalies here and there where a guy won't quit no matter what but it just doesn't work out for him. But, the overwhelming majority of guys who don't make it simply don't want it bad enough to put up with the pain of doing what it takes day in and day out to become a SEAL.

You have to have cultivated the "never quit" mentality and made up your mind that under NO circumstances will you quit . . . *no matter what.*

As the weeks go by, you will swim and run farther and faster, do more and more PT, and continue to improve both individually and as a team. During First Phase however, the "monster in the closet," so to say, is the impending test that every man who wishes to become a SEAL must successfully complete—Hellweek.

Five and a half days of continuous training with no exact comparison in any other special operations training program. During that week, you will sleep less than four hours total and will remain cold, wet, and sandy the entire time. Just the thought of it crushes the spirit of most men. In the case of BUD/S Class 239, we would ultimately start the week with one hundred and one students still left.

Most of them quit.

By the end of our Hellweek, only thirty-seven remained. It was one of the coldest Hellweeks on record, with the air temperature at night dropping into the teens and the water hovering around fifty degrees. There was literally freezing rain, hail, and snow all week. It was so cold that one classic Hellweek evolution, the "steel pier" (an evolution where you strip down to your underwear and lay directly on a steel pier allowing the frigid cold to pierce through you in an utterly miserable manner), had to be canceled due to legitimate fear by the Instructor Staff of having students die.

When we heard the fateful and cherished words, "Hellweek Secure," I heard someone yelling my name. As I looked over to my left, on top of the sand berm one of my best friends in the Teams, Johnny, and the SEAL Team FIVE Commanding Officer and

Operations Officer stood there with an American flag unfurled and waving in the wind . . . for them to go out of their way to be there for me and seeing them with the flag made for a great moment.

I jogged over with the energy I had left, "Good job, man. Get that foot looked at and get some rest," Johnny said as we shook hands (I had endured a small hairline fracture of my foot on Monday night but pushed through and ran on it all week). The Team FIVE Commanding Officer gave me a grin and nod of approval before giving me a hard slap on the shoulder. No words were needed.

We had done it—we passed the ultimate test of will and commitment to become a SEAL.

Hooya.

2

THE BIRTH OF THE FROGMEN—SCOUTS AND RAIDERS, NCDU/UDT, AND THE HEROES OF D-DAY

The fires of war stand as burning embers of crackling light, poised to set aflame the righteous indignation residing within the souls of great men. In the early morning hours of December 7, 1941, 353 airplanes of the Imperial Japanese Navy flew over the skies of Pearl Harbor and launched the attack on the United States that marked it forever in the heart and soul of America as "the day that will live in infamy." The unprecedented strike on American soil catapulted our great nation into one of the deadliest conflicts of all time.

Immediately following, while the smoke from the ships at Pearl Harbor still rolled into the sky, American commanders of the United States Army and Navy began plotting a strategy for retaliation against the Japanese that would carry our troops to the far reaches of the Pacific. Even the most cursory look at the geography of the region dictated the likely use of Amphibious Warfare as a primary means of putting American troops on the ground. And, although the United States Marine Corps had been developing amphibious tactics alongside the mighty United States Navy, the technology involved in this type of an assault was barely past its infancy and finding a way to ensure the success of such operations became a top priority—and so the need for a specialized unit of men to scout ahead of the landing force was born. The "Frogmen," as they became known, were about to embark on journey to help create a new era of warfare.

Before there were Navy SEALs or Underwater Demolition Teams (UDT) or Naval Combat Demolition Units (NCDU)—there were Scouts and Raiders (S&R). Initially formed as a joint Army-Navy beach recon unit approximately eight months after Pearl Harbor, the first Scouts and Raiders underwent intense training at the Amphibious Training Base (ATB), in Little Creek, Virginia. As is still true today, the training was harsh and intended to push the men past all their limits, both mentally and physically.

Essentially, the top brass had recognized the need for a beach reconnaissance force and sent a select group of Army and Navy personnel to begin the Joint Amphibious Scouts and Raiders Training. Initially assembled at the ATB on August 15, 1942, these

⩘ **Early Frogmen working with explosive charges**

brave men underwent gruelingly long days and were to eventually undertake missions such as hydrographic reconnaissance, assault wave guidance, and beach recon once ashore.

It is hard to do complete justice in a short work to the answer of this question: Why must the training be so difficult?

In some ways the answer is simple—the conditions a combat swimmer could face in war are so harsh and require such a strong mental fortitude to successfully handle, that the training must push the mental limits of each student beyond what they thought their breaking point was until they realize that with the right motivation and under the right conditions, as taught in training, "the body is capable of ten times more than the mind will usually allow." Swimming into an enemy held beach with sometimes no more than a combat knife, mask, and a pair of fins is not a task for the fainthearted. Add to the obvious danger the fact that the water could be freezing cold, you may have to work continuously with little or no food or any kind of comfort for hours and hours at a time, and sometimes go days without rest, and then one can begin to understand as to why the training must be brutal and it must be relentless.

As the development of the training continued, in January 1943 it was decided that the Scouts and Raiders School should be moved to Fort Pierce, Florida. That year was one of various transitions in how all the training was structured, but one thing stayed the same—it was hard. Much of the SEAL program of today is based upon, now called Basic Underwater Demolition/SEAL training (BUD/S), got its start during these early years in the Scouts and Raiders School: extensive running, swimming, calisthenics, obstacle courses, and the infamous "Log PT," were all used to harden the men and prepare them for the daunting tasks ahead. In time, the extreme nature of the training proved highly successful in preparing the men for the environments they would encounter. Sleep deprivation, continuous physical training, and extreme cold were all tools for the instructors to test the mettle of the students. Although the training has evolved over the decades, the SEALs still use a variation of this same challenge to determine who really wants to be a SEAL and who merely thinks he does.

Each trainee had to be a volunteer and the first ten to sign up were exceptionally athletic men taken from the U.S. Navy Physical Training Program, which was headed up by Commander Gene Tunney, the former heavyweight boxing champion and man who was known for beating Jack Dempsey twice. As it would turn out, one of those men, the now legendary Phil H. Bucklew, went on to earn the Navy Cross twice and was later deemed the "Father of Naval Special Warfare." Every SEAL trainee begins his journey at the Phil H. Bucklew Center for Naval Special Warfare in Coronado, California.

The first major change to the program took place when a young lieutenant by the name of Draper Kauffman was tasked with forming what would later be known as the first Naval Combat Demolition Unit. In July of 1943, Lieutenant Kauffman decided that the course was simply too long and must be condensed because WWII was in full swing. He felt the main element that needed to be addressed with the students was their commitment and desire to join his new unit, so he chose to make the very first week of training "Motivation Week," which the men quickly began to call "Hellweek." To this day, the term "Hellweek" is synonymous with "the hardest military training on the planet" and typically is conducted during the fifth or sixth week of BUD/S First Phase of training.

Kauffman, fully aware that many men might not survive the initial training, believed that if he could weed out those not really motivated to join this

⌃ The infamous "mud flats" of Hellweek. It is still the same today

special unit then it would be a relatively easy task to train those who endured the skills needed for the job. As is still the case, most of the men who started Hell-week do not finish it and quit under the relentless assault of cold water, sand, and constant training with almost no sleep during the entire five-and-a-half day ordeal. It is considered to be the ultimate test of mental strength and endurance and will challenge anyone attempting it to reach deeply into their spirit to ascertain just how bad they want to become a Frogman.

The reality was that anyone making it through the training was likely to be sent into combat almost immediately following completion. This brought a sense of urgency and seriousness to the course even beyond what would be normally present in times of peace. Therefore, it wasn't long before the Navy's Scouts and Raiders were put to work.

Officially, the very first group of Scouts and Raiders were commissioned in October of 1942, a team which included Phil H. Bucklew. The new combat swimmers already started to see combat by November of 1942 with the Operation Torch, the first landings of the Allies on the coast of North Africa. Later, the Scouts and Raiders supported various amphibious landings in Sicily, Salerno, Anzio, and southern France.

On July 7, 1943, the second group of Scouts and Raiders was formed, code-named Special Service Unit Number One, as a combined operations force. By September of 1943 they had already completed missions at Finschafen and New Guinea, and later, in Gasmata, Arawe, Cape Gloucester, and the east and south coasts of New Britain. Every mission was completed without any loss of personnel and minimal casualties.

As is common in many places involving government service, conflicts began to arise over how the unit would be utilized operationally, and soon after any non-Navy men assigned to the unit were reassigned to other units within their service. After this separation, the unit was renamed the 7th Amphibious Scouts, and their mission profile began to expand significantly.

Now, instead of merely guiding the assault boats, the elite combat swimmers would also go ashore with them, set up buoys in various channels, erect markers for incoming craft, take offshore soundings, maintain voice communications linking the troops ashore with incoming boats and ships, and even handle combat casualties and destroy beach obstacles. Over the course of the war, the 7th Amphibious Scouts participated in more than forty amphibious assault landings.

Almost all Scout landings were done at night during the new moon—the darkest time and easiest to remain concealed. This was also a time in which the Navy was experimenting with the capabilities of the men in this new unit. The Scouts would be brought to a lagoon by submarine and then paddle ashore in rubber raiding craft. Once the island or location was secured, the men would signal the submarine with a secret code, which would then come in the next night to rendezvous with the team and pick them up. (The Goodyear Tire and Rubber Company invented the inflatable rubber boats for this specific purpose.)

Once ashore, the men would bury the boats in the sand and begin their reconnaissance mission, often taking them well inland. Although their main priority still remained the clearing of an area prior to the main naval landing, which significantly enabled the assault force to take over the beachhead and then push beyond it. When they did go inland, it was common to remain ashore in a covert status for up to seven days, during which a "take no prisoners" mentality was maintained.

In order to prepare for these covert missions, the men had been trained in martial arts, and were armed primarily with the Thompson submachine gun, Colt .45 pistol, and combat knives. The practice and range of martial arts was not widespread as it is today and focused on judo and an earlier form of jiu-jitsu that included chokes, throws, joint locks, nerve strikes, bone breaking, and sentry removal techniques.

The extreme level of danger that went along with the Scouts and Raiders program continued to make it a strictly volunteer assignment—the Navy brass did

↑ **A combat swimmer with a satchel charge—cold, dangerous work**

not think it was justified to order a man into the unit. Moreover, a non-volunteer was unlikely to make it through the training required. In these early years, it would not be uncommon for a team on a covert operation to go in with twelve men and only three to five of them come back alive. There are even stories of only one man making it out alive.

The third and final Scouts and Raiders unit was deployed to China to fight alongside the Sino-American Cooperative Organization (SACO). It had been decided by the President of the United States that this mission was so important that the unit had to expand its ranks. To that end, Chief of Naval Operations Admiral Ernest J. King, Annapolis Class of 1901 (where he graduated forth in his class), ordered that the Scouts and Raiders increase its numbers to 120 officers and 900 enlisted men. These men were selected out of any place in the Navy in order to find enough to put through the training. World War II continued to be a time of rapid evolution of what would eventually become the Navy SEAL Teams.

Once selection and training of the men was complete, they formed the core of what Admiral King envisioned as a "guerrilla amphibious organization of Americans and Chinese operating from coastal waters, lakes, and rivers employing small steamboats and sampans." It would not take long for the men of this third Scouts and Raiders unit to begin their dangerous work.

Multiple elements of the Third Scouts and Raiders started conducting surveys of the upper Yangtze River in the spring of 1945 and were heavily involved in conducting a three-month survey of the Chinese coast from Shanghai all the way to Kitchioh Wan, near Hong Kong. However, much of the force also remained garrisoned at Camp Knox, in Calcutta, India and essentially remained ready should the need for them arise.

As we continue to take a close look at the development of these early Frogmen, one thing will continue to arise—as the evolution of each unit takes place there is typically a crossover period while one unit morphs slowly into another until the former is finally dissolved. As war raged throughout Europe in the early 1940s and the Germans continued to make advances, it became apparent to the Allies that stopping Hitler would require a monumental combined effort to achieve a complete victory. Allied commanders eventually decided that a two-pronged invasion of Europe—by air and by sea—would be the most likely avenue for success. It was absolutely imperative that the German war machine was stopped cold in its tracks. The forces of the Soviet Union, after being badly mauled in the German invasion in June 1941, would soon begin to mount a ferocious offensive against Nazi forces on the Eastern Front.

In order to better understand many of the initial combat deployments of the Scouts and Raiders, it is partly necessary to take a step back and look closer at a few specific operations, as well as to try to understand from a more strategic point of view what was happening with the war around this time: as the engagements heated up in Europe and the Pacific, Allied leadership continued to seek out ways to stop the German advances which continually threatened to overrun Europe. Additionally, the German Afrika Korps, commanded by "the Desert Fox," Field Marshall Erwin Rommel, continued to make steady advances in North Africa with one primary mission: secure the oil and resources of Libya, Tunisia, Morocco, Algiers, and Egypt. Hitler and his most trusted advisers believed that if his army could take control of such resources then his march toward total domination could press on unhindered. Historically, the beginning of the end for the Afrika Corps was British General (and subsequently Field Marshall)

Bernard Montgomery's offensive in the Second Battle of El-Alamein in October of 1942.

The Soviet Union, desperate to take some of the pressure off of their troops, proposed a landing in southern Europe by combined British and United States soldiers by the end of 1942. Churchill and Roosevelt, while in agreement that Hitler and his forces must be contained, disagreed on the timing and method of such a move. Instead, they offered a counter-proposal to land troops in French-controlled North Africa, believing that such a strategy would allow the Allies to have a stronger position in the Mediterranean area, as well as to help ensure Hitler did not gain control over the oil reserves of North Africa. It was hoped that such a move would force the German Army to divert substantial amounts of men and resources to assist in Africa, thereby softening their position on the Eastern Front, which would give the Red Army much-needed relief.

Once the final concept was agreed upon, planning in earnest could truly begin. The most obvious sites for an Allied invasion of German-occupied territory would be Morocco, Algeria, and Tunisia. American commanders believed that their forces could put themselves in position to execute a classic "pincer operation" against the Axis powers in the region due to the fact that the Allies already had control over much of the rest of North Africa. One major problem existed: the Vichy French controlled much of the region with 125,000 army troops, approximately 200 tanks, and just over 500 aircraft.

According to some sources, the ace in the hole for the Allies was the work of American Consul

Robert Daniel Murphy in Algiers. Murphy had been stationed at the consulate for some time and had reason to believe the Vichy French forces would not fight against the Allies. He had been developing a keen information network during his tenure in country and felt strongly about his position. After all, the French were former allies of the United States. Furthermore, the Allies believed the Vichy French had everything to gain by supporting the Allies and very little to lose. In order to allow this delicate situation to play out, Allied troops were ordered to not fire upon the Vichy unless they fired first.

As the British and American fleets were making final preparations to land troops in Casablanca, Oran, and Tunisia, the men of the Scouts and Raiders anxiously awaited orders to assist the landing force. The time to put all of their training to the test had finally arrived.

One of the original Scouts and Raiders, Petty Officer Matthew Kormorowski-Kaye, discussed some of what they experienced in his exceptionally rare personal journal:

For the first time I learned of two Scouts and Raiders that failed to return from a scouting mission before the Sicilian invasion. Both were Ensigns, both had kayaks. Both had the same mission, that of scouting the beaches prior to the invasion. It's been considered that they missed their return rendezvous and decided to paddle their kayaks to Malta. Since they never arrived, it's possible that they were strafed and were lost at sea. Their names were Ensign Kenneth E. Howe and Ensign Carmon F. Pipro.

[Author's Note: I was informed in October 1991 that Ensigns Howe and Pipro were executed as spies when captured while scouting landing sites in Sicily as part of Operation HUSKY. Ensign John G. Donnell was killed in a bombing raid one month later, almost to the day.]

'Pack your gear, we're moving out,' the word finally reached us. 'Where are we going?,' 'Don't know, just pack.' The question always received the same answer. Italy, with so many Nazi sympathizers, many would dearly love to sell information of importance. We left by truck to the docks of Naples. Our crew consisted of Ensign William Morrisey, Joe Coveallo (coxswain), Joe Crowley (signalman), Ernie Chyz (gunner) and myself as motor-machine-gunner. We boarded an "LST mid-afternoon and were given reasonably private quarters. The rest of the day we watched troops and trucks coming aboard. With its wide doors open, the LST (Landing Ship Tank) seemed to simply swallow anything that entered it. It was an invaluable piece of support equipment.

One evening, we quietly slipped out the harbor and began to cruise rather aimlessly about the Mediterranean. Little by little, more ships of every type began to form around us and a convoy had its birth. Ensign Morrisey gave us our briefing and pointed to the boat we were to use. Our objective: the south of France, the playground of the French and now the Germans also. Our beach was called 'Blue Beach' and lay east of Nice and west of St. Raphael. Blue Beach had a sandy bottom with a gradual slope to the beach. No rocks, little surf. I don't know where the information came from but it was ideal for landing craft.

Blue Beach was shaped into a crescent with a hill on the right, ending at the water's edge. The left side of the beach was marked with a concrete pillar that was a support for a concrete railway bridge that ran from right to left about fifty yards from shore. Directly behind the sand tapered 400 to 500 yards where the seaside homes were built. These multiplied until they actually became the outskirts of a town. A blacktop road rose from the sand heading to the town, taking a long gentle turn to the left. The road disappeared from view among many homes and buildings.

Our mission was to find Blue Beach before dawn and then lay to and wait to escort the assault waves to their proper landing area. H-Hour was just after dawn.

Ensign Morrisey pointed to an armored LCVP (Landing Ship Vehicle, Personnel) with a pointed bow that was on davits. We were eager to see what we were going to rely on so we climbed aboard and inspected the boat from bow to stern. The boat appeared in good condition. Ernie had twin fifties in his turret and I, a thirty caliber air-cooled Browning. The bilges were clean and dry, at least we could not see the sea slipping swiftly below us. Coveallo got the bright idea to start the engine to see if it ran. A few minutes without cooling fluid would not hurt the engine. With the engine running at half throttle, it was obvious that something was wrong. A vibration and rumble shook the entire boat. After inspecting the screw, we decided that the shaft was bent. As soon as any demand was placed on the boat, the shaft would probably snap. We would become sitting ducks.

Someone thoughtfully had fastened a new shaft inside the boat as a spare. I suspect it was known that the shaft would have to be changed. With only a few hours of daylight left, we decided to attempt to remove and replace the shaft. Over the side went Ernie Chyz, a line tied around his waist. We realized later, if he fell, the line would probably kill him instead of helping him. We had already removed the key and five bolts that bound the shaft to the engine. Ernie removed the screw and handed it up. We pounded out the shaft, inserting the new one and with the new screw secured, the sun sank below the horizon.

In minutes, it was pitch black so that we had to grope our way off the davits. On either side of the gunnel, rocket racks had been installed, twelve on each side. By the faint moonlight, we loaded the rocket racks, brought up the radio and ammunition for the machine guns.

We flicked on the radio and heard static. Our code name was 'Sugar Baker' (Scout Boat Blue Beach). Since radio silence was in effect, we could not test the transmitters and except for the static, the receiver was silent. Our guns were loaded, and we grabbed a bite to eat and arranged our personal gear. No sleep that night. At around 3:00am our LST slowed, we boarded our boat and were lowered to the water. Joe Coveallo started the engines and put it in gear before we touched the water. Immediately, we cruised alongside at the same speed, unattached. As we increased speed, we soon found ourselves alone in the blackness. Things never went so smoothly.

The cold salt-water spray in my face felt good. Ensign Morrisey was constantly checking our RMP, the compass and his watch. After about 3 hours, we throttled down as we made out the silhouette of the distant shore about 600 yards ahead. We approached land barely idling the engine to minimize noise and all eyes searching the shore for our memorized landmarks. Our training now began to pay off. Intelligence must have reliable information on our beach. It would not do to miss it. Such things as gun emplacements, roads and beach conditions were all a part of the considerations when this particular area was chosen.

It was still dark but a little predawn light helped us distinguish a small horizontal line. The sun was about to break over the horizon as we slowly inched our way towards the line on the shore. With our eyes straining, it soon became evident that it was the bridge we were looking at. Like the many times before, Ensign Morrisey brought us in right smack in the middle of our target area. We edged closer and closer, to about 300 yards.

There was no mistake, we were at the right place at the right time. I was surprised to see the bridge so close to shore, it could not be more than 100 to 200 feet from the water. We detected no visible moving lights. All was still except for the idling throb of our engine. Joe would put the engine in neutral and as we drifted, Joe would put it back in gear until we were back in our normal position, the west flank of the beach of the invasion beaches.

Over and over we drifted, as silently as possible, we used our engine only to come back to our position. Still no fire from shore. Our eyes now turned toward the sea hoping for a glimpse of the Higgins boats that *must be circling slowly. As each boat loaded with troops left the transport, it would join its group and circle, waiting for the rest of the boats to join in. Each circle of 7 or more boats would dissolve itself into a horizontal line and like a wave would make its speedy dash toward the beach.*

The boats would have 100 feet between each other leaving room for the boats heading back to the transports for another load of troops. After a number of such waves had landed their troops, larger landing craft would follow LCI's (Landing Craft Infantry) and LST's. The LST would discharge artillery, tanks, trucks and other heavy equipment. The last two types would land after a safe perimeter or large circle of ground was taken and held by the assault troops of the preceding waves from the Higgins boats. When the heavier landing craft would begin to land, our job would be over, for by then, the landing spot would be obvious to the landing craft at sea.

It seemed to take forever for the daylight to break. Soon however, the blackness turned to gray. We started to distinguish dark shapes on the horizon. The numerous ships of the convoy were there, about two to three miles out of range of any large artillery pieces. The sea was as smooth as glass, but on the horizon a thin white line appeared that should not have been there. We stared and could not imagine what it was.

Ernie thought it was a solitary wave. He was correct. One and just one wave about two feet high stretching from horizon to horizon, made its way toward us, lifted our boat, passed under and broke on the shore. An omen? I thought so. I had a brooding feeling all was not well but this was forgotten in the next few minutes.

Ernie Chyz was the first to notice. The first wave was starting its run to the beach. Flecks of light appeared on the horizon and the naval bombardment began. A series of events started materializing all at the same time. The flashes of the naval guns on the horizon, the whining of shells over our heads toward the beach, the arrival of our left LCT its cargo hold filled with rocket racks, the first three assault waves approaching at full throttle, with the first wave about 500 yards from the shore, the LCT firing its first rack of rockets.

These landed on the beach at water's edge. They were in a perfect position and began firing rack after rack of rockets, each exploding a few feet ahead of the preceding rack, effectively exploding any land mines.

By now, the town had awakened, daylight had arrived. The first wave, on our starboard all guns firing, began to pass our position, boats perfectly aligned. Ernie spotted Ensign Burgess (our old small boat officer) on the left side by the incoming wave. All heads were down below the gunnels except for Ensign Burgess. He wasn't about to make a mistake and stood fully exposed. Ensign Morrisey gave the word to fire one rocket to find our range. The hot blast of rocket exhaust hit our faces and we curiously watched where it landed.

A perfect hit on the Railway Bridge we were to avoid. I glanced at Ernie who was grinning from ear to ear, said, 'Don't look at me, I didn't do it.' 'The LCT did it,' I yelled back. Ernie agreed that the

LCT now heading back to sea must have done it. Someone will catch hell from the Admiral. We were much closer to the beach by now so that when Joe Coveallo pushed the button, all the other rockets cleared the bridge and landed close together in an area still untouched. About seven rockets did not leave the racks and we later slipped each into deep water.

About now, Ernie started firing his 50 caliber machine guns over the heads of the assault troops. Almost at once, a stroke of ill fortune. The firing pin on his right gun broke, followed by a failed ejector on the left gun. He was stuck in the turret with his now useless guns, 'a seat on the 50 yard line.'

Ensign Morrisey had Joe wield the boat around so our stern pointed toward the beach. This gave me a 180-degree line of fire. My gun fired perfectly. I swept the beach from left-to-right and right-to-left. At each end, I would raise the muzzle so that my line of fire was hitting higher and higher until I was hitting the buildings on the gradual incline. Soon small splashes began to appear around our boat. I thought the splashes were spent bullets, until the antenna of our radio, next to my head disappeared with a twang.

With less than 100 yards from the beach, the firing upon us was hardly spent ammunition but very much alive. I searched for some sign of movement or smoke from any of the buildings above the beach. Whenever I thought I saw something, I would fire. A machine-gun is not very accurate, especially when fired from a bobbing boat. It would be enough if it kept the enemy pinned down, preventing them from firing on our assault force.

The invasion into North Africa was officially dubbed Operation TORCH and it ultimately did accomplish the mission it set out to do by providing troops to seek out and further engage the German forces led by Rommel, ultimately leading to his withdrawal. Navy Scouts and Raiders participated in this invasion as well as other extremely dangerous landings in southern Europe as the Allies turned their focus away from the Africa campaign.

After the Axis Powers were defeated in North Africa in May of 1943, Churchill and Roosevelt had some major disagreements about how to proceed. Churchill believed the invasion of Italy was the most logical next step and deemed it "the soft underbelly of the Axis." With a fair amount of wrangling between him and Roosevelt, Churchill finally convinced FDR that such a move could effectively take Italy out of the war. Intelligence reports had indicated that popular support for the war amongst the Italian people was dwindling severely and therefore a major push in that region could break their will to fight.

Weeks and months passed and in 1944 as planning continued and a final decision was made about the location of the upcoming invasion: Normandy, France. The United States Navy had been hunting German U-Boats throughout the Atlantic, and aircraft carriers in the Pacific had led combined force efforts to track down and engage the Imperial Japanese Navy. But now for this operation, it would be a matter of returning to the coastal waters and doing anything possible to get troops ashore to make a final push for Berlin. It was believed that if the Allies could capture Berlin then the German war efforts would be brought to a complete halt, forcing an unconditional surrender.

The SEALs predecessors, the Scouts and Raiders, would play a major role in ensuring success. However, the Navy also began to see the need for a more expansive role in the usage of explosives. To that end, the Navy commissioned the Naval Combat Demolition Units (NCDUs).

The NCDUs were the U.S. Navy's initial effort to develop a unit that could assist with waterborne demolition operations. What was needed were men who not only knew the fundamentals of explosives, but who were also able to work in the unforgiving environment of the water. As became obvious with the Scouts and Raiders, waterborne operations entail a complex set of problems that are quite different from those encountered in typical land operations. First off, the water is often cold and the salinity can wreak havoc on even the most durable equipment. Being cold in the water is far different than being cold on land—full immersion into freezing cold water can shake you to the bone and cause your core temperature to dramatically drop to dangerous levels much faster than simply standing in the cold air. That meant any unit that would conduct such waterborne operations would have to have men ready to endure that specific kind of torment.

Lieutenant Commander Draper Kauffman (later Admiral Kauffman), before taking over the school in Fort Pierce, was called in to organize this first-ever Naval Bomb Disposal School in Washington Navy Yard. Kauffman received the Navy Cross for successfully disarming an unexploded bomb in Pearl Harbor, providing the American scientists with its first enemy bomb to study. The school he organized was the forerunner of the currently still active Naval Explosive Ordinance Disposal School. His efforts led directly to his appointment as the first Commanding Officer of Naval Combat Demolition Unit One and the subsequent command of the training center at the Naval Amphibious Training Base, Fort Pierce, Florida.

The NCDU training at the amphibious training base under Kauffman's leadership continued to be the site of some of the hardest military training in the world and the first to introduce the now infamous "Hellweek" as the first week of training. Kauffman's interest in making the training as short as possible was simply pragmatic, so the guys could be ready for war as quickly as was feasible.

Once the men completed the newly expanded training at Fort Pierce, they immediately began preparing for upcoming duty in the Atlantic theater. And, in the early morning hours of June 6, 1944, the men of the Naval Combat Demolition Teams were about make their mark on history.

OPERATION NEPTUNE

JUNE 6TH, 1944

0625 HOURS

The calm before the storm can be the worst part and it takes nerves of steel to endure those moments where seconds feel like minutes and minutes feel like hours. For the men of the relatively new Naval Combat Demolition Units, those seconds ticked by as they prepared for one of the most dangerous tasks of Operation Neptune–the amphibious landing portion of the famed invasion of Nazi-occupied France, Operation OVERLORD.

A brisk fifty degrees is nothing compared to water hovering around the same temperature. It cuts through you down to the bone and tests the mental endurance of even the toughest of men.

Such is the life of a Frogman.

Ensign Lawrence Karnowski, the Officer in Charge of Naval Combat Demolition Unit Forty Five (NCDU-45), disembarked from the small mechanized landing craft with his men into the freezing waters off the shore of Normandy, satchel charges in tow. His team was given the task of clearing sector "Easy Red" of obstacles in an effort to make way for the waves of assault teams and landing craft following them into the shore.

It is hard to describe the misery of being cold and wet with no hope in sight of your condition changing. The men of the Naval Combat Demolition Teams endured it that day while being shot at and bombarded from German positions all along the coastline. The sound of shots flying past them and mortar shells exploding all around in an effort to stop the Allied advance rang in their ears. But these early Frogmen pushed on undeterred despite the odds and facing death every moment that passed.

By 0650 hours Karnowski and his men had detonated their first satchel charge and cleared about 100 yards of the girders and twisted steel blocking the way of the landing force. Almost immediately after this, German machine guns and artillery began to zero in

⌃ **UDT Frogmen coming ashore to conduct an inland raid exercise**

on their position and fired volley after volley at the courageous NCDU men, hoping to cut them down. Karnowski's team took cover behind some of the remaining obstacles and prepared to continue planting their charges.

Unwilling to remain pinned down, Chief Millis grabbed a roll of Primacord and began sprinting in the shallow waters from obstacle to obstacle, wiring many charges before being cut down by enemy fire. Seeing his teammate go down, Petty Officer Second Class Meyers raced out to Chief Millis's body and continued setting more charges in preparation for a second detonation.

Men of the 1st Infantry Division began wading ashore as the NCDU team continued their deadly work. Smoke and the smell of gunpowder filled the air as the shelling continued. Ensign Karnowski saw one of his men take a round to the leg and another get sliced by shrapnel. With complete disregard for their own safety, Karnowski and teammate Petty Officer Svendsen swam out to rescue the injured men and carried them up the shore and into a position of cover before heading back out to finish the job.

Less than five minutes later they had detonated their second shot and opened another gap in the German line, allowing fresh troops of the 1st Infantry Division to continue coming ashore. Karnowski began prepping for a third detonation but the incoming soldiers made it impossible to accomplish this without great risk of injuring their fellow Americans so he rallied his troops and swam ashore to assess the wounded, personally digging foxholes for them and directing immediate first aid.

By 0730 hours, due in large part to the heroic efforts of Karnowski and the men of NCDU-45, the Army infantry soldiers began to storm the German positions past "Easy Red" and clear out the bunkers, further enhancing the ability to land more troops and push inland. NCDU-45 had managed to clear the largest gap of Omaha Beach, enabling Army Combat Engineers to eventually make "Easy Red" the primary egress point coming off the beach, thereby enabling American troops to maintain a much-needed foothold for the invasion.

Karnowski and the men of the NCDUs can easily be credited with ensuring the success of the landing. Without their heroic efforts, the casualties ashore could have been astronomically higher, and although we can never truly know for sure, the German forces may have been able to hold off the invasion and maintain their foothold on the beach. To understand the gravity of the situation, one would have to envision how the war may have progressed had the Allies failed at Normandy. It was truly a critical moment in history and their actions clearly paved the way for victory.

From the standpoint of the strategic importance, the NCDUs now could clearly be seen as a vital national asset. In time, the Allied commanders would further learn how best to utilize these brave men in war.

By April 1944, a total of 34 NCDUs had collected in England in preparation for Operation OVERLORD. For the assault, each six-man NCDU was augmented with three U.S. Navy seamen brought down from Scotland to assist in handling demolitions, and the resulting nine-man NCDUs were integrated with Army combat engineers to form thirteen man gap assault teams. The NCDU men suffered thirty-one killed and sixty wounded, an overall casualty rate of fifty-two percent. D-Day still remains the single bloodiest day in the history of Naval Special Warfare, although it is important to note that not one NCDU man was lost to improper handling of explosives.

The Naval Combat Demolition Units at Omaha Beach ultimately were able to blow eight complete gaps and two partial gaps in the extensive German defensive positions despite the extremely harrowing conditions and great adversity the men faced. Unfortunately, they did sustain a very high rate of KIAs and wounded.

Utah Beach had been much less fortified, so the men who assaulted that position were met with less intense enemy fire. This allowed the men to clear almost 650 meters of beach in only two hours and another 800 meters by the afternoon. Even so, the team assigned to Utah Beach did suffer casualties: six killed and eleven wounded.

For their combined actions on that bloody day, the NCDUs at Omaha Beach were awarded the Presidential Unit Citation, one of only three presented for military actions in the Normandy landing. Notably, the men at Utah Beach earned the only Navy Unit Commendation awarded for heroism in action.

In order to even further understand what sets these warriors apart, we must look even deeper into the history of the Teams and begin to weave together the many elements in the years and decades after that fateful morning on June 6, 1944. Let's begin that journey by taking ourselves to this other stage in the evolution of the SEALs–the Underwater Demolition Teams (UDT).

While the men of the Navy Combat Demolition Teams trained in Europe in preparation for their fateful missions on D-Day in June of 1944, the war raged on in the Pacific theater with each side taking heavy loses. As is the nature of war, sometimes it is the loss of life stemming from a costly operation that pushes the leadership to make the necessary course corrections to prevent repeating the same mistakes. The NCDU teams didn't get much rest and found themselves engaging in combat operations not long after Normandy during Operation ANVIL (and later Operation DRAGOON). Many of the surviving members of the units involved came from the unit on Utah Beach and were handpicked to reinforce new teams coming out of Fort Pierce in order to prepare for the final Allied amphibious assaults in Europe. After these last few landings, the war in the Atlantic became strictly a rush towards Germany in a final effort to crush the Nazi's and capture Berlin. At that time, all men graduating from Fort Pierce were sent to the Pacific theater and organized into what had become the Underwater Demolition Teams (UDT).

In the case of the evolution of the UDTs, it was the invasion of Tarawa in November of 1943 that changed their course forever. American leadership had pinpointed the Tarawa Atoll as a highly valuable strategic necessity for the continuation of the campaign in the Pacific theater. Admiral Chester Nimitz, Commander-in-Chief of the Pacific (CINCPAC), believed wholeheartedly that the route to victory lay in the taking of the central island chain through the Marshalls, Carolines, and Marianas. Tarawa was deemed a crucial link in that chain.

Nimitz had selected Vice Admiral Raymond Spruance to command the 5th Fleet, with Rear Admiral Richmond Kelly Turner to command the newly formed 5th Amphibious Force. Major General Holland "Howlin' Mad" Smith was asked to command the 5th Amphibious Corps. Each man knew that in order to achieve victory in the Pacific the American forces would have to quickly organize the men of these newly formed units and push them to the limits of their endurance.

As the planning continued, American forces had already begun scouting missions to collect valuable intelligence about the Japanese fortifications and garrison strength. When the scouting reports came in it was determined that the shallow draft Higgins boat landing craft the Marine Corps were using would be able to clear the reefs surrounding the island. It had a draft of approximately four feet and the aircrews conducting flyovers agreed that there would be at least five feet of water over the reefs. However, the day of the invasion, the planners had overlooked a small but vital piece of information: the small island's neap tide.

A neap tide is the result of the moon and the sun being at ninety degrees from each other relative to the Earth, which happens twice per month in the first and third quarter. The counteracting gravitational force causes the water to settle and prevents the usual rise. Normally, this may not be much of an issue, but when you are counting on a landing craft just making it over the obstacles in your sea-lane, this phenomenon poses a deadly problem.

Arguably, it was this mistake in not taking the tides into account, which led directly to the formation of the UDT in the Pacific.

The Battle of Tarawa—a battle that, rightly has gone down in the halls of legend, took place from November 20 to November 23, 1943, in the Gilbert Islands. Deemed absolutely critical to the war effort, the Tarawa Atoll became the focal point of the first major offensive action of the United States during the war in the central Pacific region. Additionally, it was also the first time the American forces were met with such an exceptionally high-level resistance. Other landings had been conducted, but with less opposition from the Imperial Japanese forces. However, the Emperor and his most trusted military leaders believed strongly that the Americans must be stopped at Tarawa.

As part of Micronesia, the Gilbert Islands had become a colony of the British Empire in January 1916, but were later taken by the Empire of Japan early in the war in December of 1941. Almost two years later the men of the United States Marines would prepare to take control of the territory with the hopes of providing the Americans more access to various locations that could essentially serve as forward deployed operating areas as well as airstrips for combat aircraft. It would prove to be an extremely bloody business; the Marines sustained casualties that far surpassed the campaign to take Guadalcanal in terms of sheer time—the losses incurred over the six months taken to capture Guadalcanal were incurred at Tarawa in approximately seventy-six hours.

The air bases from this "island hopping" campaign would place the United States in a much stronger position to take further offensive action against the Empire of Japan. We must recall that the ability to project power using the U.S. Navy was exceptionally limited compared to the warships and airpower of today. This fact placed much greater importance on establishing land dominance throughout the region.

On July 20, 1943, the Joint Chiefs gave specific direction to legendary Admiral Chester Nimitz to prepare his battle plans for the offensive operations in the Gilbert Islands. One month later, Admiral Spruance traveled to New Zealand in order to meet with the new commander of the 2nd Marine Division, General Julian Smith, in order to work with the division's commanders on the plan for the coming amphibious assaults in the area.

For the Scouts and NCDU men, most of their action had been in the Atlantic theater and the concept for employing a combat swimmer with waterborne demolition skills was still quite in its infancy. But on the tiny island of Betio, many factors come together when significant loss of life clarified the needs and skills the Frogmen would have to develop.

OPERATION GALVANIC

ISLAND OF BETIO, TARAWA ATOLL

NOVEMBER 19, 1943

1710 HOURS

Rear Admiral Keiji Shibazaki, Imperial Japanese Navy, a highly experienced combat officer from the campaigns in China, peered through his set of binoculars from atop a bunker near his command post, surveying the defensive emplacements he and his men had worked tirelessly to construct in the previous months. He reflected on the sentiment he shared with his troops the day he took command of the Japanese garrison made up primarily of hardened troops from the Imperial Marines: "It will take one million men one hundred years to conquer Tarawa." His effort to rally his troops had spurred them on with fierce determination to be ready for any American attempt to take this highly strategic airfield.

However, the seasoned admiral failed to take into the account the grit, determination, and courage of the equally fierce United States Marines.

Scanning the area out to the horizon, Shibazaki made a mental note to himself about how proud he was of his men and the work they had done to prepare to oppose an assault. His garrison of nearly 4,800 men had fortified the island with almost 500 pillboxes and countless machine guns, grenades, and artillery. However, the greatest advantage for Shibazaki's forces may have been nature herself: Betio was surrounded by massive razor-sharp coral reefs extending hundreds of yards out from the shore. This deadly combination had turned the small island into the ultimate challenge for any amphibious landing.

As the sun began to set, the hardened Imperial Marines checked their weapons, prepositioned ammo boxes, and ensured the supplies for each bunker were in place. A series of interconnected tunnels had been built to assist the troops' ability to move from bunker to bunker without exposing them to enemy fire. After months of preparation the only thing left for them to do was wait for the inevitable attack.

OFFSHORE THE ISLAND OF BETIO

NOVEMBER 20, 1943

0900 HOURS

The massive American flotilla consisting of seventeen aircraft carriers, twelve battleships, eight heavy cruisers, four light cruisers, sixty-six destroyers, and thirty-six transport ships had sailed into the waters off the small island of Betio three hours earlier and begun shelling the Japanese emplacements with the thunderous sixteen inch guns of the U.S. Navy's premier battleships. Waiting onboard the transports were members of the crack 2nd Marine Division and the Army's 27th Infantry Division, bringing the total troop count to around 35,000. About thirty minutes behind the original schedule, the landing force commander ordered his men to commence their assault and launched the first wave.

With the Marines enroute, the Navy ships had ceased bombarding the island for fear of friendly casualties, but this also allowed the Japanese defenders the moment of solace needed to man their weapons and attempt to mount a counterattack on the incoming small boats. And, it didn't take very long for the Marines to realize that the neap tide was about to make their day infinitely harder.

Time and time again, the small Higgins Boats got caught up on the razor sharp coral reefs making it impossible to reach the shore. Machine gun fire began tearing them up and the troops of the landing force had to make a critical decision: stay inside and wait with relative cover or jump out and wade ashore. Most chose to take their chances with the coral-filled waters. Only the "Alligator" boats, with a slightly smaller draft, were able to make it ashore.

Any amphibious assault is treacherous enough, but adding the imposing danger of wading through chest-high waters as withering enemy machine gun fire relentlessly came at you and cut down your friends and teammates must have been overwhelmingly daunting—but that is the essence of the warrior spirit—to keep going when no one else would.

The Marines and infantrymen that day had warrior spirit in abundance.

Despite the great courage and eventual victory of the American forces at Tarawa, the toll taken was high. Thousands of men died fighting their way up onto the bloody beaches and then inland over the course of the next seventy-six hours until literally only seventeen Japanese troops out of the original 4,800 members of the garrison remained. The close quarters fighting, sometimes even with bare hands, was brutal and intense.

Even in victory, a good leader will evaluate the performance of his team and determine how an operation could have been better. In the case of the Tarawa invasion, one primary question dominated during the post-operation analysis: how would the landing had gone if some form of combat swimmer had been available to clear the way for the landing craft and provide pinpoint accurate intelligence of the conditions approaching the beach?

In a way, the Underwater Demolition Teams were born in that moment.

MARCHING FORWARD—
UDT IN KOREA

The end of World War II brought with it relative peace and stability despite the tensions between East and West, which ultimately led to the Cold War era. However, a short five years later, Communist-backed North Korea decided to launch a sneak attack on the South. Utilizing Soviet and Chinese tanks and equipment, the People's Democratic Republic of Korea (PRK) pushed south, easily routing the unprepared southern defenses and driving them back to Pusan in the far southeast of the peninsula. South Korean and American troops established a perimeter 120 miles around Pusan and fought to hold the line while policymakers in Washington and around the world pondered what should be done.

General Douglas MacArthur, legendary hero of WWII, was appointed the Supreme Commander of a United Nations force that included 300,000 Americans, 95,000 South Koreans, and approximately 45,000 soldiers from various nations around the globe. As MacArthur studied the situation, he eventually devised a plan to launch an amphibious landing at the port of

Inchon. The plan, should the landings prove successful, was to spearhead an assault through the city and push to Seoul where they could cut off the supply lines of the People's Democratic Republic of Korea (PRK) fighters. For the men of the Underwater Demolition Teams (UDT), this meant prepping for pre-invasion reconnaissance duties and hydrographic surveys.

However, the Navy Frogmen knew they were capable of doing much more.

Beginning with a detachment of eleven personnel from UDT-3, UDT participation expanded to three teams with a combined strength of 300 men. During the "Forgotten War" the UDTs fought heroically, beginning to employ demolition expertise gained from WWII and began using it in an offensive role. The men continued to use water as cover and concealment as well as their primary insertion method; the Korean War era UDTs targeted bridges, tunnels, fishing nets, and other maritime and coastal targets.

All hell was breaking loose and President Harry Truman was on the radio two or three times a day talking about the Korean problem and what we as a nation were going to do about it. UDT-1 and UDT-3 were on high alert and prepared for war.

A UDT-3 ten-man detachment was in Japan training at Chigasaki Beach—a real plush assignment until the powers that be wondered what they could do with a bunch of Frogmen to help the Korean cause. By early July they decided UDT could become commandos and interdict rail traffic supporting the enemy. Little did they know that the Frogmen of the UDT were about to prove they were capable of much more than anyone realized.

Early on, Petty Officer Third Class (BM3) Warren Foley became the first Navy casualty of the war when wounded while attempting to blow up a tunnel. In late July the detachment was joined and absorbed by Team ONE which had been rushed out from Coronado. To round out the Korean commitment, Team THREE went aboard the USS *General William Weigel*, departing San Diego the afternoon of August 16 for what turned out to be a non-stop twenty-knot ride to Kobe, Japan, arriving on August 28, 1950.

The UDTs refined and developed their commando tactics during the Korean War, through their extreme grit and focused efforts on demolitions and mine disposal. Many of the men also accompanied South Korean (ROK—Republic of Korea) commandos on raids in the North to demolish train tunnels and other strategic targets. This work was unfortunately frowned upon by many higher-ranking officials because they believed it was a "non-traditional use of naval forces." This sentiment would prove to be a problem that would plague the Naval Special Warfare community in the decades to come as well.

Due to the nature of the war, the UDTs were required to maintain a low operational profile. Working alongside the CIA, other significant missions included transporting spies into North Korea and the destruction of North Korean supply lines used to reconstitute the North Korean Army. This clandestine work with the intelligence community was in many ways a perfect matchup: the Frogmen paired their combat skills and mindset with the more subtle work of the American spies. It proved to be a very effective and fruitful partnership.

As part of the newly minted Special Operations Group (SOG) established by the direction of General MacArthur, the UDTs successfully expanded their operations to conduct demolition raids on a variety of targets all along the Korean coast. Over time, these Frogmen became highly specialized in these new missions. Nighttime coastal demolition raids against railroads, tunnels, and bridges became the norm—it was a time a great change for the UDT.

The "Naked Warriors," a moniker given to them during WWII, were assigned these perilous tasks because, in the words of UDT Lieutenant Ted Fielding, "We were ready to do what nobody else could do, and what nobody else wanted to do." Later, Lieutenant Fielding was awarded the Silver Star for his actions in Korea, and was later promoted to the rank of captain.

Frogmen were part of a multitude of missions, which are rarely documented. On the September 15, 1950, UDTs directly supported General MacArthur's Operation CHROMITE, the amphibious landing at Inchon. UDT-ONE and UDT-THREE provided personnel who went in ahead of the landing craft, scouted mud flats, marked low points in the channel, cleared fouled propellers, and hunted for mines. Four UDT personnel also acted as wave-guides for the Marine landing.

Soon after, in the early days of October 1950, the UDTs also began to support mine-clearing operations in Wonsan Harbor where frogmen would locate and mark mines for minesweepers. It was extremely dangerous work, with one wrong move causing certain death.

Despite their incredible work, on October 12, two U.S. minesweepers, the USS *Pirate* and USS *Pledge*, were sunk by North Korean mines, further highlighting the need for the UDT men to continue hunting them down relentlessly. Fortunately, the UDTs were able to rescue twenty-five sailors from the sinking vessels. The very next day, Petty Officer William Giannotti conducted the first ever U.S. combat operation using an aqualung (an early attempt at creating a SCUBA apparatus) when he successfully dove on the *Pledge*, marking it for deep-water Navy divers using the more traditional dive suit of the era so they could retrieve and destroy any classified information.

For the remainder of the war, UDTs conducted beach and river reconnaissance, infiltrated guerrillas behind the lines from sea, continued mine sweeping operations, and participated in Operation Fishnet, which ultimately devastated North Korean fishing capability. An army which cannot feed itself is doomed to fail—and the UDTs hampered their food supplies so terribly that the PRK troops simply could not operate at peak effectiveness.

These veterans of the UDT had a profound effect on the development of the Teams, which is difficult to fully credit. Many of these vets became UDT instructors and were the combat-tested leaders who later went to Vietnam, further

⌃ **Demolition done right—clearing the way for the assault craft**

establishing their reputation as some of the greatest warriors in history.

As it turned out, there was much work that needed to be done over the course of the three-year war: day and night reconnaissance of enemy positions and movement to prepare for the raids on enemy supply lines and railroads. It was the first time since their inception that the UDTs had truly taken the fight inland.

The stage was now set for General Douglas MacArthur's "masterpiece of amphibious warfare," an invasion of the unlikely port of Inchon with her thirty foot tides. Now for this new kind of war, which some called a "police action," the UDTs mission was quickly changed to cope with the strange set of circumstances that was Inchon. The tides alone made the assault a difficult one, but as always, the Navy and Marines were prepared to overcome and adapt.

The UDT units were technically part of the legendary 1st Marine Division, Reinforced, during the invasion. Due to their extraordinary grit and determination, the Frogmen later received the Presidential Unit Citation for "extraordinary heroism against enemy aggressor forces in Korea from 15 September to 11 October 1950" and the Korean Presidential Unit Citation "for the invasion, evacuation, and reinvasion of Inchon."

A well-deserved award, earned at great cost with the blood, sweat, and tears of the now legendary Navy Frogmen.

The landing and subsequent push to Seoul as part of Operation CHROMITE proved to be a brilliant strategy and flawlessly achieved its intended objectives. MacArthur's 10th Corps secured the city and provided much-needed relief for the forces protecting the perimeter around Pusan. Arguably, though, the hardest work was yet to come for the American troops as the PRK defenders in the east began falling back to reinforce their lines in the north. A way would have to be found to further cut off the supplies fueling the North's war effort.

The men of Underwater Demolition Team's ONE and THREE happily obliged.

While America and its United Nation's allies conducted the war, then U.S. Secretary of State Dean Acheson, serving under President Truman, continued to work behind the scenes to solidify the strength of the United States' position around the world. As the chief architect of the North Atlantic Treaty Organization, Secretary Acheson helped make great strides in strengthening our ability to defend against Soviet aggression. However, when it came to Korea, he famously said:

"If the best possible minds had set out to find the worst possible place to fight this damnable war . . . the unanimous choice would have been Korea."

Korea was a rough place to fight, not only due to its location in the world relative to America, but also due to its notoriously harsh conditions—a seemingly perpetual winter which eventually gives way to a very short but mild Spring and very hot and humid Summer. An excessively mountainous terrain mixed in with the generally unfavorable climate makes for extremely challenging conditions for even the most hardened soldier.

However, as the People's Democratic Republic of Korea (PRK) in the north moved on the South in its pre-planned sneak attack across the 38th Parallel, the geography and weather conditions became a secondary matter . . . it became time to act.

Strategically speaking, North Korean aggression into the South was a key example of why the United States' leadership feared Communist propaganda. Left unchecked, it was believed that this kind of aggression would become more and more commonplace around the world, making it harder for America to maintain a dominate position of strength and could ultimately lead to America being the only bastion of freedom left. President Truman and his military leaders all agreed that such a situation was absolutely unacceptable.

This sentiment led directly to the creation of the Truman Doctrine in early 1947. The concept essentially was one in which the United States pledged to contain Soviet aggression by supporting nations around the world in danger of falling under their umbrella of power. An early example is Turkey and Greece in 1948, which the U.S. supported with financial aid to help their struggling economies in hopes of empowering them to make a stand independently or at least deter aggressive action through the existence of more military strength.

President Truman had told Congress, "It must be the policy of the United States to support free people who are resisting attempted subjugation by armed minorities or by outside pressures." Additionally, he set forth two fundamental principles in his eighteen minute speech: first, that the United States "should assist other free nations to work out their independence in their own way"; and second, that such assistance should come in the form of economic and financial aid so that economic stability could be maintained within each country. In response, the Republican controlled Congress agreed to send $400 million to Turkey and Greece but no military forces.

The effectiveness of this policy was immediate and succeeded on multiple levels. Also, it eventually led to the North Atlantic Treaty Organization, which was officially established on April 4, 1949. The NATO treaty signaled a major shift in American foreign policy, in that the document stated in Article 5 that an attack on any member of the alliance would constitute an attack on all members–a commitment to direct military intervention and use of force.

No matter what policy was put into effect, the men of the UDT were prepared to do what no one else could.

WONSAN, SOUTH KOREA

FEBRUARY 15, 1951

2-MILES INLAND, 0145 HOURS

The bitterly cold night air surrounded the men as they crept closer to their objective: a heavily used rail station on the outer edge of Wonsan. Lieutenant David Jacobs glanced over to his teammate, Petty Officer Tommy White, and pointed at his watch while mentally rehearsing how he planned the next ten minutes to play out. It was dark but the moon was especially bright and illuminated their target well.

Also along for the mission were two UDT veterans, Petty Officers Bob Wilson and Edward Hightower, who made last second adjustments to their gear and prepared to move. Each man knew instinctively that maintaining stealth was an absolute priority and without it the team would be met by an overwhelming enemy force. As was standard in any kind of special operations mission, remaining undetected as long as possible was a matter of life and death.

The men could hear the roar of a flight of the Navy's latest and greatest jet, the F-9 Panther, flying well overhead and bound inland for continued night-time raids. In all, the Panther pilots flew an estimated 78,000 sorties over the course of the war and scored a great number of air-to-air kills. An interesting note, the Panther was also the first aircraft used by the Navy's elite Blue Angels flight demonstration team.

As the planes flew overhead, Lieutenant Jacobs gave the nod and began his trek forward, scouting for any sign of an enemy patrol. About a hundred feet later he motioned for Petty Officer Wilson to scout forward while the rest of the team crept ever so slowly toward the railroad ahead. Jacobs had known Wilson for years and knew if you needed someone to take position as the point-man then it would be difficult to find anyone better. Wilson had grown up in Texas but his dad had taken him to hunt big game out west in Colorado every year when he was a teenager. It proved to be extremely valuable experience and had honed his instincts for stealth and survival.

⟰ **Vintage Frogmen heading into shore for a recon mission**

Wilson was good. Moving like he was born to live and operate under the cloak of darkness, he made his way closer to the team's destination, which was a well-known rail switch that redirected freight cars to the north and out of the city, along with a control substation. If the switch and substation could be disabled or even better, destroyed, then the supply cars heading up the coast to help fortify the PRK troops would be delayed at worst or cut off for weeks at best. Either way, it would be a victory and could directly impact the enemy and their capacity to wage war.

Thanks to the around-the-clock war effort, the night was not nearly as silent as it would normally be at this hour. The ambient noise of trains, cars, and American air raids all helped to make the approach to the target easier. It would nearly be impossible for anyone to hear the Frogmen's approach, and only if they were noticed visually would the alarm be raised.

The team continued forward until all the men found themselves just short of the enemy substation. A lone PRK guard puffed on a cigarette, lazily clutching his rifle as he barely kept awake. Lieutenant Jacobs motioned to Petty Officer White and gave the signal to take him out. No silencers, no night vision . . . just a Navy Frogman and his saltwater encrusted yet exceptionally sharp blade combined with nerves of steel.

A silent knife kill has in some ways always been held as the gold standard of sentry takedowns. It is a tricky business and works best when you are able to strike the killing blow before the target even realizes what is happening. As the team stood at the ready for all hell to break loose, White crept up on his prey and slipped in behind him. Seconds later, the guard was a crumpled mess on the ground, his spinal cord severed just below the sixth vertebrae.

The coast now clear, White and Lieutenant Jacobs took up overwatch duties while the other two men began setting up the charges. Wiring them to blow simultaneously, the Frogmen set up the C3 charges on the tracks and control station before carefully prepping the detonation cord. Once the job was done, it was time to blow it and move quickly to the extraction point.

At precisely 0234 hours, the forty-five pounds of high explosives blasted the substation and ripped apart the tracks—at precisely 0234 hours and a few seconds, the Frogmen were on the run for their lives.

"Who the hell came up with this plan, anyhow Lieutenant?" Petty Officer White joked as the team ran and maneuvered around the edges of the city.

Lieutenant Jacobs smiled, "Hey, you know they pay me the big bucks around here for a reason."

"Yes, sir, I don't suppose you plan on sharing that bonus officer's pay?"

"For sure, as long as we are still alive at the end of the night," Jacobs said with a grin as he tried to get his bearings.

The men could still hear the alarm sirens and commotion of other guards yelling in the distance as they continued their evasion route. Just over a mile to go and they would reach the rubber boats they had left secured under Pier 23. No one dared say the words, "*I hope the boats are still there when we get to the pier*," for fear that voicing their thoughts might invoke some kind of ancient curse that would bring their fears into reality.

At about a quarter-mile from Pier 23 it started becoming abundantly clear that the Frogmen might have to fight their way through to the boats. Fortunately, American aircraft were continuing to fly overhead en-route to their targets further inland, giving the men an exceptionally useful form of built-in distraction as they stealthily moved in the shadows. However, multiple squads of PRK troops were running around on and near the pier, setting security and doubling their patrols. If they discovered the Frogmen as they crept forward then Lieutenant Jacobs and his men would undoubtedly have an even more adventurous evening.

"Everyone circle out to the right and stay close to the edge of the bridge," Lieutenant Jacobs whispered as they all eyed the flurry of movement ahead.

"Roger that, " White replied with a nod.

"It doesn't look good, Lieutenant . . . I think we may have a fight on our hands," Wilson chimed in as he instinctively glanced down at his weapon and checked the chamber.

Jacobs reflected for a second before responding, "I think you're right, but let's try to get the jump on them and then head straight to the boats."

Pier 23 was located just past the connector bridge upon which the men of UDT-3 were currently maneuvering. When the UDT men had come into shore, the pier had been lightly guarded by only a few lone sentries on what seemed to be a routine patrol. Now, dozens of PRK troopers were scurrying about, completely changing the suddenly dire looking situation. But, Lieutenant Jacobs figured that if they could get a bit closer they might be able to take out a whole group before having to make a final dash for the water.

Petty Officer White had been thinking the same thing and already had a fragmentation grenade in hand. Hightower and Wilson scanned the area and looked for the best position to set up an ambush. Crates of equipment and supplies lined the pier and were stacked two or three high. At a very minimum, they could use them for concealment despite having no way to determine which crates to use for cover without a much closer inspection.

"Hey, stick with me, my friend." Jacobs whispered to Wilson as he grabbed his shoulder after realizing his teammate was slightly drifting off into another world, lost in his thoughts.

"Got it, sir . . . was just thinking of my daughter back home. I'm ready."

The emotional weight of leaving behind the family you love the most can take a heavy toll and each man deals with it in his own way. Some choose to set it aside, creating a mental fortress within their mind where they put such things until the time to allow its hallowed doors to swing open has finally come. Others use it as fuel—fuel for the fire within, a form of emotional oxygen that causes the embers of love and of hate to burn even more brightly than ever before—once ignited can give you energy to draw from to accomplish what you must. It is a slightly perilous method because while passion helps push you past normal limits, it must be disciplined and focused or it can run out of control.

Once the team was in its final position and satisfied they weren't going to get a better chance, White pulled the pin and tossed it right toward a small group of PRK soldiers; it landed right in the dead center of their formation. Seemingly at once the PRK troops all looked down, but before they had time to register what was about to happen the grenade exploded full-force and tossed each of the men into a heap on the ground, riddling them with shrapnel and killing them instantly.

"Nice toss, Tommy!"

"Thanks LT, but I think we're about to have a lot of company."

Two-dozen PRK troopers began shouting and running straight over to investigate and when they got close enough, the Frogmen opened fire on them in unison from their positions of cover and concealment. One down—two down—three down. Rounds from the UDT men's weapons continued to rip through the enemy and cut them down.

"Move, move! Stay close to the guardrails and keep pushing down the pier!"

All the men began to maneuver from crate to crate as the firefight erupted with furious intensity and each side started burning through ammo. Knowing their safe haven would be the water, the Frogmen did as Jacobs ordered and stuck close to the edge of the pier, hoping to eventually make it to their boats and escape into the night. Rounds ricocheted all around but the Navy men continued to take down the PRK troopers one by one.

"LT, drop!" Petty Officer Wilson shouted as he ran over to tackle his team leader to the ground. He had caught a glimpse of a PRK soldier creeping around their right flank and almost getting the drop on his lieutenant. A short burst from his M3-A1 "Grease Gun" (a submachine gun) stopped him in his tracks.

"Thanks, my friend . . . now could you get the hell off of me," Lieutenant Jacobs said as both men shared a laugh.

Sometimes in battle, a little levity can go a long way.

Back on his feet, Lieutenant Jacobs took a look around and still didn't like what he saw. Despite killing the almost two dozen PRK troops, it was obvious that many more were headed for their position. And just when things had started to look better, it took a turn for the worse.

"Grenade!"

Petty Officer White yelled for his team to take cover as he dove toward the steel guardrail. The heat from the explosion singed his eyebrows and shrapnel filled the air, hissing past him and his teammates like angry hornets. One piece managed to embed itself deeply in White's right thigh.

His teammate, Petty Officer Kevin Hightower, had it much worse—a large metal fragment sliced his bicep nearly in half and a smaller one was lodged in his neck, just missing the carotid artery by a mere inch. His breathing was labored but he remained conscious.

Lieutenant Jacobs rushed over immediately to his downed teammate, "You're gonna be okay, my friend, it's just a scratch."

It wasn't. One wrong move and the metal could shift just enough to sever the artery and that would be the end. But, it is the job of a good teammate to help his buddies push on no matter how bad it may get. In this case, the age-old standard for battle medics was appropriate—although it's unlikely that a man as tough as Petty Officer Hightower would go into shock, it can be exceptionally effective to downplay a man's injuries in the first moments to help ensure the armor of his mind doesn't come crashing down upon him.

Wilson and White rushed over within seconds and began assisting the lieutenant in treating Hightower. They quickly stabilized his neck and placed battle dressing over the wound in an attempt to prevent the shrapnel from moving. After successfully treating the wound, the primary problem facing the men now was carrying out their teammate before getting overrun by the enemy.

Hightower refused to follow instructions to lie still, but rather inhaled deeply and sat up on his own power, eyes wide and reaching for his weapon.

"Where are those little bastards . . . I'm gonna kill every last one!"

The Frogmen all shared glances and grinned at each other before Lieutenant Jacobs broke the moment, his low baritone voice filled with the gravity of the situation, "Glad you're alive, I was starting to think we were going to have to carry your hairy ass out of here."

"Nothing doing, sir . . . I'm walking out of here on my own two feet."

"Good man—now let's get the hell out of this hellhole."

Each man locked and loaded a fresh magazine while preparing to move. As they raced down Pier 23 it became apparent that another squad of PRK soldiers was moving down about seventy-five meters away. Lieutenant Jacobs looked over the guardrail and decided their best option, not necessarily the one he wanted, was to make a leap into the darkness and into the frigid waters below.

"Well, fellas, I think if we're going to get out of this mess we're going to have a make a jump for it."

The rest of the team glanced around at each other briefly before giving their sign of approval, "We are with you, LT."

"Hightower, have Wilson wrap that neck again fast and you guys jump together . . . Wilson, you know what to do."

He knew exactly what to do—never leave your swim buddy—ever.

Both men nodded and, with everyone ready to go, each jumped the railing and plunged into the frigid waters below.

The shock of the cold water was something the Frogmen were completely used to from hundreds of hours of training and operational experience, but it still always took a few seconds to adjust to the sudden change in temperature. As noted earlier, being out in the cold air is one thing while being totally immersed in frigid water is very much different indeed. It can cause your core temperature to drop dramatically in a heartbeat.

After surfacing, each man got his bearings and swam near each other to circle up in the water, taking a second to ensure everyone got through the jump intact. Wilson and Hightower had remained locked together and although it was a struggle, Hightower was determined to swim under his own power. Fortunately for the team, their rubber boats were right where they left them, about twenty meters away. The men swam directly to the boats and within a couple of minutes the Frogmen were comfortably aboard and ready to make a break for it under the cover of darkness, enveloping them like a shield on this moon-lit night.

The PRK troops made a last ditch attempt to find the men who seemed to have inexplicably vanished, but it proved fruitless. Before they had time to fully understand where the Frogmen had gone, Jacobs and his men were hundreds of meters away and out of reach.

Another solid victory for the men of the UDT.

Missions like this one marked a unique point in the transformation of the UDTs, making land-borne actions more and more commonplace. In addition, the Frogmen had started working more and more with U.S. Intelligence, creating another shift in their use and capabilities. If the men of the UDT could conduct inland reconnaissance and gather their own intelligence, then that information could then be utilized by the CIA and other military assets in planning or carrying out a multitude of operations. In many ways, these missions carried out in Korea as well as previous work alongside the CIA's predecessor, the Office of Strategic Services (OSS), proved to be a major catalyst for the shift into SEALs that would follow years later in the jungles of Vietnam.

4

FORGING THE FUTURE—
SEALs IN VIETNAM

In 1962, President John F. Kennedy established SEAL Teams ONE and TWO from the men of the already existing Underwater Demolition Teams (UDT). The situation arising from the failed Bay of Pigs operation along with the ramping up of potential hostilities in Vietnam led to a stronger belief in the need for upgrading the Unconventional Warfare (UW) capabilities of the United States military forces. Newly minted SEAL Teams initially faced multiple struggles during their development from UDT to fully trained and operational SEALs. The new focus on land and unconventional warfare meant a complete overhaul of the skill training pipeline and a fresh look at everything—from individual selection to how the Teams would be organized.

However, it didn't take long for the SEALs to get to work. Alongside their CIA counterparts, the SEALs began training the South Vietnamese frogmen very early in the war and started conducting reconnaissance missions, which further highlighted the need for dependable, real-time intelligence.

After some negotiating with the CIA-directed intelligence personnel and U.S. commanders in the region, the SEALs convinced those in charge of the need to allow them the latitude to collect their own intelligence and use it semi-autonomously to plan their own missions. Once this was established, the SEALs were able to put their skills and expertise to use far more effectively despite some concern over the idea.

Ultimately, Navy SEALs are both thinkers and shooters, not just one or the other. This fact was highlighted over and over during the Vietnam War as members of the SEAL Teams continuously adapted and outmaneuvered the enemy. A combination of individual discipline, toughness, and bravery, mixed with hard training and a willingness of the chain-of-command to trust and allow the SEALs to plan and

≈ **A Vietnam-era SEAL machine gunner watches for the enemy**

execute their own missions made for an exceptionally deadly combination.

In order to better understand the lead-up to the war in the hot and humid jungles of Vietnam, it is necessary to look back to the previous two decades of history. The fallout of world politics after Japan and Germany fell to the combined Allied power was still easy to identify.

The major allied victors of WWII, the United Kingdom, the United States, and the Soviet Union, all agreed that Vietnam belonged to the French. However, as the French did not have the means to immediately retake Vietnam, the major powers came to an agreement that British troops would occupy the south while Nationalist Chinese forces would move in from the north. The Chinese troops entered the country to disarm Japanese troops north of the 16th parallel on September 14, 1945. When the British landed in the south, they rearmed the interned French forces as well as elements of the surrendered Japanese forces to aid them in retaking southern Vietnam, since and British and the French did not have enough troops to do it by themselves.

At the urging of the Soviet Union, Ho Chi Minh initially attempted to negotiate with the French, who were slowly reestablishing their control across the region. But, in January of 1946, the Viet Minh won elections across central and northern Vietnam. Then, on March 6, 1946, Ho signed an agreement allowing French forces to replace Nationalist Chinese forces, in exchange for French recognition of the Democratic Republic of Vietnam as a "free" republic within what was known as the French Union, with the specifics of such recognition to be determined by future negotiation.

The French entered Hanoi in March 1946 and by November of that year they ousted the Viet Minh from the city. Soon after, the last of the British forces departed the country, which left Vietnam solidly in the hands of the French. After only a short time, the Viet Minh began a guerrilla war against the French Union forces, marking the official beginning of the First Indochina War.

The war quickly spread to Laos and Cambodia, where communist sympathizers organized the Pathet Lao and the Khmer Serei, both of which were modeled on the Viet Minh. On the global scale, the Cold War began in earnest, which essentially meant that any partnership that existed between the Western powers and the Soviet Union during WWII disintegrated. A complex game of cloak-and-dagger operations went forward on a grand scale and over the course of the next three decades a race between the United States and Soviet Union to see who could stay ahead technologically was also catapulted forward at breakneck speed.

The lack of available weapons severely hampered the Viet Minh, but this situation changed by 1949 when the Chinese Communists clearly won the civil war in China and were free to provide arms to their Vietnamese allies. Upon receiving aid from the Chinese, the Viet Minh quickly took advantage of the major turn of events and began ramping up military operations across the country.

In January of 1950, the People's Republic of China and the Soviet Union officially recognized the

Viet Minh's Democratic Republic of Vietnam, based in Hanoi, as the legitimate government of Vietnam. Immediately following, the United States and Great Britain recognized the French-backed state of Vietnam in Saigon, led by former Emperor Bảo Dại, as the legitimate Vietnamese government.

As we have discussed, the outbreak of the Korean War in June 1950 convinced many Washington policymakers that the war in Indochina was an example of communist expansionism directed by the Soviet Union. The American policy derived from the Truman Doctrine made it clear that any expansion of Communism around the world was essentially a direct threat to the United States and free peoples around the world. Now, the stage would be set for America to attempt to intervene any time the Soviets clearly made a move in that direction.

During his first months in office, President John F. Kennedy had already begun to realize that there was a real need to expand the role of unconventional warfare and various special operations missions as a way to counter a growing trend of guerrilla war in hotspots around the world. During a speech to Congress on May 25, 1961, President Kennedy made clear he had a deep respect for the already established Army Special Forces and committed to spending over $100 million to increase the capabilities of units involved in Special Operations worldwide. While Kennedy is typically credited with creating the Navy SEALs, technically speaking he merely gave what could be considered a formal acknowledgement to the process that had been evolving since the men of UDT in Korea.

President Kennedy's stance on the matter had also been heavily influenced by Admiral Arleigh Burke, his Chief of Naval Operations, who had specifically pushed for the former establishment of guerrilla and counter-guerrilla combat units capable of operating in any environment—Sea, Air, or Land. This is the moment where the transformation of UDT to SEAL took a major step forward and all SEALs were direct successors of the Frogmen of the UDT. Many of the early transitions were veterans of Korea with extensive experience in clandestine and special operations missions. It would be many years before the full change would take place, however, because the U.S. Navy still believed strongly in the need for UDT Teams in the Amphibious Force. In fact, it wouldn't be until 1983 when all UDT men formally became SEALs.

As noted previously, the first two SEAL Teams were officially formed in January 1962, with one stationed on each coast: SEAL Team ONE at the Naval Amphibious Base Coronado, California; and, SEAL Team TWO at the Naval Amphibious Base Little Creek, Virginia. The newly commissioned SEAL Teams were to conduct clandestine missions with a focus on maritime and riverine environments, but, it wouldn't be long before their areas of expertise would continue to expand.

New SEAL trainees would begin with Underwater Demolition Team Training and typically serve some time training specifically with the UDT units. Once the men completed the initial training they would undergo SEAL Basic Indoctrination (SBI) training at the infamous Camp Kerry high in the Cuyamaca

Mountains. Once a student completed his training at Camp Kerry, he would then finally be assigned to a SEAL platoon and begin a typical platoon workup.

Field training was intense and included all manner of weapons, demolitions, unarmed combat, guerilla tactics, and unconventional warfare. This style of warfighting is all about thinking in a new way and learning to apply maximum force through relative superiority. The fundamentals of speed, surprise, and violence of action are the hallmarks of a SEAL direct action raid and are just as vital today as they were in the jungles of Vietnam.

During these early years of the SEAL Teams, some of the very first missions they conducted were against communist Cuba. The SEALs would deploy from submarines and head into shore to conduct beach recon in preparation for a proposed amphibious invasion of the island, much like their predecessors had done in other hot spots around the world. Unofficial reports also allege that the SEALs secretly escorted a CIA operative ashore in order to allow him to obtain photographs of Soviet nuclear missiles as they were offloaded. Such missions continued to strengthen the direct ties between the SEALs and the intelligence community over the years.

President Kennedy and the commanders in the Pacific recognized in the very beginning that the relatively small nation of Vietnam was a potential hot zone for guerilla and unconventional warfare. Frogmen from the UDT were already conducting hydrographic surveys of the coastline by the beginning of 1962 in preparation for conflict, which would soon involve U.S. troop commitments. The "advisory" role of the U.S. military in Vietnam was transformed into full, direct involvement in combat with U.S. Army, Marine Corps, and Navy forces during the Johnson Administration. In 1964 there were only 16,000 American military in Vietnam, but this rose to 553,000 by 1969. At approximately the same time, the United States military force the Military Assistance Command Vietnam (MACV) and Navy SEALs (in March 1962) were already being deployed to South Vietnam as advisors. Their primary mission was to train the Republic of Vietnam soldiers in unconventional warfare and tactics similar to those developed by U.S. military forces.

It would not be long before the SEALs would continue building their longstanding operational partnership with the Intelligence community as well. By early 1963, the SEALs and CIA were conducting covert operations in North Vietnam, targeting Vietcong sympathizers and military personnel. Code-named the "Phoenix Program," SEALs and CIA operatives would track down, capture, and when necessary, eliminate or "neutralize" the enemy infiltrators. Although controversial in nature, the program was arguably a success and further strengthened the ties with the CIA.

This initiative was a CIA organized and led effort to root out and neutralize Communist sympathizers and Viet Cong leadership in South Vietnam. Early on it started with Provincial Reconnaissance Units (PRUs) and expanded over time into the Phoenix Program. Some of the most successful operations of its kind were conducted by SEALs recruited into the PRUs.

As the SEALs continued training their South Vietnamese counterparts, the Doc Nguio Nhia, it was not uncommon for some of the Vietnamese to begin joining them on patrols and missions throughout the region. They had trained them in all the fundamental skills as well as combat diving and maritime operations—and it paid off. Initially deploying around Da Nang and eventually in the Rung Sat Special Zone, the SEALs conducted interdiction missions against enemy supply lines as well as infiltration and intelligence gathering. Even with today's sophisticated technology, it is difficult to beat the intelligence value of actual "eyes on" a selected target. For that reason and others, the SEALs and other special operations units have always been an exceptional asset for intelligence gathering on the enemy.

When force was necessary, which was often, the combat with the Vietcong involving the SEALs was intense and fierce. SEAL Teams do not use traditional infantry tactics, which can call for artillery strikes to soften up a target for long periods before storming in and taking over an area—instead they prefer to strike quickly and up close. For many Vietcong soldiers, once they caught a glimpse of the "Men in Green Faces" it was already too late.

A new detachment of Frogmen from SEAL Team One was sent in to the Rung Sat Special Zone in February 1966 with specific orders to conduct high-risk direct action missions against the enemy in the region. Over the course of the next few years, the SEAL presence grew significantly and ultimately eight SEAL platoons would eventually rotate into the country on a continual basis.

Operating from a forward base in Nha Be, the SEALs also began to serve as advisors for the local Provincial Reconnaissance Units (PRUs) and continued conducting covert operations into North Vietnam, Laos, and even Cambodia. SEAL Team TWO had specifically developed a relationship with these South Vietnamese warriors and worked closely with them side by side.

In 1968, the North Vietnamese and the Vietcong conducted a major attack on the South dubbed the "Tet Offensive." *Tet* refers to the Vietnamese lunar new year. The idea was to strike on a holiday, when the American and South Vietnamese forces were on considerably less that high alert. And, aside from the obvious desire to take as much territory as possible, it was the hope of the enemy leadership that the offensive would lead to a breakdown of support for the war by the American public. In that way, it was highly successful and protests in the U.S. began to increase substantially. However, from a strictly military standpoint, the North Vietnamese army took massive losses, which has led many to declare the action a major loss for the communists.

By the time President Richard Nixon declared his plan for "Vietnamization" in 1970, whereby the United States would begin its withdraw from the conflict and turn over full responsibility for the war effort to the South Vietnamese, the Navy SEALs had demonstrated their valor time and time again in harrowing accounts of deadly engagements with the enemy. Officially, the last SEAL advisor left Vietnam in March 1973—and the South fell to the communist forces two years later. However, the Navy SEALs left an indelible mark on the pages of history and were among the most decorated combat units in the entire war. Overall, the SEALs were awarded two Navy Crosses, forty-two Silver Stars, 402 Bronze Stars, two Legions of Merit, 352 Commendation Medals, and three Presidential Unit Citations, and three SEALs received the Congressional Medal of Honor for heroism in the face of the enemy. A total of forty-eight SEALs were killed in action in Vietnam, but records indicate an estimated two thousand enemy kills by the Frogmen.

Truly, the "Men in Green Faces" were a legend in the making.

⚹ **SEALs on patrol in the jungles of Vietnam**

RUNG SAT SPECIAL ZONE
VIETNAM, JULY 28, 1966
0706 HOURS

Lieutenant Dan Owens did one last check on his Stoner 63A light machine gun, patted his Ka-Bar combat knife, and adjusted the belt holding up his Levi's. His Leading Petty Officer (LPO) gave him a once-over, checking for anything missing or out of place, and applied a finishing touch to his black-and-green camo face paint.

"Damn sir, you look like a real killer now . . . You sure you don't want to head back home and go try your luck in Hollywood? I'd hate to see that pretty face of yours get all messed up out here," his LPO said with a big grin.

His platoon commander and now close friend smiled, "Shoot, you're supposed to be the ladies' man. Maybe when we get back you can go try out for that show on Broadway you keep talking about taking your girlfriend to—I'm sure she would love seeing you in some fancy tights."

The men shared a mutual laugh and strode on toward the boat waiting to ferry them up one of the many rivers littering the region. Two other SEALs and a South Vietnamese Kit Carson Scout accompanied them in the boat as well and had somewhat grim looks on their faces.

"Hey boss," one of the men started as he looked to the lieutenant, "our scout here says he has a bad feeling about this one . . . and you know what happened last time the hairs on his neck stood up."

This one would be another "snatch and grab" mission: infiltrate an enemy position, preferably completely undetected, sneak into a hooch that hopefully would be the temporary residence of a high-value intelligence target, and drag him back for interrogation. As simple as that may sound, there was nothing simple about it.

First of all, there was no guarantee of reaching the enemy camp undetected and yet the success of the mission many times rested on the simple idea that the SEALs could reach the target before anyone knew they are even in the area. When successful, it could have a withering effect on the target's morale for him to wake up in his pajamas with a green-faced Navy SEAL staring into his eyes with malicious intent.

Second, the planning for numerous operations were based on nothing more than "actionable intelligence," which basically meant the information might be true at the moment when you got it, but it probably wouldn't be long before it isn't worth anything. There was no time for complex planning and hovering over maps for long periods of time deciding what to do. The team leader needed to get the information, process it quickly, and trust in him and his men's ability to adapt, overcome, and achieve victory or success no matter what the circumstances.

Fortunately, that kind of tenacity and raw willpower exists in great abundance with the U.S. Navy SEALs.

Finally, adding to the complexity was a common problem for warriors of every era, the modern one being no different: communications—or the lack thereof.

During the Vietnam era, SEALs barely had comm gear better than their WWII and Korean War predecessors. The thick foliage of the jungle added to the problem along with the fact that the gear was heavy and battery power was always limited. What that translated into was simple–if you got into trouble it could be a while before anyone even knows it, let alone could come to your aid.

Lieutenant Owens nodded in affirmation of his teammate's comment, but they all knew it was time to roll. He gave the signal to the boat crew chief to fire up the engines and move out. It would be a tight time schedule tonight.

The men of SEAL Team ONE, Delta Platoon, were accustomed to the heat, insects, mud, and the occasional alligator that had become a part of daily life while operating in the now-infamous Rung Sat Zone. While most American's went on with normal pursuits, the men of Delta Platoon readied themselves for yet another patrol into the bush.

As the boat coasted up river they neared their insertion point and slipped into the shallow water. Binh-Chi, their scout, linked up with the SEAL point man and led them off into the jungle. At night, every sound seems to be magnified, making the task of remaining undetected all the more difficult. It took patience and a special kind of mental resilience to successfully navigate the treacherous area when at any moment you could literally bump into someone—or something—that would alert the whole area to your presence.

The SEALs and their scout slowly crept through the winding path of thick vegetation. Snakes and other critters were a constant concern, but the men knew they had to try to shut out such thoughts and focus on the task at hand. Minutes turned into hours as the men made their way to the destination.

Speaking was not necessary. Hand signals and sometimes even a simple nod at the right moment in the right direction was enough to communicate intent. These hardened men patrolled night after night and knew each other almost as well as they knew themselves. Over time you can almost hear the thoughts of your teammates.

On this night the moon was pretty bright, making it slightly easier for them to see where they were going. The human eye is remarkable at adapting to low-light conditions, but it is still helpful to have a little ambient moonlight to assist. Of course, that also meant the enemy had a similar advantage, but all in all it balanced itself out.

After approximately three-and-a-half long hours, the team had finally reached its intended position. Binh-Chi signaled for the men to come forward to the edge of the clearing. Just past the foliage was an area about thirty meters in diameter with three small hooches. One was a slight bit bigger than the other, so the SEAL officer determined that it was likely that was some kind of command post . . . or at least was where the highest-ranking enemy would sleep.

The smell of a cooking fire still permeated the clearing and dirty clothes lined a makeshift laundry area. As the scout and SEALs began to move forward,

Binh-Chi froze in place and put up his hand, gesturing for them to halt.

A small mutt of a dog wandered about the encampment, sniffing around for food scraps. Although no direct threat to the men, one dog can make a whole lot of racket if it starts barking and then the night could quickly take a turn for the worse.

Petty Officer Miller then tapped his platoon commander on the shoulder and nodded as he looked off to the west side of the clearing. A lone sentry wearing loose fitting black pajamas, wicker hat, and carrying the typical AK-47 slung over his shoulder. He puffed slowly on a hand-rolled cigarette. The lieutenant nodded back and pointed at one of his SEALs, giving him the sign to get to work—sentry takeout work.

As he began to creep forward, his teammates took up hasty ambush positions just in case they were discovered and everything began to fall apart. This was not Petty Officer Miller's first rodeo, as they say, but it was better to be ready. He pulled his Ka-Bar slide out of its sheath and gripped it strongly in his right hand. Sentry engagement is a risky venture even for a seasoned veteran SEAL, but it was the best option to solve the current problem. Fortunately, the mangy dog had scampered off, leaving the NVA soldier as the only current security threat.

The SEAL controlled his breathing and engaged in a quick mental visualization drill as he got closer and closer to his target. *Left hand will grab him and cover his mouth while I plunge the blade vertically into his exposed neck . . . with a slicing motion the knife will exit out the front, severing the vocal cords, making him unable to scream and give us away.*

Moments later, the NVA soldier lay on the ground bleeding out. He was unconscious in seconds and would die soon after.

The SEALs moved in toward the assumed command hooch and prepared to snatch up their intended target. In many ways, this was always the moment of truth because it was almost impossible to capture someone without creating quite a bit of commotion. Killing them was always easier. But, this target was wanted for interrogation and was believed to be behind numerous plots to assist the Vietcong with infiltrating American or South Vietnamese controlled areas. It was almost time to find out just how much he knew.

With an intimidating glare, the lieutenant picked the target up off his bed, one hand around his throat, and slammed him into the ground. The other SEALs could practically hear the wind get knocked out of him as Binh-Chi began to explain in his own language about how his night was about to go from bad to worse. Petty Officer Janson, another top man in the squad, tied him up quickly and they all prepared to move.

Men, AK-47s in tow, emerged from each of the other hooches but were quickly killed by the SEALs before they could even fully process what was happening. A quick search of the area turned up some more good intelligence to bring back to the command center.

"Hey boss, looks like we've got some maps and logbooks in here," Petty Officer Janson said while stuffing whatever looked important into a bag.

Lieutenant Owens nodded in confirmation. "Round up whatever you can find in a hurry—we are moving out of here in two minutes."

"Roger that, LT."

Inside of the two-minute mark, the SEALs had found a plethora of intelligence information and a fairly large stash of cash. Not bad for one nights work.

Just as the men prepared to move, the radio operator relayed to the command center that they were moving for extraction. Boat in, helo out. A Seawolf pilot had been lingering on standby waiting for the call.

Binh-Chi knew this area like the back of his hand and happened to know that there was a clearing less than a mile to the southeast that would serve as a good spot to do a hot extract. It was a good thing too, because the brief but loud fight had drawn the attention of an NVA patrol now closing on their position.

Lieutenant Owens did a mental check of each man and gave the signal to move out. As the SEALs disappeared with their captive into the jungle, the

≈ **SEALs on riverine patrol**

NVA patrol had already been on the radio to request assistance. A company-sized unit was already in the area and on its way to attempt to intercept. The SEALs decided speed was the better option at this point over stealth and picked up the pace. Petty Officer Miller heard the familiar hiss of a snake as he stepped on its head but kept moving. The jungle always just felt alive because of the thousands and thousands of critters all over the place.

"Contact, right!" one of the SEALs shouted as they navigated the tough brush. An NVA patrol began taking shots at the men but could not have expected the hailstorm of rounds that erupted moments later from the SEALs.

With the practiced response of a well-oiled machine, the SEALs opened up on the enemy and took turns between laying down withering machine gun fire from the Stoner and expertly delivered marksmanship from the men with the CAR-15s. One SEAL dropped a grenade on the NVA position from his M203 just to make a point. *Mess with us and you're going to pay!*

The explosion rattled the remaining enemy that weren't killed outright and made for an opportunity to keep moving. The SEALs, prisoner in tow, now ran through the vegetation until seeing the clearing up ahead. A welcome feeling of relief came when the SEALs heard the unmistakable sound of the helo on fast approach. Moments later it was on the ground with the crew chief yelling for them to move out and jump onboard.

"Thanks for the ride," Petty Officer Janson said to the pilot as he jumped into the crew section of the grey U. S. Navy helicopter and helped his teammates climb aboard.

The Seawolves, as they were known, were the Vietnam version of what today is known as Task Force 160. Seawolf pilots will fly anywhere, anytime, in any conditions to assist in a SEAL operation—consummate professionals and brave flyers all.

Another good evening of work for the SEALs.

Missions like these were routine for the men of the SEAL Teams during the Vietnam era and in many ways all future SEALs owe the dawning of their reputation to these men. In a very short period, UDT Frogmen, primarily a maritime-only force, had made the transition to become a Sea, Air, and Land unit—from which the title SEAL is derived.

The complex global political situation influenced the timing of their creation as well. For the United States, the primary doctrine adopted against the Soviet regime was one of containment: the Domino Theory essentially stated that if smaller nations fell to communist influence, then the surrounding states would eventually fall as well. It was decided that watching this happen without attempting to intervene was not an acceptable course of action.

Accepting the advice of his military commanders, including the legendary Admiral Nimitz, President Kennedy decided to establish special forces units with the primary mission of counterinsurgency and disruption of the enemy using covert and clandestine tactics and techniques. This decision was a fateful one for the future of Naval Special Warfare and led directly to the SEALs becoming what they are today.

Initially, the newly formed SEAL Teams played an advisory role in Vietnam, training and helping organize South Vietnamese forces. Over time, their role continued to expand and by 1966 the SEALs were operating continuously behind enemy lines, conducting raids and interdiction missions, as well as the capture or kill missions like the one discussed in this chapter. These early SEALs had much less training time than the SEALs of today before deploying and it wasn't uncommon for a man to finish BUD/S and find himself in the hot, humid jungles of Vietnam only months after finishing his basic SEAL training. This point cannot be stressed enough in order to really get the proper perspective. SEALs of today take almost two and a half years to create and prepare for their first deployment and that assumes no major setbacks in training, such as injury or unforeseen timing and logistics issues with advanced training and schools.

In a way, this exemplifies the courage of the Vietnam-era SEAL—relying primarily on their wits and a will of steel, utilizing older equipment and comparatively very little tactical training, they forged a path that all special operations units can learn from on their own walk along the warrior path. In fact, it really is incredible what they achieved and brings into focus a fact that has been proven over and over throughout the ages of war: it is primarily the man, not the equipment, which makes the warrior what he is and must be—a man disciplined and hardened by trials of fire, and dedicated to a code of honor much bigger than himself alone.

The SEALs in Vietnam provided us examples of this kind of heroism time after time.

Small arms fire filled the air as a small fire team of SEALs from SEAL Team ONE, Bravo Platoon, held on to whatever they could as Lieutenant Bruce Moffatt took a hard right turn in the jeep they had just "borrowed" a few moments before. The flashes from American rockets still lit up the sky and the stench of death permeated the air like a thick cloud as troops from the 1st Cavalry Division made a final push to clear out the area in and around Quang-Tri City to the west.

Petty Officer John LaToof, usually the first to lighten the air with his slashing wit, was grim faced and clearly not in the best of moods. "Sir, I think our guy went down that way," he said as he pointed towards a now semi-bombed-out building about a hundred yards away.

"Roger that, hang on!"

The SEALs were after a very specific target: Lieutenant Colonel Tuan Vinh, a South Vietnamese officer . . . an officer who had become a traitor.

Lieutenant Colonel Vinh, it had been discovered, was feeding intelligence information about troop movement and force strength to his Vietcong infiltrators, information which had been used to kill three American advisors and capture another. Lieutenant Moffatt and his SEALs weren't about to let him escape now.

The SEALs ducked instinctively as more bullets flew through the air near their position moments before coming to a halt in front of what was an ARVN stronghold—or at least used to be. Now it was riddled with bullet holes and fires burned outside the main entrance.

"There must be something awfully important inside there for him to risk us catching him inside," Petty Officer LaToof quipped as the SEALs vaulted out of the vehicle and ran toward the entrance.

"Agreed, let's go," the lieutenant said with malice in his voice.

Once inside, a staircase on the right led upstairs and the SEALs bounded three steps at a time to try to close the gap.

"Look out!" shouted Petty Officer LaToof as he and the lieutenant nearly ran into a small group of NVA fighters.

The team opened up and for the next few seconds the entire passageway was sliced with lead flying all around them. But, the SEALs were just a little bit faster and much more precise than their enemy. Moments later all four of the NVA soldiers were lying on the ground, dead or bleeding out.

Pressing on, Lieutenant Moffatt ran up the next flight of steps, turned left, and saw the open door of what appeared to be an office of some kind, his fellow SEALs right on his heels. As they entered the room it became increasingly clear why the LCOL turncoat had risked coming back to his old HQ.

A somewhat small vault sat on the floor next to his desk, the door now wide open. LCOL Vinh stood next to it with a stack of papers in one hand and a makeshift match in the other. He looked the SEALs in the eye and in broken English said, "I had no choice."

Petty Officer LaToof stepped up without hesitation, drew his pistol, and shot him in the head.

"He had it coming, LT."

Lieutenant Moffatt nodded in agreement, "Let's take a look at what he was after and get back to base."

As it turned out, the vastness of LCOL Vinh's treachery was only barely known. In his hand was a stack of documents outlining names, locations, informants, payoffs, logistics and personnel movements, and various other critical information relating to the highly classified Top Secret Phoenix Program.

"Hey LT, come take a look at this," Petty Officer LaToof said as he waved him over.

Lieutenant Moffatt walked over and began taking a closer look at what appeared to be a list of names with some kind of map sector designations followed by monetary information similar to an accounting slip. After a few moments it started to come together.

"This is a list of regional commanders in charge of various Vietcong assets within their sector and the payoff amounts," the lieutenant grumbled as he felt his anger building.

As the SEALs finished gathering up whatever intel they could find, it became apparent that the battle to retake Quang-Tri, although a decisive victory for the American and South Vietnamese forces, was not quite over. An explosion outside the building gave them a sharp reminder that they needed to move out.

Earlier in the year, the NVA had made a massive push into the South to take Quang-Tri, especially

Quang-Tri City, which had both strategic and symbolic value because it was viewed as an important center of power for the South Vietnamese. Quang-Tri City had always been a prime target during the Tet Offensive.

The SEALs ran out of the building and jumped into their jeep amid the sound of small arms fire all over the area. After taking a brief second to get his directional bearings, Lieutenant Moffatt stepped on the gas and headed southeast toward Landing Zone (LZ) Betty, about ten kilometers away. Once there they would catch a helo back to Camp Carroll, a Marine Corps artillery base near the Demilitarized Zone. Bravo Platoon had established a good rapport with the Marines at the base and had a small area of the barracks to themselves. It provided the SEALs with essentially their own safe house where they could rest between ops and prep for upcoming missions.

Not a bad setup, especially when you are spending a lot of your time sleeping in a thatch hut and wading through snake-infested rivers.

Petty Officer LaToof was on the radio trying to ensure their request for a ride back to Camp Carroll was on its way when another explosion rocked their position and blew out the rear left tire. Lieutenant Moffatt managed a heroic effort to keep the jeep from rolling over and the SEALs jumped out just in time to realize they had driven into a hasty ambush by NVA soldiers fleeing Quang-Tri City.

"Take cover!"

Using the damaged jeep as cover, the SEALs took up firing positions and began to light up the area with a massive volume of fire.

In a last-ditch effort by the NVA attackers, one of the enemy launched an RPG which flew past the SEALs, exploding in the distance behind their position. Undaunted, the lieutenant and his men continued their counterattack. Petty Officer LaToof took a grazing shot to the shoulder but kept fighting. One by one, the SEALs took down the enemy fighters. Nearly as quickly as it had begun, the firefight was over and the men immediately went to work changing out the damaged tire. Within a few minutes, they were back on the road toward their pickup point.

Once they reached the LZ, the SEALs took up defensive positions and waited for the familiar sound of a Seahawk helicopter. Moments later, they were onboard and heading to Camp Carroll. One of the Seahawk crewman noticed Petty Officer LaToof's bleeding shoulder from the bullet that grazed him.

"Are you okay?" the crewman asked, clearly concerned for the veteran SEAL.

The solidly built and tough-as-nails SEAL just grinned, "Just another day at the office, my friend."

For a SEAL, pain and fatigue were merely part of the job—a part of the warrior's life.

Although the Vietnam War was increasingly unpopular at home, the SEALs in-country continued to do amazing work day after day, week after week, month after month during the entire course of their time in those hot jungles. It cannot be overemphasized how well the men of Naval Special Warfare adapted to the situation there and carried out successful missions time and time again. Before the end of the war, the SEALs were responsible for taking out over two thousand NVA and Vietcong soldiers, rescuing dozens of POWs, and capturing many key members of the political infrastructure. This is an impressive record, especially when so few SEALs overall were ever in-country at one time and only approximately five hundred were ever part of the war at all.

Arguably, one of the most impressive elements of the actions of the SEALs in Vietnam was just how quickly a new trainee could find himself in combat operations. As we have mentioned, today's SEALs have a very long buildup throughout the initial training pipeline, which can take up to two and a half years to complete. During Vietnam, the BUD/S program was slightly shorter and the post-BUD/S training might only last a couple of months before the men were shipped off to war. A trainee could walk through the doors at the Naval Special Warfare Center in Coronado and less than six months later be dropped into the jungles of South Vietnam.

SEAL veterans who were there also operated with a large amount of autonomy when compared to other units in the region. A young SEAL officer or senior enlisted man could find himself directing assets including air power and riverine units in support of his team's mission. It was not uncommon for these warriors to be given a task and then allowed to simply "get it done." This kind of freedom can only work when you have a true professional who is dedicated to the mission and holds the highest standards of honor for himself and his team. The success of the SEALs in Vietnam is a direct testimony to the effectiveness of this lethal combination.

Even today, all SEALs know that it was the heroism, courage, and success of these men in Vietnam who went before them who really paved the way for future operations and gave them the reputation as some of the fiercest fighters in America.

⌃ **The men of UDT-11 and UDT-12 recovering NASA Astronauts after capsule splashdown**

5

LESSONS LEARNED— OPERATION URGENT FURY

Long-time congressman Ronald Vernie "Ron" Dellums (D—California) took his position on the House Floor to deliver a speech in opposition to President Ronald Reagan's supposition that the new airfield under construction on the small isle of Grenada could be used for military operations. The congressman had recently returned from a fact-finding trip to the island at the invitation of then prime minister of Grenada, Maurice Bishop.

He adjusted his tie and took a small sip of water before beginning, "Based on my personal observations, discussion, and analysis of the new international airport under construction in Grenada, it is my conclusion that this project is specifically now and has always been for the purpose of economic development and is not for military use."

A few nods from his fellow Democrats in the party spurred him on, "It is my thought that it is absurd, patronizing, and totally unwarranted for the United States government to charge that this airport poses a military threat to the United States' national security."

Applause from supporters within the House of Representatives brought a smile to Congressman Dellums face as he yielded the floor to one of his fellows. However, other Congressional members were very wary of his analysis of the situation.

A few months later, on October 12, the house arrest and subsequent murder of Prime Minister Bishop brought their fears into focus as the Cuban-led military coup put the entire island of Grenada into a state of chaos. Martial law was declared and members of the Provisional Revolutionary Army (PRA), headed up by communist-backed General Hudson Austin, took control of the government.

Suddenly, President Reagan's belief that the construction of the new airfield was potentially the precursor to something more than "economic development" was fully justified. General Austin was a member of the New Jewel Movement (The New Joint Endeavor for Welfare, Education, and Liberation—a Marxist-Leninist movement) of Grenada, and now that he had assassinated Prime Minister Bishop in a bid for power he was also the de facto chairman of the newly established Military Council. It was a classic power-grab, one that would soon trigger a response from American forces.

The island of Grenada, as part of the British Commonwealth, was technically still a constitutional monarchy—Queen Elizabeth II as head of state—and its government headed by its prime minister, Governor General of Grenada, Sir Paul Scoon. By law, Sir Paul was an appointed representative of the queen on the island. He did not support the takeover of the government, had secretly requested American intervention, and hoped that somehow, with the support of President Reagan and American military intervention, a democratic government could be reinstituted and strengthened. Sir Paul was a well-liked and respected man who maintained a good relationship with the United States during his tenure.

However, one of the primary issues initially following the coup was the immediate imposition of a twenty-four hour curfew by General Austin's forces with orders to shoot anyone caught violating it on sight. For the American students at St. George's School of Medicine, this posed a very basic problem—food and water were scarce and any attempt to gather them would now be a potentially deadly gambit. This fact alone was a major factor in the decision to move quickly to combat operations. Now that American lives were directly threatened by the provincial military council, President Regan had a stronger position from which to act unilaterally.

Complicating the matter, however, was the lack of tactical intelligence both during the planning phase and execution phase of the invasion. Scant information was available about the PRA force strength, capability, and supplies. Senior military commanders pored over all available information, taking a close look at all the potential factors from the geography

⌃ **SEALs conducting a daytime freefall jump from a C-130 Hercules**

and layout of the island to which American military forces were available to undertake an invasion. After much deliberation, it was decided that a multi-pronged assault would be the best strategy.

One element of Navy SEALs from [redacted] would parachute in off the coast, take their Zodiac boats to go ashore and then seize the airfield while two more elements would come in via helo and simultaneously take the primary radio tower and the governor's mansion where Sir Paul Scoon was hunkered down. U.S. Army Rangers would airdrop in and relieve the SEALs at the airfield and U.S. Marines would land to the north and push southward, taking strategic points along the way. Unfortunately, despite the overall success of the operation, almost nothing went according to plan.

OPERATION URGENT FURY

ISLAND OF GRENADA

OCTOBER 25, 1983

The familiar sound of the rotors of the UH-60 Black Hawk helicopter washed over the men of SEAL [redacted] as they prepared to fast-rope into the chaos below. Continuous gunfire erupted from seemingly all directions and the whole area near Governor-General Scoon's mansion was a mix of eerie lights from the vehicles below and the voices of Provisional Revolutionary Army troops shouting commands.

It was pure, unadulterated havoc—just like situations the SEALs had faced time and time again in training.

Petty Officer Second Class Mitchell stepped up to the rope dangling into the darkness below and prepared to slide down. A moment before heading into the fray, a 7.62 caliber round slammed into his elbow.

"I'm hit . . . I've been shot!"

His teammate, legendary Vietnam-era SEAL Chief Brian Mason, stepped up and took a quick look at the wounded arm and gave the younger SEAL a slightly incredulous look, "Well, what the hell do you think happens in war?"

Right. Great point, Chief.

The other men just grinned as their teammate jumped onto the rope and slid down, followed at about one-second intervals with the rest of the boat crew. Once on the ground the men fanned out quickly, returned fire briefly with short, precise bursts from their CAR-15 rifles, and then took off at a dead sprint for the Governor's Mansion. The mission was simple: secure Sir Paul Scoon and his family and get them to safety.

Chief Mason directed two of the SEALs to take up security positions just outside the mansion while the main element breached the front door and began sweeping the inner rooms looking for hostiles as they searched for the governor. As the SEALs searched the building, the PRA troops focused their attack and continued to barrage the area with small arms fire. A SEAL sniper, Petty Officer Larson, took up a position on the second floor and began using precision fire to methodically take down the enemy fighters, but every time he did, it seemed like another member of the PRA would take his place.

After a thorough search of the mansion, Lieutenant Rodgers finally found the governor hiding inside a locked room in the basement. After Sir Paul heard the American accent of the SEALs he had opened the door, "Sir, we are Navy SEALs and are here to rescue you and your family. We will keep you safe."

"Thank you, thank you!" the governor said, with obvious relief in his voice.

While the SEALs from Lieutenant Rodgers' squad locked down the area surrounding the mansion, another element of men from SEAL [redacted] simultaneously took over the radio tower building. Long-time SEAL veteran, Chief Washington, directed Petty Officer Smith, a new junior enlisted man on the team, to go out near the road nearby and stop any traffic coming through the area.

"Head out there and shut down that road," he growled in his deep baritone voice.

Petty Officer Smith nodded and responded,

"Roger that, Chief," checked his shortened M60 machine gun and ran out to get the job done.

A few minutes later, a large truck came lumbering toward the newly formed checkpoint and the young SEAL began to wave them off. The driver, looking a little bit nervous, immediately began to back up and turn around. Just when Petty Officer Smith thought the truck would simply go on its way it came to an abrupt halt and began to slowly back up right toward his position.

"What in the hell is this guy doing?" he murmured under his breath as he watched the truck roll slowly toward him.

It came to a stop, but Petty Officer Smith's instincts were lighting up like a Christmas tree and he took an aggressive grip on his weapon as he readied himself. In a flash, the back canvas flaps covering the entryway into the back of the truck flew open, revealing a large group of PRA soldiers. After a brief moment to register what was going on, the young SEAL opened up on the truck and let loose an enormous volume of fire. Body parts and blood went flying all over the back of the truck as about twenty of the enemy soldiers were cut down by the massive amount of lead shredding them to pieces.

Chief Washington came running out to see what was going on, "What in the hell happened—it's a damn bloodbath in there."

After Smith briefly relayed the incident, the older SEAL nodded in approval.

"Well, son of a bitch, you just might end up with the most kills of this whole cluster of an operation," he began before adding, "get back inside and take up a good defensive position—I have a feeling we're gonna have a lot of company."

An understatement, as it would turn out.

As the SEALs at the governor's mansion and radio tower continued to repel continuous waves of enemy attack over the next few hours, Marines from 2nd Battalion, 8th Marine Regiment, continued their push south after taking Pearls Airport near the northern coast of the island. A platoon of SEALs from SEAL Team FOUR, under the command of Lieutenant Mike Walsh, had chosen to do an air assault instead of a classic amphibious landing due to the recommendation of Walsh's SEALs who had reconnoitered the beach. A classic SEAL mission, hydrographic reconnaissance is taught early on in BUD/S and refined as training progresses.

Meanwhile, the Rangers of the Alpha and Bravo Company, 75th Ranger Regiment, were having their own problems. The C-130 troop transport had encountered navigational issues and was thirty minutes late of the planned insertion timeline. To top it off, Point Salines International Airport, the intended target, had multiple obstructions on the runway thanks to the PRA forces attempt to prevent the American forces from landing. This pushed the Ranger commander to order a low-level parachute drop mid-flight en route to the airport. Normally, a static-line low-level jump will be from approximately 1,250 feet, but because the aircraft was late to the drop zone, the Rangers would have to jump in full daylight, raising concerns from the commander that his men would remain vulnerable too long from that height. The Rangers were ordered to jump from 500 feet. A 500-foot jump is barely higher than some "BASE jumps" made off high cliffs by sport jumpers. This is not so much of a problem unless you are loaded down with gear. And, in this case, the Rangers were jumping in with over 100 pounds of equipment, which can make for a very rough landing.

Even so, the Rangers of the 75th jumped in and maneuvered north to take the airport, meeting moderate resistance along the way. Accurate and precise fire support from AC-130 gunships and U.S. Navy A-7 Corsair's helped ensure the Rangers' success as the day progressed.

As day turned into night at the governor's mansion, the SEAL Teams continued to repel the enemy assault. However, they had two major issues: their communications gear was damaged and they were running dangerously low on ammunition. Lieutenant Rodgers ordered the men to ration their ammo the best they could and continue using precision fire to hold back the enemy. Although calm and cool under fire, the lieutenant knew they needed to get some kind of communications with the commanders in the States who had no way of knowing how the SEALs mission was progressing.

Just when it appeared there would be a lull in the action, the SEALs heard the sound of an armored personnel carrier, in this case, a Russian-made BTR-60 with a 30mm gun mount, beginning to approach their position. The normal tactical response to such a problem was the easy to operate and immensely popular M72 Light Anti-Tank Weapon (LAW). The LAW fired an unguided, 66mm rocket officially capable of penetrating eight inches of steel plate, which is usually enough for light armored vehicles.

However, the SEALs did not have a LAW rocket on hand due to the other squad of SEALs having been waved off when their UH-60 helicopter started taking major small arms fire on the way into the area. The SEALs at Sir Paul Scoon's mansion knew they were in trouble and needed close air support—fast.

Their radios simply would not work and they had did not have any backup communications available. Just when the SEALs thought they were completely without options, the governor spoke up.

"Lieutenant Rodgers," he began with a thick mix of British and Caribbean accent, "my personal telephone is upstairs in my office and should still be functional should the militants have been absent minded enough to forget to cut the connection."

The SEAL officer glanced over to one of his men in charge of communications, visibly seeking his opinion.

"It just might work, sir—we should definitely give it a shot."

Less than five minutes later, the central communications dispatcher at the Special Operations Command Center received the call and routed them through to the Command Staff.

"Good evening, sir, it has been a hell of a day so far," Lieutenant Rodgers said as the sound of small arms fire continued in the background.

Major General Richard Sholtes, Joint Special Operations Commander, was present for the call. "It is good to hear from you Lieutenant, we've been a little concerned here with the lack of contact."

"Sir, we have had some problems but the governor is under our protection at this time. We've continued to hold off the enemy with sniper fire but I believe they are preparing a counterattack with light armored personnel carriers."

"Understood, we'll ensure the air units in the area have your coordinates—stand by and we'll get you some air support."

"Roger that, sir."

The young SEAL Officer personally made his way to each of his men's emplacements to relay the message: the proverbial cavalry was on its way.

Soon afterward, a lone AC-130 Spectre gunship flew into position as the main gunner locked onto the target and lit up the enemy BTR-60 with its powerful 20mm Vulcan Cannon.

The ground shook as the heavy depleted uranium rounds of the 20mm cannon destroyed the enemy

≈ A SEAL training for night ops—most missions are done under the cover of darkness

vehicle and tore into the surrounding area. PRA troops nearby were killed instantly and the rest were left terribly shaken. It was then the SEALs knew they would definitely last through the night.

At the radio tower, the situation had taken a major turn for the worse as a large PRA contingent stormed the area in a last-ditch attempt to retake the communications building and force the SEALs there to withdraw. The enemy soldiers and their APCs continued to rake the building with small arms and 30mm cannons. As the SEALs continued to fight, the building was literally beginning to fall apart all around them and they soon knew the team would have to extract.

"If we don't get out of this hellhole we're dead," Chief Washington said in his typical no-nonsense and matter-of-fact manner.

Petty Officer Smith gave a grim look to the grizzled SEAL chief and they nodded in agreement. It was time to move no matter what risk that might pose.

In any tactical situation one must balance the mission objectives with the danger faced and potential cost to the team. Professional warriors like the SEALs are prepared to take any risk as long as there is a solid purpose to it. A good team leader or commander will never throw away the life of his men or subject them to great risk, especially when the chances of success are small, without a good reason. However, sometimes action is necessary no matter how risky or how much danger is involved. In this case, the SEALs knew they were out of good options and it was time for a "tactical withdrawal."

The men stacked up on a back door to the radio tower and prepared to make a run for it. *We are dead men for sure,* Chief Washington thought as he got ready to open the door.

"No matter what happens, head for the water and we'll regroup there," he yelled above the noise of the massive gunfire all around them.

Navy SEALs work long hours to become comfortable in the water, so much so that it becomes a safe haven for them. There are many good units who understand and have good skills in land warfare, but the SEALs also make the water their home.

The men nodded as the Chief kicked open the door and began to sprint across an open field toward the coastline. Bullets were flying everywhere and he took a shot in the arm that nearly tore it off at the elbow. Another round blew off the heel of his right boot, but fortunately didn't hit the foot. After a brief tumble, he grabbed his other elbow pad and used it to make a quick bandage for his right arm, which was now barely hanging on. Despite the pain, he kept his composure and kept moving.

"Damn Chief, that arm is a wreck," Petty Officer Smith observed after they made it over the ridgeline.

"Yeah, it's gonna need some attention once we get out of this mess."

The SEALs made it to the water and began to swim parallel to the shoreline. But, it didn't offer much protection unless they got much further out. After a bit of time, they came across an outcropping with some vegetation and rocks that offered them temporary sanctuary.

Holed up in the outcropping, the SEALs redistributed their ammo and what meager rations they had left and hunkered down. They made sure everyone had some ammo for their sidearm, a knife, and a bit to eat. They hadn't slept for almost three days and although they were temporarily out of sight, they all knew they would eventually have to move and look for a way to get out to sea.

"Hey, Smith, take Johnny with you and go see if you can find some boats or something to get us out to sea," the SEAL Chief said through the pain. If you don't find anything make your way out as far as you can and wait for the rescue aircraft to spot you." SEALs feel pain like everyone else, but learn to manage and compartmentalize it in a way that allows them to push on past any normal human limits.

Part of what drives the men past all reasonable limits is the training, but in many ways it is the SEAL ethos and culture that inspires them to keep going even further than they even realize they can when they begin the journey. The "Never Quit" mentality is drilled into every trainee relentlessly until it is burned into your psyche. You learn to continuously raise the bar of what you expect of yourself and your team and a deep sense of honor and commitment to the warrior code brings it all together. The strength of the SEAL brotherhood and the actions of the men who came before you also push you to want to ensure you are living up to their example and beyond.

Chief Washington and the rest of the squad waited it out awhile, but U.S. Navy A-7 Corsairs began pounding the area nearby in an attempt to wipe out the Grenadian forces. Unfortunately for the SEALs, those bombs started dropping way too close for comfort near their location. Washington then shared what was likely a mutual sentiment, "Well, this bullshit of a day just took yet another turn for the worse—let's get the hell out of here."

The SEALs with him managed a grin despite the nasty situation they were facing and nodded in approval. After taking a final moment to gather themselves, the Frogmen made a break for it and ran straight to the water. It was unlikely the other men were coming back, so they had to assume they headed out to sea and it was time for them to do the same.

Six hours later, a C-130 aircraft went flying overhead and spotted a flare launched by the SEALs to grab its attention. Before long, the C-130 crew marked their position and radioed for the nearest ship to come pick the SEALs up. Miraculously, the other men Chief Washington had sent off to search for a boat had ended up in nearly the same patch of water out at sea.

Back at the governor-general's mansion, the SEALs had continued to repel much smaller counterattacks by PRA forces and remained hunkered down until daybreak. Although it didn't go exactly as planned, essentially they had accomplished their mission of finding Sir Paul and keeping him safe. A few hours after first light, the Marine Corps units moving south from Pearls Airfield finally made it to the location, relieving the SEALs and assisting in an evacuation.

By this time, Marine Corps and Ranger units had also secured the two student campuses on the island where American medical students lived and studied. The young students were beyond relieved when the Americans came to their rescue. As the hours passed, the remaining PRA forces were either killed or captured by the elite American forces.

Unfortunately, despite the overall victory and success of the operation, the U.S. forces did suffer some tragic losses during the initial hours of the invasion. Of note, twelve U.S. Navy SEALs had orders to parachute in forty kilometers off shore and then use their small CRRC boats to rendezvous with navy ships in the area before heading off to the island to assist in the raid. However, weather conditions had abruptly taken a turn for the worse and the SEALs jumped into rough seas with twelve-foot swells. Even for these highly trained warriors the conditions proved to be fatal and four of the brave men drowned. The other SEALs of the unit had catastrophic mechanical problems with the boats and despite a heroic effort to continue the mission under terrible conditions, ultimately were unable to make it ashore.

However, the aftermath of operation URGENT FURY proved to be a great opportunity to learn.

The chain of command immediately realized that interoperability and communications between units from other services was almost completely zero and there was no quick way to resolve the issue. Additionally, the SEALs on the ground, many of whom were veterans of the Vietnam era, saw the operation as a good reminder that no matter how good you think you are, it is imperative that you do not underestimate your opponent. The PRA troops had fought hard and nearly killed many more of the elite SEALs. Although most of the men made it home, those who were there took the lessons in stride and ensured the men at each respective team got a reminder during debriefing that there is no room for complacency.

For the SEALs, their motto—"Earn your Trident every day"—came even more clearly into focus.

As a result of the lessons learned, Congress passed the Goldwater-Nichols Act a few years later in 1986, a bill which provided the most sweeping changes to the organizational command structure of the military since the National Security Act of 1947. The new legislation created the Chairman of the Joint Chiefs of Staff, which intended to counter inter-service rivalry by placing one commander in place to direct the overall strategy of an operation instead of having to go independently to each Joint Chief. Also, the chain of command was streamlined further by placing the Chairman of the Joint Chiefs directly under the Secretary of Defense, reporting straight to him, and placing the Secretary of each service in more of an advisory role.

The first test of the new system took place in 1989 when the U.S. military was yet again called into action in Panama. Dubbed Operation Just Cause, the conflict provided another opportunity for the SEALs to prove their immense value in securing our nation's vital interests abroad—it also served as another step toward shaping the SEALs of the future.

Soon after Grenada, the SEALs would again prove why they are America's deadliest warriors.

SEALs killed in Grenada, but not forgotten: Machinist Mate 1st Kenneth J. Butcher, Quartermaster 1st Kevin E. Lundberg, Hull Technician 1st Stephen L. Morris, and Senior Chief Engineman Robert R. Schamberger.

6

SHAPING THE FUTURE– OPERATION JUST CAUSE

Former CIA Case Officer, James "Cowboy" Smith, walked into his living room just as the regular programming was interrupted by the familiar voice of his former boss, George H. W. Bush. At this moment, President Bush was explaining to the American people why combat operations in the small Central American nation of Panama were justified.

Smith took another sip of his evening tea and thought to himself, "*I knew it was only a matter of time . . . they should have listened to me.*"

As he listened to the president's speech, it became clear that something major had triggered the situation, but the seasoned former intelligence operative wasn't totally buying the explanation. He thought back to the many cables he had sent back to headquarters, which, as far as he was concerned, painted a grim picture of the future stability of the

Panamanian government. A sentiment, he reflected, that was based on first-hand knowledge of the dictator himself: General Manuel Noriega.

"General Noriega's reckless threats and attacks upon Americans in Panama created an imminent danger to the 35,000 American citizens in Panama. As president, I have no higher obligation than to safeguard the lives of American citizens," President Bush said from his desk inside the Oval Office during the live broadcast."

Within a minute of broadcasting the speech on TV, Smith's phone was already ringing.

"You called this one a long time ago, buddy," a familiar gruff yet cheery voice said over the phone.

Smith nodded to himself, "Noriega started going off the rails years ago . . . do you remember all the dirt we had piled up on him? Crazy drug parties, throwing rivals out of his plane at 10,000 feet, and doing whatever it would take to maneuver into position to take over."

"I remember—we should have taken him out when we had the chance."

The veteran CIA operative smiled in agreement as President Bush continued his speech to lay out his case for military intervention. The United States had concluded that General Noriega must be taken into custody for his crimes and involvement in international drug trafficking, but the real trigger was far worse.

General Manuel Noriega: military officer, CIA informant, dictator, major drug trafficker, and all-around criminal.

For many years General Noriega was a highly valued CIA asset—highly valued and highly paid. Some reports show he was paid $100,000 annually, which was later increased to $200,000 for his long-term cooperation and information on various local and international groups of great interest to the United States. However, when the opportunity came for him to make a political move and take power, he didn't hesitate to use his position to make the pieces fall into place.

Most people know that the nation of Panama holds strategic value due to the highly useful Panama Canal. However, what most people do not know is

≈ Operation Just Cause—20,000 people were displaced as the chaos erupted around them

that there exists a record demonstrating an understanding of the usefulness of the region dating as far back as 1534. Charles V, Holy Roman Emperor and King of Spain, ordered an expedition to survey the "Isthmus of Panama" to explore the possibility of building the canal to ease passage for Spanish vessels traveling to and from Peru. However, it would literally be centuries later in 1914 when the U.S.-owned region of Panama would finally open a fully functional canal after multiple attempts by various nations to achieve a similar creation.

Now, the Panama Canal was wrapped up in the complexities of modern geo-politics and General Noriega made sure to profit from it.

In 1984, as the de facto ruler, Noriega allowed the first elections in sixteen years to take place in Panama, but when the vote looked like it would be a landslide victory for former President Arnulo Arias the dictator forcibly put a halt to the count. After what was believed to be a massive fraud, the government announced a victory for Arias's opponent, Nicolas Vallarino. This and the revelation that Noriega was behind various political and personal assassinations led to a severe downturn in the relations between the U.S. and Noriega.

Tensions continued to build until 1989 when another election was held and it became clear that Noriega had intended to declare his choice for president, Carlos Duque, no matter what the outcome of the vote. However, when it became clear that Duque would lose three to one in the election he refused to go along with Noriega's plan. Rather than let this come to light, Noriega chose to void the election and name Francisco Rodriguez, a longtime associate, as the new president. The United States did not recognize Rodriguez as the legitimate president.

The scenario resulted in the imposition of economic sanctions by the U.S. and eventually led Noriega and his followers to declare a state of war between Panama and the United States, which later was a primary factor in the decision to invade by President Bush. Nevertheless, the final push President Bush needed to order the invasion actually surrounded a situation that occurred in December 1989 concerning a young Navy SEAL officer and his wife.

SEAL Lieutenant Adam Curtis had just flown his wife in country for a visit down in Panama a few days prior on December 16, 1989. Lieutenant Curtis had been assigned to SBU-26 (Special Boat Unit), which had gained a reputation for being the "rulers of the rivers" in the area. The men of SBU-26 kept the waterways of Panama under tight control.

After arriving at the airport, the young SEAL Officer had decided to take his wife out to a nice dinner before heading back to base. As the political situation in Panama continued to heat up it made life increasingly dangerous, especially for the American's stationed at nearby bases. Lieutenant Curtis and his wife Bonnie finished dinner and began to head back to the base but had gotten turned around and the driver made a few wrong turns, which led to them ending up right outside a Panamanian Defense Force (PDF) checkpoint.

Ahead of them was a car full of Marines who had been stopped by the PDF security forces. Lieutenant Curtis waited to see how it would all play out, and moments later the Marines made a run for it. The PDF opened fire on their vehicle, killing Marine Corps 1st Lieutenant Paz with a shot that hit him in the back. Knowing he wasn't in a position to help in any way, Lieutenant Curtis pulled the car up and awaited what he thought would be simple harassment and some inconvenient searching of their car.

It turned out to be their worst nightmare.

The PDF security pulled them from their car and began to beat the SEAL officer with their rifles and simultaneously rough up his wife, Bonnie. Before they knew it, the couple was arrested and taken to a nearby prison for interrogation. What started out as a simple night out to dinner had quickly become essentially a POW situation.

With one American serviceman dead and another being held for interrogation, the final pieces were in place to give justification to take down Noriega. President Bush was now ready to make the call to invade and restore order and democracy.

Another provocation was the case of an American citizen, Kurt Muse, who had been part of an underground radio broadcast speaking out against Noriega. He had been arrested and thrown in the notorious Panamanian prison, Carcel Modelo, months earlier by the PDF. Muse later recounted the ordeal saying that although he was not physically tortured, he was put into solitary confinement and was in fear daily as he listened to the screams of fellow inmates.

"You died a million deaths—horrible people doing horrible things to their own people," he was quoted as saying after his rescue by Army commandos during the initial stage of the invasion.

A technicality in a treaty signed years previous had allowed for the treatment of a spouse of an American citizen who served in the government by an American physician while in custody. Since Muse's wife was a Department of Defense employee, he qualified under the terms of the agreement and was receiving daily visits by an American doctor who later helped him smuggle a letter to President Bush out of the prison. Amazingly, the letter actually made it to the White House.

For the SEALs, a large problem had developed: an intense debate over the proper planning and strategy for the mission they had been given—disable Noriega's personal plane and boat to prevent his escape.

A combat swimmer operation to disable Noriega's personal yacht was reasonably straightforward, but the raid on Paitilla Airfield raised numerous concerns. Senior Navy leadership, including command elements from the Naval Special Warfare community, had called for a large strike force of SEALs, forty-eight in all, to complete the assault on the airfield. Such a plan would require multiple SEAL platoons to work together in a highly volatile combat environment in a way and using methods that were not traditionally utilized by the SEAL Teams.

SEALs normally like to operate in smaller teams, sometimes as small as two to four men, but frequently squad-sized groups of eight men will be used. During this period, they normally would not ever work in groups larger that a full platoon of around sixteen SEALs. It was generally assumed that large-scale missions like airfield seizure would be best suited to U.S. Army Rangers, who could drop hundreds of men on a target and take it over lightning fast with overwhelming force and firepower.

A handful of senior SEAL officers who took part in the initial planning, vehemently disagreed with the mission concept and offered multiple alternatives which they believed better suited the SEALs fundamental approach: surprise, speed, and violence of action. They argued that attempting to maneuver approximately fifty SEALs under the given circumstances was tantamount to operational suicide.

Their alternative plans were all some form of classic SEAL-style operations: sneak in, use technology, speed, and relative superiority to their advantage to destroy the potential getaway aircraft without ever being noticed. Then, use the ensuing chaos to their advantage to whittle down the PDF soldiers and lock down the airport.

Despite a valiant stand against the chain-of-command, their approach was ultimately overruled and the multi-platoon task-force concept was implemented with the men of SEAL Team FOUR assigned the assault. In those days, SEAL Teams had regional assignments and so each would focus on specific tactics relative to their assigned tasking. SEAL Team FOUR was officially the SEAL Team tasked with Central and South American operations. The men began to rehearse immediately and attempted to quickly overcome the tactical pitfalls of the strategy they were ordered to utilize.

It would turn out to be a deadly mistake for the SEALs.

OPERATION JUST CAUSE

PUNTA PAITILLA AIRFIELD

DECEMBER 20, 1989, 0045 HOURS

Bravo, Delta, and Golf platoons reached the edge of the airfield and hustled out of their CRRCs (Combat River Raiding Craft) amid the sounds of American airpower already overhead and inflicting heavy casualties on the PDF forces. Intel had suggested that the airfield at Punta Paitilla would have light resistance and be an easy approach for the SEALs. However, bright lights shined all over the area making concealed movement a near impossibility. Combined with the airstrikes already underway, the SEALs crucial element of surprise was already lost.

Determined to push ahead, the SEALs moved towards their rehearsed positions. Bravo platoon would move the light aircraft on the field onto the runway, Delta platoon would take control of the towers, and Golf platoon would go straight for the hangar. Two Air Force Combat Controllers would join them and assist in linking the SEALs with an AC-130 gunship loitering overhead, which was prepared to offer major fire support as needed.

As Golf platoon got closer to the hangar, a series of more bright lights came on further exposing their position. A gruff-sounding PDF soldier yelled for them to drop their weapons.

"Negative, you drop your weapons immediately!" came the reply from a Spanish-speaking SEAL in the platoon.

Within seconds, the PDF troops opened up with an astounding volume of fire, killing four of the

SEALs outright and wounding many more. It was already apparent that the plan forced upon the men was a tactical disaster.

"We've got major casualties . . . request immediate assistance!" the SEAL radioman said over the command net.

Delta platoon's commander ordered his SEALs to rush forward and reinforce Golf platoon immediately. Technically, Golf's mission was only to disable the aircraft in the hangar, but it had turned into a firefight for their lives. It took the men less than a couple of minutes to reach the hangar to assist, but in a gunfight seconds can feel like hours.

Using light machine guns and standard CAR-15s, the SEALs returned fire with precision and began taking out some of the PDF soldiers. But it was obvious that taking out Noriega's aircraft with "minimal collateral damage" was quickly becoming an impossible task. Chief Don McFaul was already wounded but courageously continued fighting and running from man to man to render medical aid.

"Get that AT-4 ready to go . . . we're going to blast that plane to hell," the SEAL Chief said as he pointed to one of his remaining unwounded teammates. Calm, cool, and collected under fire, Chief McFaul was a pillar of professionalism and the warrior spirit.

One of the SEALs readied the rocket launcher and took cover behind the fallen SEALs as he prepped his shot. He'd only get one chance.

Moments later, the rocket streaked across the runway and slammed into the side of Noriega's aircraft, going off with a massive fireball and rocking the entire hangar area. Smiling to himself, the young SEAL looked over his shoulder and said, "How about that Chief?"

But, right before the blast, Chief McFaul had taken raking fire to the chest from one of the PDF soldiers and died almost instantly while dragging his teammate, Petty Officer Moreno, to safety. In his final moment, Chief McFaul had valiantly laid on top of his wounded teammate to help ensure his survival.

Although later successful, the Air Force Combat Controllers were never able to establish communications with the AC-130 overhead during the short but intense fight for the hangar. The after-action report indicated that the radio and communications traffic in the area had been so concentrated that they were unable to lock into their signal and maintain a connection.

Communications failure in war only adds to the chaos and ultimately degrades a team's ability to fight cohesively thereby reducing overall combat effectiveness. However, the superior training and iron will of the SEALs drove them on to success even when everything was seemingly falling apart around them.

Concurrent with the attack on the airfield, a SEAL combat swimmer team executed what could be considered a picture perfect limpet mine attack on Noriega's patrol boat, the *Presidente' Porras*. The blast from the mine tore the small ship apart and practically shook the walls of the nearby Panamanian buildings, rendering the vessel completely useless and unrecoverable. It is considered to be the first ever SEAL mission to successfully execute a mine attack on an enemy ship of battle.

Additionally, there was another little known element in action during the opening hour of the invasion. A group of SEALs and members of SBU-26 were tasked with investigating sniper fire from a nearby bridge. SEAL Chief Don Mann (author) literally ran from his quarters at Fort Amador toward Rodman Naval Base carrying his weapon and equipment when a jeep full of Army soldiers saw him and asked, "What in the hell are you doing?"

"I'm a Navy SEAL Chief and I have to get to Rodman now!" he said in his matter-of-fact manner, trying to somewhat mask his excitement.

The men were astounded to realize that the seasoned SEAL was planning on making the four mile run on foot with full gear before they came along.

"Uh, right, well damn Chief, get on in—we'll get you there!"

Minutes later Chief Mann was at the pier boarding the patrol craft (Patrol Boat River, PBR), which was a lot like a decked-out Boston whaler armed with a .50 caliber machine gun and MK19 grenade launcher. As the wind blew past their face and the boat sped to their destination, Chief Mann couldn't help thinking to himself, *You know, this really is kind of an insane mission . . . we are heading into check on a possible enemy sniper who probably has cover from an elevated position.*

Even with those thoughts running through his head, SEALs are ultimately men of action, and men like that don't like sitting on the sidelines, so insane mission or not, it felt good to get out and do something productive like take out an enemy sniper.

The SEALs got closer to the bridge and started immediately taking sniper fire. After a bit of work to zero in on his location, the SEALs went full throttle and maneuvered the patrol craft toward the enemy position. Upon seeing the overwhelming firepower they were about to bring to bear on him, the PDF sniper quickly lost heart and decided to make a run for it.

With all their primary missions now accomplished, the remaining SEALs on the ground regrouped, hunkered down in the hangar, and prepared the wounded men for medevac transport. A mission that many senior commanders had deemed a "walk in the park" had turned into a successful but deadly evening for the SEALs.

In the aftermath of the mission, controversy about the plan continued and led to a fair amount of

⌃ **Members of Special Boat Team 22 conduct an exercise with the SEALs**

infighting among some of the SEALs leadership. Although technically a success, it is generally agreed upon that the decision to use such a large force of SEALs in a way that did not maximize their effectiveness through traditional stealth and speed tactics was a primary factor in the loss of life. Some veteran SEALs stood fast by their belief that the raid on Paitilla airfield should never have been a SEAL mission at all and instead should have gone to a unit like the Army Rangers, who are better equipped for such a task.

Regardless of the loss of life, ultimately the operation was a success. And, the outcome of the invasion of Panama did ultimately lead to new lessons learned and served as another reminder that proper planning and communications are crucial to minimizing casualties and achieving mission objectives.

Noriega was captured soon after major combat operations were complete and flown back to the United States to face trial for his role in the international drug trade. He was sentenced to thirty years in prison and later extradited to France where he was put to trial for additional criminal charges and convicted. The Panamanian government, however, later requested a special conditional release of Noriega from the French prison so he could be extradited to Panama, where he would face charges of human rights violations.

Now, at eighty-three years of age, he lives out his days at the Renacer prison nearby the jungle areas of the Panama Canal.

For the SEALs, Panama served as yet another training ground for future operations. Hard lessons were written in the blood of SEALs who held to the highest ideals of honor and the warrior code: LT John Connors, ENC Don McFaul, BM1 Chris Tilgman, and TM2 Issac Rodriguez paid the ultimate price, but in doing so allowed their fellow SEALs to learn lessons that would help continue to mold the men into the fighting force they are today.

In the years ahead, such valor would continue to be common among the U.S. Navy SEAL Teams.

7

HEROISM IN ABUNDANCE—NAVY SEALs IN SOMALIA

In the fall of 1991, the country of Somalia was experiencing horrendous internal strife that led to literally hundreds of thousands of deaths of the country's citizens. Various warlords vying for control of the resources within the region were constantly in a state of war with one another. This infighting devastated the agricultural base of Somalia and although nations throughout the world began to send food to the war-torn country, vast amounts were hijacked and stolen by tribal leaders. Some reports say as much as 80 percent of the food was taken in this way and never reached those in need.

American leadership in Washington, D.C., under President George H. W. Bush decided that a more direct role was necessary and began planning a massive relief effort. Operation Provide Relief was officially launched in August 1992 and consisted of ten C-130 transport aircraft and four-hundred aid workers who ultimately delivered approximately 48,000 tons of food and medical supplies. However, without military power stationed in the region to supervise, it proved difficult to ensure the starving Somali people were properly cared for, and unfortunately the death toll rose to a massive 500,000 with another 1.5 million forced out of their homes.

To combat this problem, the next step issued by the President was dubbed Operation Restore Hope—officially known as United Nations Security Council Resolution 794.

The lead up to this entire situation can be traced back in part to January 1991 when Somalian President Mohammed Siad Barre was overthrown in a civil war that broke out between the established government and various tribal factions vying for control. Most of the official Somali National Army completely dissolved and many of the soldiers were absorbed into the regional forces or were recruited by one of the warring factions. Lawlessness thrived and people began to suffer on a greater scale.

Of all the factions, a few were able to establish the primary positions of power, the main being the United Somali Congress (USC). Later, the USC split into two primary factions: one led by Ali Mahdi Muhammad (who eventually became president), another led by the notorious outlaw Mohamed Farrah Aidid.

In all, four main groups were present—the USC, the Somali Salvation Democratic Front (SSDF), the Somali Patriotic Movement (SPM), and the Somali Democratic Movement (SDM). This situation in Somalia serves to highlight the difficulty faced when attempting to intervene on a humanitarian level in a foreign nation. With no centralized government with which to negotiate and coordinate a relief effort, it can be exceptionally chaotic. This makes for a wild and unpredictable situation, one primed for violent outbreaks.

Operation Restore Hope consisted of a large contingent of United States Marines of the 15th Marine Expeditionary Unit. The Marines charged ahead into the country and quickly secured a large area of the city of Mogadishu as well as the naval port and local airport. Soon after, they were reinforced by various elements of the 7th Marines and U.S. Army's 10th Mountain Division.

For months, the American military presence helped secure the flow of badly needed supplies, but the units present were not given a directive to engage in seek-and-destroy operations against the warring factions. So, while much more of the food and medicine flowing into the country did ultimately go to help the ravaged population, the warlords continued their fighting and still were able to manage to disrupt the relief efforts to a great degree.

During this time, the Navy SEALs and other special operations forces maintained an exceptionally high training tempo and were coming off of the victory in Iraq during Desert Storm. The old adage, "if you stay ready, you don't have to get ready" remained the constant philosophy of America's top warriors. More specifically, the men of [redacted] were training and operating all over the world. As it turns out, it would not be long before they would asked to assist in Somalia.

UN Secretary Boutros Boutros-Ghali made an official statement in March 1993 showing support for

Resolution 794 since he believed it was clear that the American presence in Somalia was indeed helping. However, the massive disarray in the country meant that no reliable central and secure government, police force, or any true standing army existed. The chaos made it difficult to achieve the kind of success the international leaders were hoping for in war-torn Somalia. With hopes of creating some kind of stability, the UN Security Council signed an authorization to enact UNOSOM II (United Nations Operation in Somalia) to supersede UNITAF, the United States-led but UN-sanctioned operation already in effect. Officially, the UNOSOM II agreement was confirmed by all parties involved, including the many warring factions within Somalia, at a conference held in Addis Ababa, Ethiopia. That is, all but one—the warlord known as Mohammed Farrah Aidid.

In response to this call for unity, Aidid utilized his control over the airwaves with Radio Mogadishu to broadcast anti-United Nations material aimed at preventing any attempt to consolidate the various factions against him in a unified effort. An order was given to shut down the radio station, but the plot to do so was uncovered by Aidid thanks to various spies he had working in the area. In addition, Aidid's people discovered the existence of a plan to conduct inspections at the radio station main building, based on UN information networks claiming Aidid maintained a weapons cache inside. Aidid had no interest in cooperating and sent a large militia unit to intercede. The subsequent attack on June 5, 1993, resulted in the death of twenty-four Pakistani troops with another fifty-seven wounded, plus three wounded American troops and one Italian soldier as well.

The next day, the UN Security Council voted in favor of Resolution 837—a directive "to locate, arrest, and prosecute the persons responsible for the death and wounding of the peacekeepers."

During the following week, American commanders made preparations for more direct action and issued orders on June 12 to begin attacking specified targets connected to Aidid in an attempt to bring him to justice. This part of the operation only lasted four days and was not successful in locating Aidid despite a highly coordinated effort and even the announcement of a twenty-five thousand dollar bounty for information that would lead U.S. forces to Aidid.

Approximately one month later, on July 12, American intelligence believed they had solid information on Aidid's current location inside a local safe house. Cobra attack helicopters led an assault on the compound, which ultimately killed sixty people, although the exact number of deaths was disputed. Aidid's interior minister claimed a great number of women and children were killed in the attack, but this was never proven. Aidid remained at large.

In early August 1993, the United States created Task Force Ranger with the specific intent of hunting Aidid and his lieutenants. The joint forces unit was made up of elite units of the Army, Navy, and Air Force: U.S. Army Rangers from Bravo Company, 3rd Battalion 75th Ranger Regiment, Navy SEALs from Naval Special Warfare Development Group ([redacted]), Army soldiers from the famed US Army Special Operations Command (USASOC), Air Force Pararescue or

"PJs," Air Force Combat Control Technicians (CCTs), and some of the finest aviators in the world from 1st Battalion, 160th Special Operations Aviation Regiment (the "Night Stalkers"). The group of highly trained warriors reported directly to the Task Force Commander, Major General William F. Garrison.

The internationally best-selling book and movie *Black Hawk Down* tells the story in great detail and is a must-read for anyone wanting to delve into the details. However, most documentaries and books about the Battle of Mogadishu focus on the Rangers, Delta Force soldiers, and a captured American pilot. Missing from this account is a substantial part of the story of the sniper element from [redacted] which was present and assisted in the rescue operation and eventual defeat of the Somali militants.

October rolled around quickly and it became clear to the National Command Authority that the best option to capture Aidid would be to send in an assault team on a moment's notice as soon as the intel officers could pinpoint his location. Warlords like Aidid are not stupid—far from it. And as such, know that remaining mobile is one of the basic tactics to use when a superior force is hunting you down.

Then it happened . . . credible information was obtained that gave the current location of Aidid's lieutenants—time to roll out. As this was primarily an Army-run operation, USASOC soldiers was selected to lead the raid on the primary location and members of the 75th Ranger Regiment would act as a blocking force, flying in and fast-roping down to surround the compound in which it was believed the men were hiding. The word in the American camp was that this would be a quick mission to snatch and grab a couple bad guys. The words "thirty minutes tops" were echoed by various senior leaders.

Four "chalks" or teams of Rangers loaded up the helicopters and prepared for liftoff. A full convoy of trucks and combat vehicles prepared to head into the city as well. The basic plan was simple: USASOC soldiers would hit the compound and grab the targets, Rangers would create the perimeter around the building, and the Ranger convoy would roll in, pick everyone up, and head back to base. Simple.

Simple, but full of potential disaster.

First of all, there exists a major rule in war—never underestimate your opponent. Be confident, trust your training, remind yourself of the importance of your mission, remember the tales of honor in generations past, which paid for the lessons of combat in blood. Do all these things . . . but still never assume it will be an easy fight.

In the story of David and Goliath there are many lessons which can be taken and applied to modern war, but that is one of them. Goliath, "a man trained in war since his youth," and physically much more powerful than the young David, was so overconfident that he chose not to wear one of the most important pieces of his armor—his helmet. This decision cost him his life.

Perhaps in some ways, the Americans that day on the hot and sandy streets of the war-ravaged city of Mogadishu made a similar mistake.

The SEAL sniper element was loaded up in an unarmored M-998 combat truck that didn't even have doors. Fortunately, the supply section of Task

Force Ranger had put some Kevlar ballistic matting on the floorboards to help with potential mines or IED devices.

It was a good thing too.

Commander Olson, the senior SEAL on-site for the operation, called his fellow Frogmen in for a quick briefing on the operation.

He began the impromptu brief in his usual relaxed yet commanding style: "Gentlemen, this will be a standard snatch-and-grab style op . . . USASOC will hit the target with Rangers from the Seventy-fifth providing their perimeter security. Once they assault the building you guys will grab the prisoners and get back to base."

Normally, the members of an operation of this complexity would get a full briefing that can take an hour or two, but the SEALs had been out on a separate mission [redacted] in the area. The clandestine work had taken up most of the previous day and continued through the current morning.

Walking up to one of his men, Olson slapped him on the back and said with a grin, "Shouldn't take long . . . Good luck and I'll see you when you get back."

The SEALs retreated to their team area long enough to do a gear check and grab some chow. Even though the mission plan was supposed to be quick, you never really know until you get out there how it will go. But the men of [redacted] were used to making the best of any bad situation and planning for any major contingency. One of the major elements that set apart the best and those who are merely great at what they do is a mastery of the basics. Every trade has that set of skills that are considered the most fundamental—in the parlance of American football, the best of the best "block and tackle well."

In the SEALs trade, it is much the same. Shooting, tactics, leadership, innovative thinking, supreme attention to detail, and of course, the fundamental things like speed, surprise, "violence of action," and courage. This [redacted], poised to go to work in the hot and extremely dangerous streets of Mogadishu, had mastered them all.

It was time for the SEALs to go to work.

OPERATION GOTHIC SERPENT

MOGADISHU, SOMALIA

OCTOBER 3, 1993

1542 HOURS

The whitewashed Olympic Hotel came clearly into view as SEAL sniper Howard Wasdin resisted the urge to hit the gas. Wasdin couldn't help but think to himself how frustrating the current situation was for them. *Dammit, I can only drive as fast as the lead vehicles will allow . . . What the hell is this, a lazy Sunday drive to sightsee?*

As the convoy seemingly crept forward, the USASOC operators had fast-roped into the target building approximately ten minutes earlier; the four chalks of Army Rangers had simultaneously gone into the courtyard and streets surrounding the compound with the intent of providing a security perimeter. Command and control assets had already made their first mistake of the day and had directed Black Hawk call sign Super Six-Seven, piloted by Chief Warrant Officer Jeff Niklaus, to the wrong location. Ranger

Chalk Four was now on the ground about a block north of their intended position and already under heavy enemy fire.

A relentless onslaught of radio traffic filled the comm systems; what seemed like a hundred different conversations were all going on at once. It was a little bit maddening to have such a massive amount of communications havoc taking place when all the SEALs wanted to do was get on with the mission.

Wasdin shook his head in annoyance as he turned to his teammate and close buddy, call sign Casanova. "I wish these idiots would just shut the hell up and clear the channel!"

Casanova nodded in agreement. "Yeah, I don't know what all the damn chatter is about—get in there and shoot the bastards and call it a day—simple."

⌃ **SEALs riding in a Humvee with heavy weapons mount**

Less than thirty seconds later he got his wish, if only for a short window, but it was not the news anyone wanted to hear.

"Man down! We need a medic! Ranger down!"

Army Ranger Private First Class Todd Blackburn, Chalk Four, missed the rope while leaning out to fast-rope to the ground. Black Hawk Super Six-Seven had been maintaining a hover at about seventy feet off the ground and the young Ranger fell the entire distance before landing in a crushing heap on the street below. Blackburn's head and back were severely injured, but he was alive.

However, little did everyone know that this "routine op" was about to really go to hell. Somali militia fighters had been getting riled up by Aidid's pronouncements over the radio about the "Imperialist Americans" and how the United States planned to destroy their homes. Mixing that message with a healthy dose of the popular local drug known as khat was a major recipe for a fight.

Aidid's men had been chewing on the leafy green plant all afternoon and were just about to slip into their manic phase, which tends to hit about one to two hours after you start chewing on the stuff. Unfortunately for Task Force Ranger, this meant that they were heading in right when the Somali's would be at their most aggressive. Anyone who has fought someone high on drugs, especially the mind-altering kinds that enhance aggression (PCP and such come to mind) knows that people can fight much harder and much longer than any normal human has a right to do when the dose is at its peak effectiveness. Fortunately, khat doesn't tend to make the user stronger, but it does make them *want* to fight.

Still, the SEALs are always ready for a fight if the need arises, which proved a good thing because all hell was about to break loose.

Hundreds of Somali fighters began surrounding the area, summoned by Aidid's men, who encouraged them "to defend their homes." Wasdin and his fellow SEALs had just rode into a storm of 7.62mm rounds flying around the area like a massive migrating horde of killer bees. The distinct sound of rounds whizzing past their heads took them to full alert—it was definitely time to fight.

The SEALs jumped from their vehicle and joined the gun battle erupting all around them. Wasdin took up a position of cover and started scanning for targets of opportunity—there were many, but target selection is always a matter of judging the greatest threat at any given moment. A Somali militiaman was taking potshots at their position and actually had a decent place to fire from, having taken up cover behind a concrete wall about ten meters up on a roof a hundred or so meters away. The highly experienced SEAL sniper, at this moment using his CAR-15 battle rifle with an ACOG (advanced combat optical gunsight) scope, allowed the red crosshairs to line up with the enemy sniper's head and paused for a split second.

Boom!

A 5.56mm round from his CAR-15 hit the target dead in the forehead, dropping him instantly as a fine red mist of blood filled the air behind him. Dead.

One down . . . another few hundred or so to go.

His fellow SEALs did the same. The thousands of hours of training were paying off again as their rounds continuously found their mark. There was one big problem, however; every time one of Aidid's men dropped, another one took his place. There was a seemingly an endless supply of bad guys coming out of the woodwork.

About the time Wasdin was admiring his handiwork with the CAR-15, one of his SEAL buddies, code named "Little Big Man," yelled over to him in his typical no-nonsense voice, "Aw hell, man . . . I've been hit."

No big deal . . . just a mere flesh wound. Or, at least that was the hope.

Wasdin took a break from the action to check on his teammate. "Hey man, let me check it out." A full once-over checking for wounds revealed the truth—Little Big Man had his leg saved by his big fat Randall knife he insisted on carrying into every mission. The guys at the team had been giving him grief about it for years, but today it paid off. The round from the Somali's AK-47 had ricochet right off the thing and left him with nothing more than a big fat raspberry bruise.

"Well I'll be damned, that ugly ass knife of yours finally paid off!"

Both men laughed as Little Big Man replied, "That's right, and you can't have it, bro!"

Seconds later it was time to get back to business as the fighting continued and the convoy prepared to move out. They were burning through ammo but nearly every shot was finding its mark so it was worth it to keep pulling that trigger. Just over thirty minutes into the battle, Wasdin heard a stray AK-47 round ricochet near him before feeling it hit behind his left knee. His SEAL friend, code-named Casanova, came over to check out the situation and calmly dropped another bad guy like it was a walk in the park. Dan Schilling, an Air Force CCT, had been in the vicinity and grabbed him by the bandolier and pulled him over out of the line of fire. Casanova, also the team medic, stuffed his wound with a bunch of Kerlix gauze and wrapped it up nice and tight. Within a couple minutes he was back on his feet and back in the fight.

Even so, Wasdin began to think to himself that he shouldn't have been hit. After all, he was a SEAL Team [redacted] sniper with years and years of training and deployment experience. At thirty-eight years old, he was still going strong and felt confident he had many years of kicking ass left in him.

The thought of being hit shook him up a little. Wasdin was used to winning and like all SEALs, hated losing. He had made it a point to win at nearly everything in his career. Somehow, it was the other guys who should get hit, not him. At that time, his ego and belief in his invincibility was so strong that it was nearly inconceivable that such a thing could happen. But, it was only a minor wound, so he'd just deal with the mental gymnastics later.

Getting back to it, the SEALs and Rangers killed dozens more of the fighters who relentlessly continued to come at them. The militiamen lit fires all around the area, specifically to stacks of tires, to create a dense, black smokescreen to protect them from being targeted and also to alert their fellow country-men to fight. Hordes of them kept coming.

As Wasdin and the SEALs got back into the fight, they happened to look over their shoulders and noticed an American truck was smoldering from the fires touched off when it was hit by an RPG (rocket propelled grenade). Part of them just shook it off, but another part, deeper down, knew that something was wrong. This was supposed to be an easy mission—a quick in and out.

The voice inside their heads started getting slightly louder telling them that all was not fine in this situation. A few minutes later, their intuition was unfortunately proven correct as a voice came over the radio, "Super Six-One is down!"

U.S. Army Chief Warrant Officer Cliff Wolcott had been the pilot in the Black Hawk helicopter, now mangled and on fire on the ground. Wolcott had been known for his exceptionally accurate imitation of Elvis Presley and even had a cartoon of Elvis painted on the side of his helo with the caption *Velvet Elvis*. Task Force Ranger's mission had quickly gone from a prisoner snatch to a full-fledged rescue mission.

The SEALs and Rangers loaded up the convoy and prepared to move, but as they got ready to hit the gas, Wasdin noticed a young Ranger prone in the street with an M-249 SAW (squad automatic weapon) pointed down an alley and letting loose short bursts of fire.

"Get up and load into your vehicle!" the veteran SEAL yelled at the kid.

Nothing.

⌃ **A SEAL manning the .50 cal**

The young Ranger didn't seem to notice; he was so focused on his mission of laying down cover fire that either he couldn't hear Wasdin or it simply didn't register. Time was of the essence and they had to get the hell out of Dodge.

Since simple verbal commands didn't seem to do the trick, Wasdin jumped out of the driver's seat of his vehicle and ran over to the young Ranger and gave him a kick in the ass, "Hey, get the hell up, we're moving!"

Eyes glazed over, the Ranger finally seemed to process what was going on, picked himself and his weapon off the ground, and trotted to one of the Humvee trucks. Wasdin ran back to their vehicle and hopped back in the driver's seat.

As they drove out of the main area, AK-47 rounds continued to fly all around. Using his left hand to steer, Wasdin kept firing his CAR-15 with his right hand as they weaved through the city streets. Having commandeered one of the Humvees, the SEAL sniper took a certain amount of comfort in the fact that the .50 cal machine gun mounted on the top was letting loose as they made their way back to the base. In combat, the sweet sound of the .50 is almost soothing—it meant that death and destruction of the enemy was most likely taking place on the other end.

A blast from the 20mm cannon of one of the MH-6 Little Bird helicopters demolished the entire wall of one of the nearby buildings, sending Somali's scattering. The pilots of the 160th Special Operations Aviation Regiment were legendary and pulled off aerial maneuvers that seemed impossible.

The sound of the blast rocked the whole area, but it also quickly brought Wasdin and his fellow SEALs to the inevitable conclusion that Aidid's people were way better equipped than they ever thought possible and were much better fighters as well. On top of that, there seemed an almost endless number willing to come join the fight.

Wasdin turned to Casanova and said, "These assholes were way more ready for a fight than I thought."

Casanova and Little Big Man nodded nearly simultaneously in agreement, "Yeah, brother, these little booger-eaters aren't fucking around out here—we better keep our head on a swivel or we are likely to take some hits."

As it turned out, Casanova could have done well as a prophet as well as a Navy SEAL.

While the SEALs kept fighting, a Combat Search and Rescue (CSAR) Team, led by U.S. Air Force

Pararescue Tech Sergeant Scott Fales, was inserted by Black Hawk Super Six-Eight at the crash site of Super Six-One. The Air Force PJs were met with heavy resistance but fought their way to the downed helicopter and found both pilots dead at the scene and with two crew members unconscious but alive. Rounds relentlessly strafed their position but they managed to drop almost a dozen of the enemy fighters with precision fire before moving the American airmen to a nearby burned-out building where they created a makeshift shelter using some of the Kevlar plates from the downed Super Six-One's wreckage.

Wasdin's internal fear meter kept rising but, as always, he managed to wrangle it under control. Growing up, like many men who choose the warrior's life, he'd had a dad who pushed him hard. Sometimes he'd thought it was too much, but looking back on it then, he was glad his dad had forced discipline on him. It had prepared him well for the trials of becoming a SEAL and the combined training and inner strength imparted through that process, in which one is forged in fire, made dealing with the stresses of combat manageable and even usable for mental fuel.

A great deal of a SEAL's training is based on this concept—place so much stress on the men that their tolerance for it climbs to extremely high levels. If it was simply a matter of getting into great shape and learning how to shoot and learn some tactics, becoming a SEAL wouldn't even be half as hard as it is—it is the constant, relentless, and never-ending pressure to perform at a high level that adds the required stress inoculation to the individual SEAL's inner being.

It is a crucial component and cannot be manufactured in nearly any other way.

The convoy continued fighting its way back to the base, but it didn't take long to realize that the chaos of war had struck. Somehow, the convoy lead vehicle with Lieutenant Colonel Danny McKnight commanding, kept making the same mistake and drove them in a circle! Now, nearly every vehicle in the entire convoy had dead or wounded soldiers in it and Wasdin and his fellow SEALs were getting pissed off.

"What the hell?! Didn't we just leave this part of the party?" Wasdin said as much to himself as his teammates.

"Yeah, man, I think we pretty much just ran ourselves in a fucking circle," Little Big Man grumbled as he checked his SEAL modified M-14. Little Big Man was also muttering to himself in no uncertain terms that he should have left that big-ass M-14 back at the base and opted for the standard CAR-15—he was out of 7.62 ammo and no one had any extra except the Somali's.

As the entire convoy started to make course corrections the firefight continued all around them. All the trucks and Humvees were full of holes and many had multiple flat tires but kept going. Many of the Rangers were in a mild state of shock and a few in a full state of shock. Hours earlier they had been hanging out in the camp, eating, telling jokes, and just passing the time. Now, they were all in the fight of their lives.

Lieutenant Colonel McKnight had taken some shrapnel and was seriously wounded, so the Air Force

CCT (Combat Control Team), lead by Dan Schilling, took tactical control of the convoy and managed to cut through the mess of communications filling the airwaves. The SEALs and Rangers were trying to get in there and rescue the pilot and crew of Super Six-One, but there was one major problem: another Black Hawk had been hit.

The Navy P-3 Orion aircraft cruising overhead attempting to provide crucial Command and Control didn't realize that they were heading for Six-One and instead vectored Wasdin and his team toward Chief Warrant Officer Mike Durant's downed helo. They knew either way they had a tough fight still ahead and it wasn't going to get any easier.

Despite the high number of wounded, the death toll with Task Force Ranger was relatively still low. The Somali militia could not say the same. Bodies littered the streets as the smoke billowed all over the city. Even so, the gunfight continued. Wasdin eventually burned through over a dozen magazines of 5.56mm ammo from his CAR-15 and the fight was not even close to over. Ammo cans from the Rangers' Humvees allowed him to top off his weapon, but in time it ran dry yet again. The carnage continued and the chaos enveloping the situation continued to spiral out of control.

The convoy briefly slowed down even more than it already had with all the twists and turns through the city, and with his CAR-15 out of ammo, Wasdin resorted to putting it aside and drawing his Sig Sauer 9mm pistol. As he looked to his left side, a member of Aidid's fighters stepped into the doorway of a blasted out building holding his AK-47 at the level. Wasdin immediately perceived the threat and went into full alert, preparing him for the lightning quick reaction needed as the Somali man brought his weapon to bear:

Breathe . . . front sight focus . . . head or upper thoracic cavity . . . two-shots . . . classic double-tap . . . trigger control.

Members of [redacted] had trained this scenario thousands of times on the range. Wasdin knew it would only be a moment and his adversary would drop—the words "I never miss" repeated in his mind like a mantra.

He squeezed the trigger and immediately felt the familiar backward jarring of the slide . . . once, twice . . .

But his prey did not fall—it was not supposed to happen this way.

In that moment in time the Somali man pulled the trigger on his AK-47 over and over, praying that one of the rounds would strike true on the American infidel. One finally did and ripped into Wasdin's right shin, nearly blowing the lower part of his leg clean off.

Damn!! This guy isn't playing around . . . FRONT SIGHT FOCUS!!

The SEAL warrior had broken a cardinal rule—don't rush the shot. He took an extra half-second to line up his eye with his front sight and pulled the trigger twice in rapid succession. An instant later the man dropped to the ground in a heap with two clean shots to the face.

Wasdin tried stepping on the gas but nothing was happening. His mind wouldn't follow. He tried again . . . nothing. Looking down, he saw that his foot was turned backward and was a mangled mess, barely hanging on by a thread.

Now he was really pissed, not just about his leg, but about the fact that it dawned on him instantly that if he'd taken the fraction of a second needed to ensure his shot was lined up he probably would have saved himself from a shattered leg bone and possible amputation. He was perplexed; such a nasty injury should hurt a whole lot more than it did, but his nervous system was on overload. Using his left foot, he hit the accelerator and felt the vehicle lurch forward.

A couple minutes later, Casanova and Little Big Man helped Wasdin climb across the center console so Casanova could drive. As the team looked at his leg wound, it was obvious that they needed to immobilize it or run the risk of the jagged pieces of bone slicing an artery and causing him to bleed out. His SEAL buddies weren't about to let that happen.

Propping his legs up on the hood, they took a couple minutes to tie Wasdin's legs together, using the left one as a brace for his mangled right one. It would help slow the bleeding, but was still a total mess.

With his usual grace, Casanova simply said, "We are going to get you home, man."

The convoy kept moving, but it wasn't long before they realized they were once again right back where they freaking started! Unbelievable. To make matters worse, another enemy AK-47 round hit Wasdin in the left ankle.

"Dude, I think your days dancing in the strip clubs are over," Little Big Man said in his low, baritone voice. That guy had a sense of humor dryer than the Sahara Desert.

Wasdin finally knew for sure they were in trouble. Now, that might sound absolutely ridiculous and crazy to the average civilian or even some military personnel, but you must understand that SEALs are supremely confident in their ability to face anything put before them. On the one hand, it grants them great courage, but on the other hand it can keep them from realizing just when the storm around them really is about to wipe them off the Earth. For the first time in the battle, Wasdin felt truly vulnerable—it was as if he had stepped into the crystal chamber and allowed the rays of a red sun to wash over him. He was human now after all.

Now fully aware of his vulnerability also led to his first major spike of fear to rise within him. It was not an overwhelming fear, but the kind of fear that forces you to face your mortality. Years of training helped keep it under control.

"We really have to get out of this hell-hole," Wasdin said through the pain. Interestingly, the left ankle pain far outweighed the pain of his nearly blown off right leg.

Tactically speaking, the whole convoy needed to get back to base and regroup and everyone knew it. If they were going to have any chance of getting back out here to rescue the downed pilots then they desperately needed to resupply, tend to the wounded, and prepare another ground assault.

About the time they started to make progress, Casanova pulled over to the side of the road where the vehicle promptly died.

Wasdin thought back to one of his favorite old films, the 1960 movie *The Alamo,* starring John Wayne as Davy Crockett. It was one of his favorite movies of all time, and Davy Crockett was by far his favorite person in the Alamo. His mind began to drift as the reality kicked in:

This must be how Davy Crockett felt before they killed him: outgunned, undermanned, and without protection. Seeing his people get wiped out while the enemy continued to advance. This is it. Howard Wasdin checks out in Moga-dishu, Somalia, on the afternoon of October 3, 1993. My one regret is I haven't told the people I love that I love them enough–during my time on Earth, that is what I should've done more.

Someone over the radio said the quick reaction force (QRF) was coming in to rescue the SEALs and Rangers of the convoy. It seemed like another bad joke with awful timing.

"Well, it's only been four hours we've been in this damn firefight with the whole fucking city swarming in to kill us. What exactly do they deem to be 'quick' when it comes to a quick reaction force?" Casanova said as he adjusted his weapon sling.

Wasdin and the SEALs kept fighting, but the injured SEAL couldn't effectively shoot anymore. Just about the time they thought it was the end, a big "Deuce and a Half" truck pulled up next to them full of fresh troops with the QRF and began getting them the hell out of there.

Casanova and Little Big Man helped transfer all the wounded to the QRF truck, but Wasdin insisted on being the last to go. He couldn't walk and was in a whole lot of pain, but he was able to register the fact that a single Ranger was standing in the middle of the road trying to coil back up a rope that had fallen on the ground. The young Ranger's eyes had glazed over and he was obviously in an advanced state of shock.

Sometimes when the mind begins to shut down you simply go into an automatic mode where you do whatever your muscle memory has trained you to do. The young Ranger was simply following protocol they had done in training time and time again . . . coil the rope and keep things organized.

Wasdin watched him in a mild state of disbelief and tried to get his attention, "Hey man, come on and get in the truck. This isn't a training op, just leave the damn rope and let's go!"

But the Ranger wouldn't budge. Now, Wasdin was getting irritated for real.

The SEAL sniper pointed his Sig Sauer pistol at the Ranger and said with a commanding growl, "I won't kill you, but if you don't get your ass in that truck right now you're walking out of here with a limp."

Suddenly, the young Ranger seemed to snap out of his mental fog just enough to get motivated to drop the rope and get in the truck. It was a good thing too because the SEAL sniper meant business.

While Wasdin and his convoy prepared to move out and head back to the base, the vehicle that had initially veered off course found itself in a real mess. Private Richard Kowalewski, a Ranger with Bravo Company, 3rd Ranger Battalion, knew that he and his teammates in the Humvee were all in serious trouble.

Having joined the Army only two days after graduating High School, Kowalewski was not your typical Ranger candidate. Instead of focusing on athletics he found enjoyment in chess, literature, and the arts. He spoke German fluently and loved Shakespeare. However, he also had the one trait all Rangers and SEALs share—a love for his country. This fact, along with an intense desire to serve, had led him to the Rangers, and now to a faraway land in Africa to fight against an evil warlord.

Private First Class Clay Othic clamped down a little harder on the bandage he had used to wrap Kowalewski's arm, "Hey, Alphabet," he started, using the nickname Kowalewski had been given since almost day one in the Rangers because his name was so hard to pronounce, "If you want I can drive, man."

Kowalewski shook his head, "I'll be okay, it's not too bad."

"I think I got the bleeding to stop for now so you're good until we can get back," Othic said with his all-business tone of voice.

Rounds still flew all around them in what had been one ambush after another since their initial mistake. *I KNEW we were going the wrong way,* Alphabet thought to himself as he allowed his mind to drift momentarily on the people and things of home. It had turned out to be one of the worst cases of making a wrong turn in history—the last thing you want to do in battle is walk into an ambush. There is an old saying in the warrior trade: If you survive one ambush just go home and retire because you'll never survive another one.

In true defiance of the cosmic rules of nature, Alphabet and his buddies had now survived at least a half-dozen ambushes in the last thirty minutes. Unfortunately, his fortune was about to run out.

Alphabet took a hard left turn and stepped on the gas as he nearly plowed right through another stack of burning tires on the corner. As he looked over his shoulder, a Somali man popped out of the shadows holding a standard Russian-made rocket launcher that was a favorite among third world countries because it was easy to use and could be purchased for a relatively low price in the worldwide weapons market.

"RPG!!!"

Kowalewski yelled to his buddies to brace for the impending impact of the rocket-propelled grenade now flying right at them. In combat, as the adrenaline dump hits your system, sometimes it can produce a "time dilation" effect: It seems like everything slows down to slow-motion.

As the rocket sped toward them, Kowalewski had a brief moment of remembering the stars as he would lay on his back and just think about life. The face of his girlfriend flashed before his eyes and he almost smiled.

Slam!

The rocket hit directly in Kowalewski's left arm, severing it at the elbow, before continuing on into his left ribs. Everyone in the Humvee expected the large orange flash of an explosion . . . but it never came. Instead, the RPG had lodged itself inside the chest of the young Ranger and didn't explode.

"Damn, someone grab him!"

The other Rangers in the Humvee scrambled to both move their friend but also to engage the enemy. Private Othic quickly jumped into the driver's seat as his buddies pulled Alphabet into the back. Had the round simply been a dud or was it still live but didn't go off?

An RPG rocket is a two-stage device: right after pulling the trigger, a small propellant launches the rocket out of the tube and then a few moments later the rocket motor will kick in and carry it to its intended target. Maximum effective range is normally around 500 meters, but a shot from less than 300 is much more likely to hit. Due to the wind stabilizer fins an RPG rocket will also turn into the wind after launch.

Either way, this RPG didn't go off the way it was made to do, and now Kowalewski was in critical condition. Everyone knew it was a miracle they were still alive, and also were keenly aware that their friend wouldn't make it if they didn't get him medical help extremely soon.

While Kowalewski was barely clinging to life and his fellow Rangers fought to get him and themselves out of the nest of enemy fighters, Wasdin and his convoy were finally on the right track and headed on the road to the base. And from there all the way back to the base was remarkably actually pretty quiet, all things considered. But once they pulled through the gates, the absolute chaos was obvious as the medics attempted to triage all the wounded, sorting through who was on death's door and needed immediate attention and who was merely in bad shape. At least forty or fifty American soldiers were being tended to by the medical teams.

"We're going to get you taken care of," Wasdin heard a young Army medic say in a matter-of-fact tone as he realized he was drifting in and out of consciousness. Fighting to stay awake and alert, his mind wandered a bit, from thoughts of the battle to thoughts of home. In the forefront of his mind were his two kids, Blake and Rachel. His devotion to the SEAL

Teams meant he probably only saw them five or six times a year. Looking back, it bothered the SEAL warrior somewhat, as he knew on some level that his absence meant they didn't get as much guidance from him as they deserved, but it was his hope that his devotion to duty and example of service would inspire them to push themselves to do great things as well.

Casanova and Dan Schilling had carried the wounded SEAL to the triage area and were hovering around waiting to hear the status. The young medic cut Wasdin's pants off and began slowly analyzing the wounds. Wasdin thought he heard him say something about how they might not be able to save his right leg, and that sparked a burst of energy.

"You have to save my leg! Please do whatever you have to do . . . please don't amputate!"

At that moment, Wasdin only thought of his ability to get back out to fight again another day. If they cut off the leg, how could he ever deploy again? How could he ever get back into the fight?

As he mentally wrestled with the dire situation he felt himself start to get angry. Angry at himself for missing that shot, angry with the bad guy who had blown his leg to hell, angry with the crazy warlord for pushing these Somali people to fight when all the Americans were trying to do was make sure starving people could eat, and mad at God for allowing him to end up hurt this bad in the first place.

One minute quickly turned into ten, and ten to sixty, and sixty to a hundred and twenty. Wasdin felt the heat of the air waft over him, but the smell of burning rubber of the city had coated the inside of his nose so that was all he could smell. After a few hours of rest, a small thread, perhaps only a single strand of thought, crept into his mind: What if I wasn't mad at God for allowing me to get wounded like this, but instead was mad at God for forcing me to see my own humanity . . . my own vulnerability?

I can't go there . . . not now . . . maybe not ever . . . I must focus on getting well and doing my duty for the sake of the team and the mission.

And so with that thought, Howard Wasdin took that thread, rolled it up, and locked it away in the fortress of his mind. Many years later, a special person God put into his life was given the key, the only key, to allowing that steel door to be opened . . . but that is another story.

In the aftermath of the battle, records show that eighteen Americans had died with seventy-three wounded in action, not including a Pakistani and a Malaysian soldier who had taken part in the rescue attempt. The State Department estimated that between 1,500 and 3,000 Somali men, women, and children were killed in the battle. However, it is important to note that in war, the unfortunate truth is that many times noncombatants become combatants: If a "civilian" picks up a rifle, straps on an explosive device, or prepares to throw a grenade, then they immediately lose their civilian non-combatant status. It is a difficult concept for many people to wrap their minds around, but it essential for the professional warrior to understand that although he may detest what he must do, the fact is that he must take action to neutralize the immediate threat posed by such a person.

Sometimes in war there are no real winners . . . only survivors.

That is not to lay claim that such action is unjust, but rather is to help to make clear the fact that one can win the battle but lose the war. The men of Task Force Ranger won the day and achieved the mission objectives in a decisive matter despite the heavy casualties. Each and every soldier fought bravely and had to dig deep into their mental reserves to find the courage and stalwart fortitude to keep fighting no matter how many losses they took. But, as is many times the case, the politics of a region and situation can turn a victory into a defeat.

And therein lays the soldier's dilemma. He is not there to make policy or to debate the merits of how he and his team are used. His existence is one of marching forward and shattering the will of the enemy in the name of freedom and justice.

The next morning, Wasdin heard the over the radio that a select group of the Army's famed 10th Mountain Division, reinforced with a small contingent of Pakistani and Malaysian army troops, had assembled in their vehicles and prepared to move out. Over a hundred vehicles, including M48 tanks from Pakistan and Condor armored personnel carriers from Malaysia, stormed back into the area to rescue the remaining Americans. Although successful in rescuing the survivors from the first crash, the second downed Black Hawk helicopter was overrun by Somali forces.

USASOC Gary Gordon and Randy Shughart had volunteered to attempt to hold off the waves of enemy troops despite knowing it was nearly impossible odds stacked against them. For many hours the brave men fought against seemingly endless numbers of Aidid's men and eventually fell to enemy fire. The Somali's had repeated attempts over and over to reach the downed helicopter before finally overcoming the USASOC soldiers. For their courage and sacrifice, both men were posthumously awarded the Congressional Medal of Honor. The Black Hawk pilot, Chief Warrant Officer Durant, was later released and returned to United States forces. Unfortunately, Private Kowalewski died of his wounds despite a heroic effort by medical personnel to save his life.

A less-known fact was that fighting did continue after the Battle of Mogadishu. Another USASOC operator, SFC Matt Rierson, was killed by a Somali militia mortar attack. No single battle had been more bloody and had contributed to so many casualties since the Vietnam War than did the battle to take down Aidid and rescue the downed American pilots. This remained the case until the famed Second Battle of Fallujah in 2004.

Technically, the Battle of Mogadishu was over on Monday, October 4, 1993. Eventually, all United States troops made it out of the city and to the United Nations base where the command element had set up its headquarters. Of note, a small group of Rangers and USASOC soldiers led by Staff Sergeant John Dycus realized that the convoy had no room left for them in the vehicles so they ran back to the base in full gear. The run became known as the "Mogadishu Mile."

General Garrison, despite the heroic efforts of the men under his command, officially accepted responsibility for the results of the battle and sent a handwritten letter to President Clinton. In the letter he stated that he did take responsibility, that Task Force Ranger had the intelligence information necessary to conduct the operation, and that ultimately their objective was met and the mission was successful despite the casualties. In fact, Task Force Ranger did capture their primary targets as intended. An important note when considering the historical significance of the operation.

In an official statement by the U.S. Special Representative to Somalia, Ambassador Robert B. Oakley, he stated:

"My own personal estimate is that there must have been 1,500 to 2,000 Somalis killed and wounded that day, because that battle was a true battle. And the Americans and those who came to their rescue, were being shot at from all sides . . . a deliberate war battle, if you will, on the part of the Somalis. And women and children were being used as shields and some cases women and children were actually firing weapons, and were coming from all sides. Sort of a rabbit warren of huts, houses, alleys, and twisting and turning streets, so those who were trying to defend themselves were shooting back in all directions. Helicopter gunships were being used as well as all sorts of automatic weapons on the ground by the U.S. and the United Nations. The Somalis, by and large, were using automatic rifles and grenade launchers and it was a very nasty fight, as intense as almost any battle you would find."

On October 6, 1993, President Clinton held a national security review and directed the Acting Chairman of the Joint Chiefs, Admiral David E. Jeremiah, to discontinue all aggressive action against Aidid's forces and to only fire if fired upon.

Ambassador Oakley was reappointed as the special envoy to Somalia. He worked for months toward a full cease fire of hostilities before eventually announcing that the United States would withdraw all military presence by the end of March 1994.

In the aftermath of the Battle of Mogadishu, typical politics was hard at work and people on every level of government and the military command structure analyzed what had taken place for weeks and months on end, many looking for someone to blame. Realizing this fact, Secretary of Defense Les Aspin resigned his post and stated that he was the one to blame for his decision to refuse Task Force Ranger's requests for tanks and extra armored vehicles.

The United States government feared for years after the Battle of Mogadishu that a repeat of the situation could take place in other regions around the world. Many people believe that this is the primary reason behind the lack of American intervention in the Rwandan genocide in 1994.

Additionally, some believe that Osama bin Laden and the Al-Qaeda terrorist organization helped train and fund Aidid's troops. CNN correspondent Peter Bergen later traveled to the war-torn area of the world and actually interviewed bin Laden, who stated unequivocally that his Al-Qaeda fighters had indeed helped Aidid.

During an interview in May 1998, bin Laden claimed that the United States withdrawal from Somalia was tantamount to weakness. He had also previously claimed responsibility for ensuring the coordination of the attack on the American troops in

Somalia, but then denied doing so. However, the terrorist leader expressed his "delight at the deaths of filthy Americans."

Little did he know that one day his demise would come at the hands of a U.S. Navy SEAL!

The Official Order of Battle of American and UN Forces involved in the Battle of Mogadishu:

Task Force Ranger

1. USASOC [redacted]
2. Bravo Company, 3rd Ranger Battalion, 75th Ranger Regiment
3. 1st Battalion, 160th Special Operations Aviation Regiment ("The Night Stalkers")
4. Combat controllers and Pararescuemen from the 24th Special Tactics Squadron
5. Navy SEALs from the [redacted]
6. CVN-72 USS *Abraham Lincoln* and Carrier Air Wing 11
7. Task Force–10th Mountain Division, including:
   1st Battalion, 22nd Infantry Regiment
   2nd Battalion, 14th Infantry Regiment
   3rd platoon, C Company, 1st Battalion, 87th
      Infantry Regiment
8. 15th Battalion, of the Frontier Force Regiment, Pakistan Army
9. 19th Lancers of the Pakistan Army
10. 10th Battalion, of the Baloch Regiment of Pakistan Army
11. 977th Military Police Company

UN Forces

1. 19th Battalion, Royal Malay Regiment of the Malaysian Army
2. 11th Regiment, Grup Gerak Khas, a Special Forces Group of the Malaysian Army
3. 7th Battalion, Frontier Force Regiment of the Pakistan Army

8

FORCE OF CHOICE—NAVY SEALs IN THE GLOBAL WAR ON TERROR

SEAL TEAM FIVE HEADQUARTERS

CORONADO, CALIFORNIA

SEPTEMBER 11, 2001, 1030 HOURS

Commander Tom Hanson, SEAL Team FIVE Commanding Officer, strode out into the inner courtyard of the SEAL Team FIVE headquarters and motioned for the men to circle in close. With a look of determination and intensity he began his speech, "Gentlemen, we all know by now what has happened this morning and I assure you that work is already beginning for us to respond to this cowardly act with all we have as a nation. It is my hope that the president will use us as the force of choice to hunt down those responsible."

Over a hundred SEALs nodded in agreement, faces a mixture of anger and yet excitement at the prospect of being given the honor of tracking down and bringing to justice the evil men who brought the Twin Towers

⌃ **SEALs stop for a moment during a Land Warfare exercise**

down. In the many years ahead, the U.S. Navy SEALs would be called upon time and time again to do just that—to hunt down the terrorists responsible and use their superior skills, courage, and firepower to prevent our enemies from ever doing it again.

Things moved quickly after that day, and the men of the SEAL Teams who had been training for years were all about to get the opportunity to put into practice everything they had learned. Initially, this meant the Teams were flying into Afghanistan to pursue elements of the Al-Qaeda terrorist network. It was extremely dangerous work, requiring the men to conduct raids through some of the most rugged terrain imaginable, pursuing their enemies into the mountains and tunnel complexes that existed all over the war-torn country. Afghanistan is a grimy place with very little infrastructure to support basic needs of its people. When you step off the plane in Kabul, the first thing that hits you is the smell—the air is permeated with the smell of death and decay, not to mention (according to rumor) that fecal matter accounts for the greatest part of it. Truly a sad state of affairs, especially when you consider that most of the population just wants to live some kind of normal life. However, the Taliban commanders and hardline Islamic militants help ensure that achieving some kind of true stability is next to impossible.

⌃ **SEALs emerge from the water with their MP-5 submachine guns**

In November 2001, a platoon of SEALs were inserted into Afghanistan and given the mission to recon and ultimately secure a potential forward operating base for U.S. Marine Corps assets with the 15th Marine Expeditionary Unit approximately 190 kilometers southwest of Kandahar. The SEALs moved in and accomplished their mission with extreme efficiency, easily accomplishing the task and taking control of what would later become known as Camp Rhino.

This would be the first official mission of the SEALs in an arduous campaign throughout Afghanistan.

As the weeks and months went on, the SEALs and their counterparts throughout special operations had an immediate impact that reverberated throughout the country of Afghanistan and is still felt today.

≈ **SEALs from SDV Team TWO rappel onto the deck of a waiting submarine**

No longer could its treacherous mountains and caves be considered an untouchable safe haven for plotting the next terror mission. One by one, the various tunnels and caves throughout the region were cleared and the Taliban and al-Qaeda fighters seeking refuge within them were scattered. Mission after mission was executed with precision, stealth, and when required, the utmost ferocity.

President Bush had laid out a very specific strategy: Hunt down the men responsible for the attack on our country and if you harbor them or provide them assistance in any way then you will be treated as part of the terrorist network. No exceptions.

From a warfighter point of view, this clarity of purpose made the task much easier—although it was imperative to establish relationships with the local population and generally show them that we are not an invasion force there to terrorize them (and rather a force for good within their country), the simplicity of the grand strategy made achieving the objectives very straightforward. Are you part of a terrorist group threatening the United States or its Allies? Are you in support of one?

If the answer is yes . . . the SEALs will hunt you down.

OPERATION ENDURING FREEDOM

NEAR THE KHYBER PASS, AFGHANISTAN

DECEMBER 1717, 2001

THE BATTLE OF TORA BORA

The following account is based on real people and events, but modifications have been made for reasons explained in this book and its endnotes. It is a scenario similar to an actual mission carried out by the people displayed:

"Well Senior Chief, what do you think of our position?" asked Lieutenant Rich Wilson as he surveyed the surrounding terrain.

≈ **A SEAL on patrol in the snow-covered mountains of Afghanistan**

The veteran SEAL took a moment to glance at what appeared to be a young mountain lion in the distance before replying in his usual grim voice, "Well, I think it pretty much sucks."

"Roger that, I'd say that's my assessment as well. Let's trek on up another hundred meters or so and see if we can't find ourselves a better perch," the lieutenant said with a smile. He always knew he could count on his friend and teammate to spare any BS and get right to the point.

Senior Chief Dave Riley, a legend within the Teams [redacted] nodded in agreement, pointing to a small outcropping of rocks and trees farther ahead, "It is likely our target will use the road near the base of the mountain pass for any attempt to escape quickly by truck—otherwise they will parallel it on foot about thirty to fifty meters out . . . either way we should have a clear vantage point from up over there."

The two SEALs made their way up the side of the small mountain until they reached their destination while the rest of the squad was ordered to descend to a lower position that would afford them solid cover for an ambush. Once they were settled in, Lieutenant Wilson grabbed his radio and checked in with the commander at the Tactical Operations Center near Forward Operating Base Rhino.

"Grizzly Three-Six, this is Polar Express, we are in position, over."

A few moments later the response came in, "Solid copy Polar Express, Vulture is moving your direction, ETA ten minutes."

The command center had nicknamed the Taliban fighters in the region "Vulture" thanks to a sly off-hand remark from a young Army communications sergeant.

As the minutes passed by each element of the SEAL squad ensured they were in the best possible position for an ambush. The air was cold but had no effect on the men as they mentally rehearsed the upcoming moments. Lieutenant Wilson leaned over to whisper to his teammate, who was making a final adjustment on the scope of his .300 Win Mag rifle, "Senior, I've got movement—looks to be about two clicks out—three trucks, heading this way up the road."

"Copy that."

The young squad leader then whispered into the comm net, "Standby, Vulture en route, repeat Vulture en route."

Barreling down the road towards their position and clearly trying to escape were three worn-out but fully functional trucks full of Taliban fighters hoping to somehow elude the grasp of the combined offensive in the surrounding region. The SEALs couldn't yet see it from their vantage point, but the men of the Taliban were clearly afraid. Between the relentless bombing from Allied jets and the persistent attack from special operations forces, their nerves were stretched to their limits.

Senior Chief Riley shifted his rifle a couple degrees to the left and found his sight picture, the red crosshairs shifting only the slightest amount with each of the SEAL sniper's breaths. As the seconds ticked by, Riley would enter into a zone of complete and utter concentration. It can feel as though time even slows down before you take the shot.

The sniper's trade is at once simple and amazingly complex. Add to the equation moving targets and the difficulty starts rising off the charts. You have to know your weapon to the highest degree, know the ballistics perfectly, understand how the elevation and temperature will affect your shot, and then somehow by the grace of God and a whole lot of skill place a small piece of lead on a target the distance of six to ten football fields away. Some guys have a special knack, an "X-Factor," that cannot be rationally accounted for in any scientific way—they just *know* when the shot is on and when to squeeze the trigger.

Inhale deeply. Hold your breath and pause.

Crack!

The driver in the lead vehicle of the convoy slammed against the seat as the back of his head practically exploded from the impact. Blood doused the other two Taliban crammed into the front, both of whom were now in a mild state of shock and frantically trying to keep their truck from rolling. Moments later, Senior Chief Riley pulled the trigger again and exhaled as the bullet ripped through the second man in the front seat.

Nothing but total and complete chaos from here on out, the veteran SEAL thought as the truck careened off the road and slammed into a snow-entrusted tree.

The second truck barely missed the first as it turned hard right and almost spun out of control. Unfortunately for them, they turned right toward the SEAL element set up to give them a welcome.

A massive volume of gunfire erupted from the SEALs as they began to cut down the enemy one by one. Arms and legs of the terrorist fighters were ripped off as the rounds sliced through the air, until some kind of explosive that was being carried by one of them was set off by the relentless barrage. A small fireball ensued and the rest of the Taliban from that truck were dead.

The driver of truck three, seeing what had already happened, hit the gas and decided to try to make a break for it hoping that enough speed would keep the SEALs from finishing them off. His luck was about to run out.

Petty Officer Jones, the squad gunner, swung around with his M249G light machine gun and unleashed on the Taliban vehicle for a solid five seconds, riddling the truck with lead and blowing out at least two tires.

"You got these guys Senior?" The lieutenant exclaimed, confident of the answer before he even asked.

"Standby."

One by one, the SEAL sniper put an end to each of the rest of the fighters as they scrambled around looking for cover near the now disabled vehicle.

Lieutenant Wilson patted his friend on the shoulder and smiled again, partly because he knew they had achieved their current mission, but also because of the respect he had for his friend and Platoon Chief, the same man who had once been an instructor of his during BUD/S. It showed in his voice, "Damn, Senior Chief, that was some good shooting . . . whenever you want me to give you a tip or two down at the range just let me know—I'm here for you whenever you need it."

The SEAL sniper grinned and kind of liked the smart-ass style of his friend and squad leader, "We better regroup and prepare to move out, but . . . let's do a quick battle damage assessment and grab any intel we can find first."

About fifteen minutes later, the SEALs had packed up and were ready to move.

Wilson grabbed his radio as they all started making their way down to check the carnage, "Kodiak Three-Six, this is Polar Express . . . targets eliminated and preparing to move—ETA ninety minutes to reach checkpoint Bravo."

"Roger that, Polar Express—keep us apprised of any changes."

The SEALs then quickly assessed the damage and rounded up whatever Intel looked intact before spreading out in a loose diamond formation and beginning the hike to the next checkpoint. During one of his sorties, an American pilot caught a glimpse of what appeared to be a small structure in a clearing about 300 meters up the side of a particularly jagged ridgeline on the mountain pass to the south. According to the pilot, the structure appeared "small but significant, with recent movement nearby."

Which, of course, could mean anything, so the SEALs had no idea what to expect. Weapons? More intel? Supplies?

Darkness slowly began to set in as the sun prepared to set. Each man in the squad of SEALs were fully alert, and despite the need to move quickly, had to maintain a close watch for any enemy activity. If they were spotted before reaching the ridgeline and beginning their ascent to take a look at the encampment, they would potentially be in perfect position for an enemy ambush.

⌃ SEALs of Task Force K-Bar investigate one of many cave complexes in Afghanistan

A pretty steep gradient awaited the men, and as they got closer it became more and more apparent that reaching a good spot to do some reconnaissance might require some climbing up the steep slope. The path up was easy to see, but that also meant it was likely to be closely watched by the Taliban, if any were still around.

Senior Chief Riley took in the situation and checked the time, "Lieutenant, we probably need to divert over this way and plan on scaling up somewhere with the best looking holds," he said as he performed a mental checklist of his gear and best options.

Lieutenant Wilson nodded and did a visual scan of the area where Senior Chief was pointing, "Right . . .

we'll know for sure when we get closer but it looks like there might be a decent path up over there."

The team made its way to the base of the mountain and began a steady climb up the side, using minimal tools due to the numerous handholds and relatively mild slope. About sixty minutes later, the SEALs found themselves on a natural ledge overlooking the small compound a little more than 200 meters away. Lieutenant Wilson pulled out his binoculars and made a slow, methodical scan of the target area.

"I see various crates, a fire pit, and some kind of makeshift clothesline . . . Whoever has been hiding out there is either still in there or is coming back fairly soon," he whispered to Senior Chief Riley.

"Let's give it some time and see if we can't get a positive ID, sir."

≈ **SEALs take over an enemy weapon cache**

"Copy . . . I'm gonna call it in—let the guys know we are planning to sit tight for a while," he replied while gathering up his comm gear.

The squad took a couple minutes to find a good, but not necessarily comfortable, place to spend the next hour or so observing the location of the suspected enemy hideout. It would be easy to just rush in and kick some ass, but Lieutenant Wilson and Senior Chief Riley thought it was best to give it a little time and see who might show up. The trouble with killing all the bad guys outright is that it is impossible to interrogate and gather information from dead terrorists. Although many of them captured over the years resist, with the right motivation even the most dedicated to their cause tend to talk at some point. The SEALs wanted to see if there was anyone at this particular camp worthy of a chat before taking it down.

After about an hour, the men started to see some activity ramp up. A large truck coming in from the south stopped at the base of the mountain and a small contingent of Taliban fighters jumped out and began to offload some cargo.

"Hey, Senior, what do you make of these guys?" Wilson whispered as he leaned over to tap him on the shoulder.

Riley took a second to check it out through the binoculars and replied, "Looks like a bunch of bad MOFOs, sir. But, those crates are no run of the mill Haji-made stuff—the markings look like Russian to me."

Lieutenant Wilson took a closer look and concurred, "I think you're right, RPGs maybe?"

⌃ **A SEAL conducting reconnaissance on a suspected enemy encampment**

"That would be my guess. Who do we have on the ready station overhead?"

"A couple F-16s are on patrol. Give me a second and I'll let them know we might have something," Wilson said as he mentally reviewed the call sign list he had memorized for the day.

After a few moments, he had them up on the comms. "Viper Nine-Six, this is Polar Express, over."

Captain Henderson, a seasoned fighter pilot, responded with her usual charm, "Polar Express, this is Viper Nine-Six, I read you . . . hope you got some work for me today—it's getting a little boring up here."

Wilson smiled, "Roger that Nine-Six, we have a large force of Taliban preparing for a big party and could use some assistance—grid coordinates 42R-TV44754306."

"Copy that, ETA five minutes . . . go ahead and light 'em up and I'll be there shortly."

Senior Chief nodded at his squad leader in acknowledgement and quickly removed his pack to get out his SOFLAM PEQ-1B Laser Acquisition Marker, better known as a "laser designator." The device illuminates the target with an infrared signature that a pilot can use to lock on their munitions and deliver them with pinpoint accuracy.

Right on time, Captain Henderson and her F-16 came into the area and after a few minor adjustments, had the GBU-12 Paveway II bomb ready to go. She banked her jet slightly left and prepared to let it loose.

"Polar Express, this is Viper Nine-Six, I have target acquisition—standby, over."

"Heads down, boys . . . our angel in the sky is about to crash the party," Lieutenant Wilson said over their internal comm net.

Over the last week the sound of an American fighter jets in the region had grown ever more familiar to the Taliban fighters, but unfortunately for them, it was usually too late. As the band of terrorists continued offloading their cargo, the last thing they heard was the roar of the American smart weapon screaming in on their exact location.

Moments later a bright flash erupted near the compound followed by the thunderous sound of 192 pounds of Tritonal High Explosive vaporizing at least a dozen of the Taliban forces and sending a shockwave strong enough to knock down trees and spray rocks in all directions. The overpressure and fiery blast created finished off anyone not killed outright.

Mission accomplished.

However, just as the hunt had begun in Afghanistan and unbeknownst to the SEALs, the pieces of a complex international puzzle were beginning to come into focus and the United States' old nemesis and dictator of Iraq, Saddam Hussein, had already begun pushing the limits of the sanctions imposed upon his country following Operation Desert Storm in 1991. United Nations Security Council Resolution 687 had been put into effect on April 3, 1991, and essentially broadened and solidified a series of other resolutions previously levied against Iraq (specifically, Resolutions 660–686). Arguably the most significant part of these resolutions was the obligation of Saddam Hussein under the Geneva Protocol to unconditionally remove or destroy all chemical and biological weapons as well as any ballistic missiles capable of striking targets beyond 150 kilometers.

In many ways, this was the prelude and opening chorus to another war in Iraq.

As the SEALs, Green Berets, Rangers, and other members of the Special Operations Command continued their work in Afghanistan, President Bush and his cabinet continued to face the daunting reality that our intelligence operatives and their international counterparts had reason to believe that Saddam Hussein had no intent of fulfilling all the obligations of the UN Resolutions. Stockpiles of weapons of mass destruction were believed to be present in Iraq and the United States began to apply increasing pressure on the international community to depose Saddam and his regime. Longtime U.S. ally, the United Kingdom, with Prime Minister Tony Blair at the helm, stood by President Bush despite continuous opposition from members of the UN Security Council and other nations in the General Assembly. It was believed that diplomacy was indeed making progress and that more time should be given to the process.

President Bush disagreed.

In the months prior to this moment, the Joint Chiefs of Staff and various military commanders within their fields had already begun the complex planning process for a full-scale invasion of and military operation in Iraq. Air power of course would be a big part of the initial battle plan, but the reality that every strategist knows and understands is that the ground forces ultimately take and hold the territory— a full victory is unachievable otherwise. However, General Tommy Franks, having just finished the initial push into Afghanistan against the Taliban, had been tasked with the job of leading the overall invasion of Iraq. A longtime student of history and warfare, he hatched a brilliant plan that would take advantage of the subtle art of subterfuge: a page right out of the classic Sun Tzu book on strategy, *The Art of War.*

Knowing that Saddam Hussein's forces would not be able to stand against multiple fronts, it was generally agreed upon that finding a way to misdirect and split his forces would make even more vulnerable to superior American firepower and simultaneously reduce the threat to our own troops. This led to a little known mission [redacted]—the mission became known as "April Fool."

[Redacted] spent months developing a relationship with a local Iraqi believed to be an Iraqi intelligence officer himself. It is an exceptionally delicate business and the slightest misstep can lead to exposure of the operative's intent, or worse—capture by enemy forces and detainment. To put it mildly, enemy countries do not tend to respond well to American spies.

However, the American spy had something extremely valuable—the United States, "Top Secret" invasion plans.

Essentially, it was hoped that the Iraqi intelligence officer would learn of the plans and offer to pay handsomely for them. The catch? The plans explained in great detail how the U.S. forces would invade through the North and West borders of Iraq through Turkey and Jordan.

Places from which American forces would never come and had no intention of doing so in the first place.

In the intelligence business, a number one priority is the ability to adapt and become whatever your target needs . . . within certain limits, of course. For example, let's say the person you are focusing on has a fascination with World War II history or even something truly unique like the etymology of a specific language. Whatever it is they have an interest in, you can use that as a common ground to build a relationship with them if you do your homework. Over time and once a high level of trust is established, it will be necessary to determine the motivations of the person. What drives them? Acquisition of wealth? Personal honor? A religious code? Family loyalty?

Most people have a motivation, that when understood, can be exploited by a seasoned intelligence operative. In the case of April Fool, the personal pride of the target that created just the right circumstances to succeed against her target—the Iraqi intelligence officer knew that procuring the potentially game-changing "secret plans" of the Americans would guarantee him a substantial promotion within Saddam's regime. And that meant wealth, status, and family honor.

All things he would be happy to enjoy in greater measure.

Amazingly, the buy went off without a hitch and the "top secret plans" immediately made their way to Saddam's inner circle. This led his military planners to immediately reposition the Iraqi armor and mechanized infantry regiments to reinforce those positions, only to find out—after it was too late—that they had been tricked. It was a classic move of military strategy involving deception and subterfuge, which when combined with our air power, opened the door for our forces to quickly begin overwhelming the Iraqis.

UNITED STATES CENTRAL COMMAND

OPERATIONS IN THE VICINITY OF BAGDAD, IRAQ

MARCH 20, 2003, 0525 LOCAL IRAQI TIME

Lieutenant Colonel Randy "Kodiak" Johnson checked the airspeed and altimeter inside the cockpit of his F-117 Nighthawk stealth fighter and nodded to himself that all looked good and all systems were a go. He looked out the right side of his canopy and could barely make out the angular silhouette of his fellow Nightsalker, Major James "Twitch" McAllister.

"Eagle Three-Nine this is Eagle One-Five, time to target is approximately fifteen minutes, how copy, over," the Flight Leader said over the tactical net as he continued to scan the horizon.

Major McAllister made a slight adjustment to his FLIR (Forward Looking Infra-Red) system, "Copy that Eagle Three-Nine . . . it's gonna be one hell of a show tonight."

The veteran combat pilot smiled to himself, *Yes, it is my friend.*

"Roger that One-Five, they will never even see us coming."

Simultaneously, in the waters off the southern coast of Iraq, the USS *Bunker Hill* (CG-52), a Ticonderoga-class guided missile cruiser, glided through sea while the crew waited in anticipation for their orders. A few moments later, Captain Farris Farwell, the ship's Commanding Officer, spoke over the 1MC, a Navy ship's public address circuit.

"God bless USS *Bunker Hill*. God bless America. In approximately ten minutes we will have strike tasking and missiles away," he said with a calm yet forceful voice.

The countdown continued as the stealth fighters raced toward their target and the missile batteries of the *Bunker Hill* were spun up and readied for launch. Intelligence reports had indicated that Saddam Hussein, his two sons, and other senior members of the Iraqi leadership were currently located inside an underground bunker on the outskirts of Bagdad. It was hoped that the strike and subsequent invasion might just take out the primary command structure in the opening moments of the war, severely disrupting any resistance.

At 5:34 a.m. local Iraqi time, LCOL Johnson and MAJ McAllister's GBU-27 Paveway 2,000 pound bombs penetrated the target compound and wreaked havoc on the area. Moments later, BGM-109C Tomahawk Land Attack Missiles (TLAM-C) from the USS *Bunker Hill* and five other ships or submarines in the task force began to slam into their surrounding targets as well.

Operation Iraqi Freedom was officially underway.

Approximately eight hours before the official

opening moments of the invasion, the Navy SEALs prepared to conduct what was considered by many to be one of the most important elements of the entire upcoming conflict: secure the primary offshore oil platforms and the pumping stations that fed them to ensure a disastrous repeat of 1991's Operation DESERT STORM would not take place. Previously in 1991, Saddam and his regime had taken a "scorched Earth" policy and allowed millions of barrels of oil to be spilled into the north Arabian Sea, creating a massive environmental disaster.

≈ **A modern SEAL in Combat Swimmer gear**

On the southern tip of the Iraqi Al-Faw peninsula sits the primary valve station feeding oil from the off-shore platforms to the rest of the country through other oil terminals further inland. To ensure the entire system was kept secure, Navy SEALs along with their [redacted] and U.S. Marines were tasked with taking over and locking down each key point in the system. Due to their obvious expertise with waterborne operations, the SEALs specifically had the job of securing the offshore platforms.

A large task force of the SEALs were inserted via high-speed boats courtesy of the Naval Special Warfare's Special Boat Unit (SBU), with whom they operate closely any time there is a need for support on rivers or seas. The team also maintained helicopter support with multiple SEAL snipers on standby as they circled the area.

⌃ **A SEAL element practices "shooting and moving" in the desert**

Timing of the operation was critical. Intelligence reports gained from airborne surveillance the day before the takedown showed only typical oil workers onboard, but as the time of the invasion drew closer the SEALs were informed that there was substantial movement taking place on the offshore platforms. Close analysis indicated that the Iraqis were reinforcing each one with security forces and antiaircraft guns. Although the SEALs never assume a mission will be easy, it was now clear that the stakes had been raised substantially. To make matters worse, they also had reason to believe explosives were being rigged all around the oil platform and wired for remote detonation.

This meant that now instead of seizing control of a group of noncombatants, the SEALs and British Special Air Service (SAS) troopers would have to contend with an enemy force of unknown size and composition and then find a way to defuse the bombs all before the entire platform erupted into flames . . . an incredibly dangerous task with potentially staggering consequences.

With absolute precision, multiple Special Boat Unit craft raced underneath the offshore platforms, allowing the SEAL warriors to debark and scale up onto the main level. Moving quickly, the men began rounding up the civilians and engaging what turned out to be limited resistance from the overwhelmed Iraqi security forces. In just under forty-five minutes, the SEALs and coalition partners had accomplished their mission despite the exceptionally fluid and complex circumstances.

Another tribute to the professionalism and skill of the SEALs.

Far to the south in the city of Basra, intense fighting had erupted and a small contingent of U.S. special operations forces, including a small number of SEALs, had engaged the enemy in fierce street battles. Saddam and his loyalists viewed the defense of Basra as a strategic imperative since it was not only home to over one million people, but also contained multiple oil fields, including the second largest on the planet—the West Qurna Field to the northeast.

The intelligence community and their counterparts from special operations units worldwide stationed in all parts of the world had been brought in and were operating clandestinely for months before the invasion—standard procedure before a major military engagement. Such small clandestine units can gather intelligence, disrupt enemy operations, and gain valuable insights about the actual situation on the ground. In the case of Basra, the coming insurgency would ignite quickly and members of the local population had been preparing for a possible American invasion for some time. Although the British forces had the primary duty of taking the city, the members of Task Force Yankee had been maintaining a presence in the shadows. A few former SEALs working as U.S. government contractors were part of the paramilitary team sweeping through the city and assisting the other Coalition forces on the ground.

However, in many ways, the majority of the work the SEALs would do in Iraq would come later, when the insurgency was in full swing. Operation

Iraqi Freedom, known as Operation Telic to the Brits, made quick work of the Iraqi Army and Armor Divisions, routing them in short order. Many Iraqis surrendered without a fight while others fought valiantly but vainly in an attempt to hold off the Coalition troops. Our combined airpower and military might was simply overwhelming, and made Saddam's attempts to convince his forces that they were winning an exercise in futility.

After the completion of the main offensive and the key elements of the mission to bring down Saddam Hussain were complete, the Coalition maintained a strong presence and began the next phase of the war: a struggle to achieve a stable Iraq with a new provisional government in place. This was an extremely difficult task when one understands the

≳ **A SEAL with a custom desert paint scheme on his rifle**

tangled and hostile relationships between factions and different sects of Islam.

It is beyond the scope of our account to dig deeply into the history and elements that fully paint the picture of everything that led to this point in Iraq and the region, but suffice it to say that it was a witches' brew of multiple motivations: nationalism, religious belief and the conflict between opposing views within the Muslim faith, family heritage, tribal loyalties, the allocation and control of vital resources, and of course, pride, wealth, and personal status. Although some Iraqis were happy to see Saddam fall from power and were thankful for American and Coalition efforts, not everyone saw things that way. Many Iraqis simply saw the Americans as invaders who were meddling in their affairs. And, from a religious point of view, they had been taught their whole lives that Americans, and Christians and Jews in particular, were evil and must be either eradicated or converted—by the sword if necessary.

Nothing else fuels a need for vengeance in quite the same way.

For the Navy SEALs and U.S. Marine Corps, it was the Iraqi city of Fallujah in early 2004 that would prove to be a battleground unlike any they had faced in decades. In the months prior, military contractors from Blackwater USA, including former Navy SEAL Scott Helvenston, had been providing high-threat security and asset protection throughout Iraq. On March 31, 2004, Scott and three other Blackwater personnel were ambushed while escorting food and supplies to various checkpoints and food banks in Fallujah. A large mob of local insurgents attacked their convoy with grenades and small arms while the contractors were transiting through an extremely volatile section of the city.

All four men from Blackwater were killed and their bodies burned and dragged through the streets to the cheers of the insurgents. Two of the men's bodies were hung from a bridge overlooking the Euphrates River. This sparked an outrage among the Americans and led to the first major attempt to push into Fallujah. President Bush and National Command Authority, at the recommendation of local commanders in Iraq, immediately ordered our ground forces to eliminate the Iraqi guerrillas in Fallujah. On April 1, Brigadier General Mark Kimmitt, the Deputy Director of Military Operations in Iraq, promised the U.S. response would be swift and overwhelming.

The 1st Marine Expeditionary Force was ordered to take control of the city, but was met with heavy resistance. As the Marines pushed further into the city, it became obvious that the Iraqi insurgents were well-equipped and fanatical in their dedication to defending their homes. An estimated two-dozen different insurgent groups were dug in around Fallujah and were armed with RPGs, mortars, grenades, and standard small arms. The fighting was constant and ferocious.

During this period, Shiite Cleric Muqtada al-Sadr led the formation of the Mahdi Army, a major local insurgent group. The Mahdi's helped convince Iraqi police units and other members of the nationalistic Ba'athist Party to simply abandon their posts. Ultimately, a cease-fire was declared which both sides used to rearm and dig in deeper, fortifying their positions. The U.S. declared that major military operations would be turned over to the Iraqi Provisional Government and the newly formed Fallujah Brigade; however, in the months following this would prove to be a disaster for the Americans. In time, the Fallujah Brigade simply disbanded and turned all the weapons the U.S. had supplied them with to the insurgency.

All these factors combined to lead to a second attempt to take Fallujah in November 2004. This time, the American forces were even more prepared to do whatever necessary to achieve a solid victory.

OPERATION PHANTOM FURY

CITY OF FALLUJAH, IRAQ

NOVEMBER 30, 2004

The following scenario depicts actual events but the names and some details have been changed for security reasons:

Petty Officer Second Class James Villareal saw a plume of smoke and fire blossom as the rockets from an overhead Marine Corps AH-1W Cobra helicopter slammed into a building about five-hundred meters ahead of him. From his vantage point, the fireball was so large it looked like the rockets must have hit a cache of explosives the terrorists had been hiding.

"Hey man, did you see that . . . I don't think any bad guys are going to be hiding out in that building anymore," he said to his friend and Teammate from SEAL Team FIVE, Petty Officer First Class Brad Workman.

Workman grinned a bit and gave him a nod, "It appears their day has just been ruined, but we better stay focused and get back on the scope."

The SEALs had been ordered to provide sniper support for the Marine invasion into the heart of the city and multiple teams had taken up residence, so to say, in various buildings around the central area. Petty Officer's Villareal and Workman were one of many SEAL sniper teams there to help take down the enemy fighters.

All around the area the SEALs could hear the crack of small arms fire followed by grenades, rockets, and bombs going off—some close, some far, but definitely all around their position. Right this moment, their job was to provide overwatch for the Marines on the ground going house to house to clear out the city. Dust and smoke hung in the air making the task of targeting a specific person much harder.

"Guardian One-Three, this is Apache Two-Six, our platoon is moving East through your sector—keep a close lookout," came the call from the young Marine Corps platoon leader over the comm net.

Navy SEAL Brad Workman immediately turned his spotting scope to attempt to get a visual of the Marines and after a few moments saw the unmistakable look of Marines in full combat gear hustling into the area, weapons at the ready.

"I've got 'em . . . check your two-o'clock, about six-hundred yards out," he whispered to Villareal before continuing to scan the area.

"Roger, I see them."

Suddenly, the Marines of Charlie Company, Platoon Alpha, dove for whatever cover was available as the distinct sound of an RPG streaked towards their position. Rock, iron, and concrete flew in every direction upon impact.

"Contact! Contact front!" yelled the platoon sergeant.

The explosion was followed by heavy machine gun fire from a building about 100 meters to the east. It was a close call for the Marines who were now preparing to leapfrog towards the burned-out former market the terrorists appeared to be hiding inside.

The SEAL sniper had a momentary flashback as he recalled his early training at BUD/S . . . *You cannot simply shoot—you must hit.*

Ingrained into the SEALs early on in training is the concept that your training is never over. As a professional warrior, it is the SEALs job to constantly push his limits and get better at every skill. "Be the best at something and solid at everything else" was a line repeated at BUD/S over and over and then reinforced at their respective teams.

For Petty Officer Villareal, there was one thing with which he was always the best—putting a piece of lead on a very small target from nearly any distance.

He took a deep breath and peered through his Nightforce scope, "I've got movement on that building about one hundred meters from Alpha Platoon— looks like a heavy machine gunner and another guy with an RPG launcher . . . what's your estimate?"

"About Five-hundred-and-fifty meters," said Workman as he dialed in the laser range finder on his spotting scope.

"Copy that . . . standby."

James Villareal shifted his weight and pulled the stock of his .338 Lapua sniper rifle tight into his shoulder as he peered through his scope at the target over five football fields away. In the snipers trade, target identification and selection is based on a sliding scale of importance that depends on the situation: soldiers with heavy weapons or rockets are often on the top of the pecking order along with enemy snipers. A well-placed shot that takes out a heavy machine gunner or rocketeer can reduce the enemy's effectiveness by an order of magnitude.

The reticle inside his scope was a crisp red, just bright enough to do its job, but not so bright as to be a distraction. He allowed himself a moment to ensure he was settled in on the enemy target before pulling the trigger. A 1,000-meter shot typically takes approximately 1.45 seconds to reach the target. In this case it was only three quarters of a second before the terrorist machine gunner was hit by just over 4,800 pounds of force.

A shot like that means he was dead before he even hit the ground.

Without missing a beat, Villareal continued scanning for the next target when he heard heavy machine gun rounds rake the building they were sitting on followed by frantic yelling over the comm net from the squad of Recon Marines down below. It sounded like one of them was both exceptionally angry and scared at the same time.

And then it happened—a loud crack in the distance accompanied by a bright flash from what appeared to be an armored vehicle. Moments later, a TOW Missile was en-route to their position: a grave mistake now seconds away from causing a massive friendly fire incident.

The TOW missile: a tube-launched, optically tracked, wire-guided missile which is typically used for anti-tank operations, but can be outfitted with various warheads, which makes it capable of being used against heavily fortified positions as well. In this case, the standard version armed with 3.2 kilograms of high explosives was flying right at the SEALs and Marines.

As the Marines from 1st Recon Battalion continued trying to wave off the U.S. Army's Bradley Fighting Vehicle, the TOW missile screamed through an open window and skidded to a halt less than five meters from the men who instantly ran and dove for cover outside the building, scattering like a bunch of wild deer. Petty Officer Villareal and Workman had no idea what was happening.

But as the seconds ticked by . . . nothing. No explosion. The TOW missile had miraculously failed to arm and just sat there in the middle of the ground floor of the building.

Realizing they had just barely escaped certain death, the recon Marines regrouped and got the attention of the SEALs above, explaining that their hiding spot was no longer safe. Fortunately, the Army unit responsible for the shot realized the error and called for an EOD (Explosive Ordinance Disposal) team as everyone evacuated the area.

Despite the close call, the SEALs pushed on unfazed and moved to another hide site to continue the mission. There were still Marines out there pushing into the city and they still needed them to help ensure as many Americans came home alive as possible. Knowing they were temporarily exposed, Villareal and Workman visually scanned the area and saw a multistory building about two hundred meters away which appeared to suit their needs.

"Well, it appears God was looking out for us on that one, man," Villareal said as they moved between various points of cover and concealment en-route to their new perch.

Workman nodded grimly, "Yeah, brother, that TOW missile would have ruined our day for sure if it had gone off . . . it's a freaking miracle we are still alive."

"Alexis and Jackie just about became filthy rich—I guess it's a good thing we got those secondary life insurance policies, but I'm not sure I'm quite ready for the wives to cash in on them just yet," he said with a laugh.

As the SEALs allowed themselves a moment to enjoy the joke, two more Cobra gunships flew overhead and lit up multiple enemy positions in the distance. It was followed closely by an F-16 fighter jet with bombs hanging from multiple pylons under its wings. The sounds of battle continued to rage on and the dust and sand seemed to fill the air more than ever. Small arms fire continued to rattle off from nearly every direction.

Once at the building, Villareal and Workman quickly made their way to the top floor and set up a new overwatch emplacement. Within a few minutes the men were up and ready to go. A quick scan of the area made it obvious that multiple Marine Corps fire teams from 1st Battalion, 3rd Marine Regiment were maneuvering all over the area clearing out structure after structure throughout the city. Since most of the civilian population had evacuated the city before the invasion nearly anyone left was a target. In many ways, it made the work easier despite the constant danger around every corner. Not that they could shoot indiscriminately, but they were far less likely to have to concern themselves with civilians. This scenario, based on the actions of actual individuals and their response to immediate events, gives a sense of how daunting was the retaking of Fallujah. In November 2004 the city was a full-on war zone with each side having only one mission—kill the enemy before he kills you.

The next three weeks were essentially a continuous repeat of this cycle and in late December the United States declared a decisive victory. After the battle, Fallujah was a shell of its former self, with bullet holes in the walls of every building still standing and fires still burning throughout every sector of town. But the Al-Qaeda militants and Iraqi insurgents had been finally routed from their positions—either killed, captured, or in some cases had chosen to flee to fight another day. In total, approximately 2,000 of the enemy fighters were KIA with another 1,500 captured. In all, 107 Americans were killed and another 613 wounded.

Though Fallujah was technically a victory, in fact one of many, the Global War on Terror was far from over and the SEALs would continue to be called upon in nearly every corner of the world. Men from the Teams continued to constantly train and prepare for their next deployment, and in many ways their biggest fights were still ahead.

Back home, President Bush, the National Security Council, and the Joint Chiefs were hard at work developing plans to continue prosecuting the War on Terror and put worldwide pressure on Al-Qaeda and its leader, Osama Bin Laden, whom it was believed had narrowly escaped the grasp of American forces during the Battle of Tora Bora. Intelligence reports remain conflicted as to whether or not bin Laden had actually been there during Operation Anaconda, but

≽ **SEALs conducting a desert warfare exercise**

many of the men on the ground were certain they had him cornered before slipping away into neighboring Pakistan.

Either way, bin Laden was still at large and considered to be enemy number one of the American people. An enormous amount of resources were diverted to tracking and eventually hunting down the man who had coordinated the worst attack on American soil since Pearl Harbor. And, as has been the case throughout the War on Terror, the Navy SEALs were right in the middle of it all.

The next ten years after the Battle of Fallujah was filled with deployment after deployment for the SEALs and other members of the special operations community. Of particular note are the widely known actions in which SEALs played the key role: The Battle of Ramadi, Operation Red Wings, and Operation Neptune Spear—all which have had their stories told in great detail in books like *American Sniper* and *Lone Survivor*, or in various documentaries on the History Channel or other networks. However, in some ways the public actions of the SEALs tend to make the general population overlook the fact that these warriors have been on the forefront of this fight day and night. There are SEALs who have literally done eight or nine combat deployments back to back with only relatively brief periods of time back home. With the average deployment lasting six or seven months, that puts some men in the zone of nearly sixty months of sustained combat operations over the last ten years— an astonishing amount of experience which provides a wealth of knowledge to pass on to the next generation of SEALs.

But, it can also take a heavy toll on the men: a toll on the body, mind, and spirit.

A Navy SEAL and his teammates train constantly, deploy, and then come home and do it all over again. Over the years the body can break down no matter how tough you are mentally. For this reason, one of the premier assets of a SEAL is resilience—mental and physical. There are professional and Olympic athletes all over the world who may be able to outperform many SEALs in specific events, whether it is running, swimming, or other athletics. But there is a criterion that goes beyond physical prowess; it is the reason that when the President of the United States needs someone to hunt down terrorists he doesn't call the Olympic Triathlon Team, the winners of a Spartan or BattleFrog Race, or champion CrossFit Games athlete.

He calls the SEALs and their special operations counterparts in the Army, Air Force, and Marine Corps.

In the end, they are called because at the heart of the SEAL ethos is the simple fact that the men are not just athletes—although many are great athletes—but they also have a mindset and spirit that is different from most: they willingly accept the fact that their primary duty includes the capability to go anywhere in the world and risk their lives in the most austere environments to engage America's enemies in war. No athlete, no matter how accomplished, must agree to do the same to be at the top of their chosen discipline.

This doesn't even touch on the other sacrifices— sacrifices paid in time apart from family and friends, forgoing other personal pursuits or endeavors, and in some cases, giving life and limb as a result of their absolute dedication to the mission. A heavy price indeed.

And so, of the thousands of missions conducted by the SEALs, any number of which deserve to have their story told, one such mission stands out in a way that demonstrates the pinnacle of what a SEAL can hope to achieve: the rescue of an American doctor from the grasp of the Taliban by the men of [redacted].

TOP SECRET INSTALLATION
[REDACTED] AFGHANISTAN
DECEMBER 5, 2012, 2345 HOURS

The following scenario is based on real events and is taken from sources including official citations, but also incorporates elements representative of actual people and the work they do:

Air Force Technical Sergeant Max Ziminski sipped on his third cup of coffee for the night and took a quick look at the monitor mounted on the far wall of the room, noting to himself that everything looked good but feeling compelled to ask anyway, "Sergeant Keller, how's our bird doing tonight?"

The young but experienced Predator UAV pilot made a quick mental note of the system status before replying somewhat dryly, "Things look good, all systems nominal."

Not a moment later, Ziminski got a call on the SATCOM phone the officer of the watch always kept on standby. He put down his coffee and hit the button to accept the call. Sergeant Keller kept her eye on the tactical screen but couldn't help overhearing

Ziminski repeat a lot of "yes, sir . . . right away, sir" over the next minute so she knew something was up.

"Keller, do quick systems check of the bird's eye in the sky and prepare for new tasking. We've got something big going on," he said while reaching for the internal comm system.

Ziminski immediately made the call to [redacted] the post commander for one of America's greatest assets in the War on Terror: a Top Secret Predator Base.

"Yes sir, they need you to call immediately . . . we have emergent tasking requiring our assistance," Ziminski said as [redacted] sat up in his stateroom and reached for his reading glasses.

Predators would be needed to help locate an American—a doctor of Afghani descent by the name of Dilip Joseph who had been on a humanitarian mission to his native land near Kabul. Unfortunately, local militants associated with the Taliban had taken notice of Dr. Joseph and decided he would make a good propaganda piece, or at a minimum, would make a substantial ransom payment that would help fund their operations.

Time was of the essence. "Sergeant Ziminski, I'll be down to the control station in five minutes. Please have the pilot on duty head toward the coordinates provided by [redacted]."

At the same moment, the Watch Commander at [redacted] was already waking up the [redacted] Task Force Commander, Commander Mike Metcalf. Mike Metcalf, a career SEAL officer, was accustomed to calls in the middle of the night, but somehow he knew this one felt different.

"What have you got for me?" The veteran SEAL said as he was already making his way to his locker to grab a uniform and get down to the Tactical Operations Center.

"Sir, an American medical worker has been taken hostage by the Taliban—they have the Predator from base Sierra One en-route to his last known location to begin a sweep," the watch commander said crisply.

Commander Metcalf quickly jumped into his uniform and ordered the watch commander to have someone wake up one of his top man, Chief Special Operator Edward Byers, and have him meet him down at the TOC. Within minutes both men were getting a complete situation report and knew they needed to start prepping.

"Commander, it won't take long for the guys responsible for the kidnapping to have him nearly anywhere in the country, so we better move fast figuring this one out," said Chief Byers with a sincere look of concern.

"Agreed, Ed. In a way the doctor is a man of two worlds, being an American citizen but with Afghani heritage—it's likely they will keep him alive as long as possible in an attempt to get us to give in to their demands."

Chief Byers nodded. "I'll spin up the guys and start prepping, sir."

Before long, the entire intel section was up and starting the tedious process of scouring through any and all leads, analyzing any data relative to the kidnapping, and contacting any local field assets who may have heard something about the situation. Meanwhile, the SEALs started going through their pre-op checklist and made sure everything was ready to go at a moment's notice.

As the next twenty-four hours passed, small bits and pieces of information started to flow in and began to allow a clearer picture to coalesce. Dr. Joseph was the medical director of a non-profit company called Morning Star Development, an organization dedicated to helping the people of Afghanistan achieve a better standard of living including medical care, education, and infrastructure. A career physician, Dr. Joseph continually hoped that his efforts would prove fruitful for the people of his native land.

Despite the influx of intelligence information and the now loitering Predator continuously scanning the region, it was a lead from a local informant that gave them the break they needed to locate the doctor. For the mere equivalent of twenty American dollars, a very significant amount of money for most Afghanis, a local man who had become disillusioned with the strict Taliban rule passed on a rumor he had heard about an "American doctor who had turned against his people" and gladly accepted payment from the [redacted] operative who had been developing him as an asset for some time. After a lengthy conversation, the informant had given up a vast amount of desperately needed information concerning the possible location of the doctor or where he might soon be taken. It was standard procedure for hostages to be moved from one location to another in order to frustrate attempts to rescue them.

A testimony to the delicate and ultra-complex world of HUMINT (Human Intelligence), the break allowed the planners to direct the Predator UAV to observe likely routes the kidnappers might use to travel through the region toward the eastern province of Laghman. One of the rumors overheard by the informant had pointed directly to the Qarghah'i District of Laghman. Within another twenty-four hours the SEALs and intel personnel had the location pinpointed.

Time to mount up.

QARGHAH'I DISTRICT, LAGHMAN PROVINCE

EASTERN AFGHANISTAN

DECEMBER 8, 2012

2345 HOURS

A barely visible crescent moon waxed high in the night sky as the lone [redacted] Blackhawk helicopter cruised along a mere twenty meters from the ground. Its cargo: a small team of Navy SEALs from [redacted].

Chief Edward Byers adjusted his helmet light and the reddish glow illuminated his detailed map of the area well enough to go over the planned route one more time in his mind. It would be a fairly rugged hike, but not a lot of climbing. His primary concern would be time to the target. Based on what they knew the SEAL element had planned for a four-hour hike in but it is always hard to make a perfectly accurate estimate. Unknown factors have a tendency to creep in and force adjustments to even the best plan.

The pilot-in-command, Major Tom "Redwood" Peters, pressed the internal comm button as he scanned out ahead using his night-vision goggles and flying along at a comfortable 130 knots. "Gentlemen, we are approaching the drop site—ETA two minutes . . . repeat, ETA two minutes."

Petty Officer Nick Checque glanced around at his fellow SEALs and traded a nod with each man signifying they were ready to go. As the team leader for this op, Chief Byers ran through a last mental checklist and prepared himself to exit. Every guy has a different way of dealing with the last moments before a mission, but typically one's mind naturally begins to transition to a laser focus and whatever elements you may be feeling—fear, cold, pain—all begin to diminish and become nothing more than something you remain vaguely aware of but is compartmentalized away until it dissipates completely. All the matters is the mission.

Major Peters pulled back on the stick and adjusted the cyclic, bringing his bird into a perfect hover, demonstrating the invariable rock-solid piloting for which he was well known. Within seconds the SEALs were down the fast rope and on the ground.

The men sprinted ten meters, spread out, and took a knee while their ride quickly disappeared into the dark, almost moonless night. After a waiting a short time to ensure their entrance into the region had appeared to go unnoticed, they quickly formed up and began the hike to their target approximately thirty kilometers away. Hills and unimproved trails added some difficulty to the forced march, but for the SEALs it was just another day at the office.

The crisp, cold air of the dark but starlit night helped regulate the body temperatures of the rescue team as they closed within a quarter mile of their target. Fortunately, the trek had been relatively uneventful, and after the nearly four hours it took to get through the mountainous Laghman Province of eastern Afghanistan, Chief Byers and his team took a brief moment to decide on the final approach. Intelligence reports had allowed the Predator UAV to pinpoint the location of Dr. Joseph. His humanitarian work, traveling around the country in an effort to train local physicians in modern healthcare skills and techniques, had been unfortunately brought to a halt by his captors.

During these final few hundred meters of the patrol, the uneven terrain continued to be the only way into the small compound ahead. Chief Byers and the other men knew that despite the fatigue of the long trip in on foot, the success of the mission would depend on using the stealth, speed, and aggression for which U.S. Navy SEALs had become legendary. As they continued maneuvering closer to the target location, the team finally was able to get a visual of the building in question. The SEALs instinctively controlled their breathing and slowed their movement in order to maintain the best chance of remaining undetected. Chief Byers gave a customary pat to the patch on his right arm of Saint Michael the Archangel, a patch handed down to him by a fellow SEAL upon entering the country on his first combat deployment. He had worn it on every mission since that time now many years and many deployments later.

No talking between them was necessary as they crept forward toward their target—a nod or simple hand gesture was enough. Time seemed to slow down as they approached—one hundred meters, seventy-five meters, fifty meters, twenty-five meters . . .

The point man, Petty Officer Checque, raised his left hand, ordering the team to freeze as he saw an insurgent guard slowly walk around the side of the compound. He knew instinctively that in this moment the effort to maintain the element of surprise could be compromised. As he took another breath, frozen in place, the guard stopped and looked intently in their direction before taking off at a sprint for the main door.

Time to move.

With the element of surprise gone, Petty Officer Checque instinctively shouldered his HK 416 assault rifle, took a shot at the guard just as he entered the building, and rushed forward. The clock was ticking now, and mere seconds would determine success or failure of this critical and dangerous mission.

Nick sprinted ahead and crashed through the front door, Chief Byers and the squad only seconds behind him. The Taliban guards had assumed that a rescue team might come and had been preparing for it. As the SEAL point man burst through the make-shift door, a guard let loose a burst from his AK-47 assault rifle and a round struck the valiant American warrior in the head.

Feeling a surge of aggression, Chief Byers pushed his way through the layers of blankets serving as an inner door for the compound and came face-to-face with the guard. With pinpoint accuracy, Byers lined up the sight picture with his rifle the way he had done thousands of times in training and on dozens of missions and killed the terrorist fighter instantly with a shot to the head.

Out of the corner of his eye he saw a man race toward the corner of the room, but the darkness prevented a positive ID: this was a rescue mission, making it imminently critical that the SEALs identify with absolute certainty whether the person was an enemy combatant . . . or the man to be rescued.

Byers rushed forward and tackled the unknown man, pinning him against the wall and maintaining control over him while reaching up to adjust his night-vision goggles to allow close-up focus. In the same moment the rest of his team burst into the room and began to call out to Dr. Joseph, asking him to identify himself. Once the goggles had refocused, Chief Byers realized the man he pinned was Taliban so he dispatched him with two quick shots to the body and one to the head.

A voice then called out from across the room, "I'm here, I am Doctor Joseph!"

Without hesitation, Chief Byers sprinted over to the man and leaped onto him, selflessly guarding him with his own body as the fight continued all around them. Looking up, he realized another guard was directly behind the doctor, but he was out of position to take a shot and so reached up and grabbed the man around the throat, pinning him against the wall. Moments later, one of his SEAL teammates, demonstrating incredible marksmanship, killed the enemy fighter from across the room with two precision shots.

Less than ninety seconds from the initial contact, all the guards were neutralized by the SEALs and they began to move to the extraction point. Rattled, but okay, Dr. Joseph was moved to the helicopter landing zone while the other members of the squad began immediate medical assistance on their fallen teammate.

"Come on man, stick with us . . . we're gonna get you out of here," Chief Byers said as he retrieved his emergency medical kit. Blood loss can be one of the primary causes of death, so once he established whether or not his teammate was breathing it was time to do whatever he could to prevent him from bleeding out.

He's not going to make it, Chief Byers thought, slightly irritated at himself for admitting the situation seemed dire and potentially out of his control.

A short time later, Major Peter's [redacted] Black-Hawk swiftly glided into position for a recovery. After the team climbed aboard the helicopter and it began the forty-minute flight back to Bagram Air Base, the team continued to try to keep their friend and teammate alive. Technically a resounding success, the extremely difficult mission now seemed bitter-sweet. Petty Officer Nick Checque died from his wound en-route.

Therein is the essence of the warrior: the willing-ness to risk everything for another life, most of which are people you have never known and will never see again.

Long live the brotherhood.

9

NAVY SPECIAL WARFARE DEVELOPMENT GROUP— AN OVERVIEW OF [REDACTED]

The most secret of missions, the highest value targets, and the most dangerous operations in the world are conducted all over the globe by members of the Navy's most elite fighting force: [redacted].

On the April 24, 1980, U.S. Forces from [redacted] commenced a mission intended to rescue fifty-two American embassy staff workers held captive in Tehran. Officially dubbed Operation Eagle Claw, it was to be one of the very first missions for the Army's new Delta Force. The mission failed.

The operational planners had broken a cardinal rule of military missions—keep it simple. Instead, the commanders developed a highly complex two-night mission with multiple aircraft and no full comprehension of the completely unpredictable environmental conditions. As is many times the case, the unknown factors that warriors encountered in the field continued to plague the already difficult mission.

Eight helicopters were forward deployed to the first staging area, call sign Desert One. Enroute to the site, three of the helicopters were disabled because of various problems encountered mid-flight: hydraulic failure, clouds of very fine sand fouling the intakes, and a cracked rotor blade. The planners had decided to abort the mission if fewer than six helicopters remained operational, even though they believed that only four were necessary.

With three of the aircraft down right out of the gate, the mission commanders recommended aborting the operation—a decision highly debated to this day by various military leaders. In the end, President Carter accepted the recommendation to abort and the mission was called off immediately.

In the aftermath of the failed attempt, it was decided by members of the Terrorist Action Team (TAT) that a Maritime Counterterrorism Unit was necessary. The TAT had been responsible for the planning of Operation Eagle Claw and recognized that had there been a naval component to the mission capabilities then there would have been potentially better options available, particularly because of the extremely difficult logistical nightmare they had faced. Commander Richard Marcinko was tapped to develop, train, equip, and deploy this new unit.

During his tenure as the Commanding Officer from 1980–1983, Marcinko had given his new team the name [redacted]. America was at the height of the Cold War with the Soviet Union and at the time there were only two SEAL teams in existence. Marcinko believed giving his team the title [redacted] would potentially confuse the Soviets and lead them to think there were more SEAL Teams than truly existed.

Marcinko was given unprecedented latitude and funding to develop his new team. It was highly rumored that the budget for ammunition and training for his SEALs ran so high that it was actually more than the budget for the entire United States Marine Corps. This meant that the newly commissioned [redacted] had essentially an unlimited amount of money for training and equipment—and they put it to use.

The men of [redacted] trained relentlessly and Marcinko was granted the power to handpick his men. Essentially Commander Marcinko went to all of the SEAL Teams, UDT Teams (which remained in existence until commissioned as SEAL Teams in 1983), and SDV Teams and snatched up whoever he

⩓ **A SEAL classic: the Desert Patrol Vehicle (DPV)**

thought fit the mold. His criteria were focused on a few fundamentals: combat experience, tactical knowledge, proven performance, top physical conditioning, and last but not least, personality.

Anytime you put together a team you have to anticipate that you will encounter two distinct personalities: the individual operators and the team overall. Each contributes to the other and Marcinko had a distinct type of personality in mind for his crew. He wasn't much of a spit-and-polish kind of guy and definitely was one to bend the rules, sometimes to a breaking point. Marcinko wanted SEALs who were going to mesh well with that philosophy and was intent on finding them.

The move was not without controversy. Many SEAL leaders had come up in the teams believing in the time-proven adage, "We don't have to be friends or even like each other to work well together." Simply put, a professional can set aside personal feelings and get the job done even if his teammates are not his best buddies.

Military leaders in every branch have dealt with this issue and each service and unit has its own solution. For the U.S. Marine Corps, an exceptionally rigid rank structure and respect for the chain-of-command is their way of doing business. Same applies in general for the Army Rangers. But the lines begin to get a bit blurry for small special operations teams because of the nature of the work and the requirement of each man to be generally more mature and more of a "think outside the box" kind of guy. That is not to say that rank is not respected in the SEAL Teams, but rather that the men share a sense of comradery that begins in a unique way when all trainees, officer and enlisted alike, go through training together side-by-side. This is one of the many factors that makes BUD/S different from some of the other programs.

Either way, for Marcinko's team he wanted guys who were rough and not bound by standard military protocol. It was a lot like a bunch of guys in a biker gang who had turned their aggression toward doing something good instead of something criminal.

After Marcinko selected the men who would become the first team members, what the U.S. Navy calls "Plank Owners," the team began coming together in very short order. They immediately started an aggressive training cycle to get the new team operational as fast as possible. [redacted] had been formally created in October 1980 and by May 1981 was declared mission ready.

The original team consisted of seventy-five shooters with another contingent of support staff. Marcinko later revealed that he wished he had more time to get the team up and running but ultimately was satisfied with the results. And he had good reason to be. The team had trained hard, many times doing back-to-back eighteen to twenty hour days to push themselves to get ready. Nothing was left to chance and the men of [redacted] spent relentless hours at the range, diving, jumping out of all types of aircraft, running tactical drills, and staying in absolute top physical shape. By the time they were declared operationally ready, they truly were prepared to go anywhere in the world and take on any mission with a focus on maritime-based operations like ship take-downs, assaults on waterborne oil rigs, and rescue missions on coastal targets.

Marcinko's role as Commanding Officer of [redacted] lasted until 1983. He turned over the command to Captain Robert Gormly. The first three years was like a whirlwind and the men who were there describe it as a "wild ride . . . and worth every second." In contrast, Captain Gormly wasn't as much a maverick as Marcinko, but commanded and received the respect of his men just the same.

Over the next few years, [redacted] continued to develop and adapt to new mission requirements. It wasn't long before they were being called upon to conduct missions beyond the initial parameters set for them. And some controversial circumstances surrounding the original founder led the Navy to dissolve [redacted] in favor of a new name and a new mission.

⌃ A SEAL scales the ladder to the target before taking it down

From then on, the famed team became officially known as Naval Special Warfare Development Group, or NSWDG for short, and their mission was stated as simply "to provide centralized management for the test, evaluation, and development of equipment technology and TTP for NSW."

Even so, the team is still known best by its original moniker, [redacted].

The new mission statement, while very modern and tech-savvy, was actually a very clever way of disguising the fact that their true purpose remained essentially the same: be the premier maritime counterterrorist unit in the world. Since the late 1980s, the unit has continued to mold itself into an even more effective and efficient combat team. Currently, NSWDG is made up of the following "Squadrons":

[redacted]	Assault Team 1
[redacted]	Assault Team 2
[redacted]	Assault Team 3
[redacted]	Assault Team 4
[redacted]	Special Reconnaissance/Infiltration/Sniper
[redacted]	Mobility and Transportation
[redacted]	Intelligence/Crypto/Electronics Warfare
[redacted]	Selection and Training
EOD	Explosive Ordinance Disposal

Each squadron is divided into three "troops" and commanded by a seasoned lieutenant commander (LCDR O-4). In addition, each squadron has a distinct personality to it with a nickname associated with it.

One aspect that should not be overlooked is the current selection process to become a member of NSWDG. Candidates for the legendary team must already be SEALs with operational experience and will begin the process by completing a series of tests and evaluations beginning with an enhanced Physical Screening Test (PST), psychological testing, an interview, and an oral review board. If the Review Board deems them fit to continue on to selection they will report to [redacted] for a nine-month-long Operators Training Course.

[Redacted] is brutal. The pace is absolutely relentless and the attrition rate is actually quite high due to the extreme level of scrutiny placed on the candidates to perform at the highest level. You must keep in mind that every student has already proven himself as a SEAL in an operational team and so the expectation level is extremely high. If a student is to be successful in making it through the demanding course it will be imperative for him to remember part of the SEAL creed: you earn your Trident every day.

Simply put, that means no resting on past accomplishments or believing you have nothing to learn. As the Selection and Training instructor cadre will prove to you *very* quickly, there is *always* more to learn. And, never forget that the business of the SEALs is a matter of life and death—a NSWDG operator will certainly be put to the test if accepted into the team

⌃ **Training at night with IR Lasers and Night Vision**

so the training must be realistic, and therefore, dangerous. Live fire exercises are the norm and almost nothing is off-limits. To be the best the team must train its people above and beyond all normal limits.

During his time in Selection and Training, the student will attend various civilian and military training courses such as advanced diving and parachuting, tactical unarmed combat, specialized driving, rock climbing, VIP protection details, and more. Every single evolution throughout training is evaluated and the student is either deemed worthy to continue or is dropped. Assuming the drop was not for safety reasons, he may request an opportunity to try out again at a later date.

Once a student finishes Selection and Training, he will be assigned to one of the operational squadrons. As noted earlier, each squadron has a personality of its own. The guys in [redacted] Squadron tend to

⌃ **A SEAL team emerges from the water**

spend a lot of their PT time in the gym, and it shows. These guys probably most closely resemble how most of the population would imagine the toughest military unit on the planet would appear.

[redacted] is a bit more conservative than [redacted] or [redacted]. [Redacted] Squadron has a lot of endurance athletes who were often exceptional runners and/or swimmers. [redacted] Squadron has a reputation as being the down-and-dirty crew. Known as "the Pirates," a lot of the guys from [redacted] who come aboard are the ones who might be in a biker gang if it wasn't for the Teams. Generally speaking the guys in [redacted] were a little further on the "non-conformist" scale than some of the other guys.

However, when it comes to skill and deadly efficiency, every man is well-trained, brave beyond measure, and lethal—no matter which squadron he is assigned.

Although the original purpose of the SEALs was to be the premier maritime counterterrorist force, over the years it has grown to be truly capable of any possible special operations mission including Hostage Rescue, Counter Proliferation of both conventional as well as nuclear weapons of mass destruction (WMD), and the elimination of high-value targets (HVTs). [redacted] stands as the go-to unit when the president of the United States has special tasking of which only these men are truly capable.

Of those missions, one of the most dramatic and most satisfying for the men is the rescue and recovery of Americans captured and taken hostage by one of the myriad of evil groups or organizations that exist in the world. It is also one of the most difficult missions the men of [redacted] perform.

To conduct a successful hostage rescue, many factors must be accounted for as the men prepare, as well as during every single phase of the mission, from learning of the need for an extraction all the way to the engagement with the kidnappers themselves. Each step in the process is of critical importance.

The training to prepare for a hostage rescue is in some ways both routine for the men as well as exceptionally demanding. Routine in that each SEAL from [redacted] has spent thousands and thousands of hours perfecting his craft and preparing on the range or in the "kill house" (a specialized, usually armored building built to train in Close Quarters Battle or CQB) with their weapon skills, in the field doing tactical combat training, or doing physical conditioning nonstop to ensure he is ready to go at a moment's notice should the need arise for him to execute the mission.

The hard part? The extreme mental concentration required to shoot, move, and communicate in a completely chaotic environment with multiple distractions. And if any *one* of your shots misses its mark then either you, your team, or the hostages could die. This is not an exaggeration.

To that end, the operators at [redacted] must train for absolute precision, judgment, and mental resilience. In the kill house, the guys are expected to put every single round within a box on the target slightly smaller than a three by five index card— even when moving and engaging multiple targets while in full combat gear. There is *zero* tolerance for

⌃ **Cold weather ops—a SEAL must be able to operate in any environment**

a missed shot and the stress level can be extremely high. To add difficulty to each training scenario, all training in the kill house is with live ammunition and team members take turns acting as the hostages where a miss could truly result in death of a fellow SEAL. But this is how it must be done at the highest levels to ensure maximum skill and confidence that when the time comes and the lives of untold hostages are on the line, you know you can make the shot.

On a cold night in January 2012 the SEALs of [redacted] would have to put this training into practice for one of the most dramatic rescues in American military history. And the Navy SEALs of [redacted] are always ready to answer the call.

Mission Profile: Hostage Rescue
Target: Captured Aid Workers In Northern Africa
Enemy Force: Somali Militants
Unit Tasking: SEAL Team [redacted]

Background:

In October 2011, an American aid worker named Jessica Buchanan and her colleague Poul Thisted from Denmark were taken captive by Somali militants hoping for a very large ransom. Jessica and Poul had been working for a project funded by the Danish Refugee Council that focused on efforts to rid the country of Somalia of thousands of land mines and to teach young children how to find and avoid them. While traveling by car in northern Somalia, the militants kidnapped them at gunpoint.

The pair was driven to a remote location in the desert and ultimately held for ninety-two days.

During their captivity, Buchanan became deathly ill and had a thyroid condition that needed medication on a daily basis, further exacerbating her already terrible situation. The leader of the Somali group told her they were merely wanted for the ransom that would be paid for her release. They were demanding a payment of forty-five million dollars in United States currency.

As the days and weeks dragged by, Jessica began to lose hope that she would ever leave the bandit camp alive and her medical condition worsened daily, partially due to the lack of medicine but also because of the terrible lack of sanitary conditions. They were forced to sleep outside, no matter the conditions or temperature; the desert can be a very cold place at night. Bugs, particularly exceptionally large beetles carrying who knows what kind of disease, plagued them each and every day, crawling over and into their sleeping mats, hair, and clothing.

What had begun for them as a mission of peace and mercy had turned into a nightmare.

Negotiations between the Somali bandits and the hostage negotiators were ongoing. In time, the team of agents and analysts were able to decipher specifically to which Somali clan the militants belonged, who their leader was, and in what region they most likely would be holding the captives. Although the final details as to how they pinpointed the exact location are classified, they were able to determine the location of the bandit camp by utilizing a mixture of traditional as well as high-tech methods and techniques.

Approximately eighty days into their captivity, Jessica had already lost twenty-five pounds and was extremely sick; her condition had deteriorated badly. She had also developed a case of a urinary tract infection but was given no antibiotics to treat it. Now, in even greater pain than she had been already, she told her captives that if she didn't get help she knew she would die out there in the desert. For her kidnappers, this posed a serious problem, not because they cared for her well-being or health, but because if she died they would lose all hope of being paid a ransom.

Her medical condition was communicated to the negotiators and the information was passed on to the [redacted] headquarters in Washington. The officials from both agencies then told President Obama the bad news. He immediately decided that something had to be done.

On January 23, 2012, days before the upcoming State of the Union address and with Jessica's life now certainly in imminent danger, the President called a meeting with an advisory team, the members of which recommended the immediate planning of a rescue operation to extract her and her colleague from the militants.

It was finally time for the SEALs to go to work.

OPERATION [REDACTED]

[REDACTED], SOMALIA

JANUARY 25, 2012

0012 HOURS

32,000 FT

The following account is based on official reports, personal experience, and the public interview of the captive, Jessica Buchanan, which aired on the television show 60 Minutes *(the names of the SEALs involved and some minor details have been changed for security reasons):*

The red glow of the internal lights inside the [redacted] transport aircraft allowed the SEALs to see just well enough to do a final gear check. Lieutenant Commander Jeff "Havok" Yeager, the on-site mission commander from [redacted], checked his watch and made a mental note: three minutes.

Each man had a slightly different mental preparatory routine before a jump. For some, they preferred to simply zone out and think about something else; for others, it was a matter of mentally rehearsing the upcoming mission over and over in their minds until they felt absolutely confident every last detail was perfectly engrained in their memory. Once on the ground it would be time to move out and execute the plan with absolutely no room for mistakes.

They were [redacted] relatively light. For some extended missions you have to pack a lot of extra gear to survive, sometimes for days on end without any resupply, and that extra equipment can start to add up quickly in weight. The SEALs had trained time and time again to move fast over long distances wearing a heavy load, but it was by far not preferable. Every last kilogram of gear better be necessary for your mission; and if it isn't you needed to consider lightening your battle kit (the term "kit" or "battle kit" is military parlance for the equipment you wear or take with you on a mission), except for equipment needed for contingencies, which must always be accounted for on a mission. There is a saying in the military: "It is better to have it and not need it than to need it and not have it."

Following that advice can save your life.

Senior Chief Nathan Parker stood up and gave the signal to rally just before the pilot came over the intercom system, "Gentlemen, we will [redacted] in thirty seconds—standby."

The SEALs all stood up and walked over to the rear of the aircraft, awaiting the familiar sound of the wind rushing in as the cargo bay door opened wide. They had each done a jump like this hundreds of times at a minimum, and for some of the old salts in the team, thousands of times. But the difference tonight was the life of one American and her colleague hung in the balance and the next two hours would determine whether the hostages would live or die.

It was dark. No moon whatsoever meant it would be a little trickier to [redacted] the landing zone, but they would hit the ground at a distance well away from the enemy encampment and hike in on foot the rest of the way. Stealth was crucial and without it there would be a high likelihood of mission failure. That was completely unacceptable to the SEALs.

Green light—Go, Go, Go!

The SEALs exited the aircraft and felt the cold air surround them like a sheath. The jump plan had called for a High-Altitude High Opening (HAHO) jump instead of a High-Altitude Low Opening (HALO) jump. Essentially, that meant that the SEALs would jump from an altitude over 12,000 feet and have more time under the canopy to fly and direct their chute, which also allowed them a much greater range. It is technically possible to fly over 40 miles, up to an hour under canopy, if necessary to reach a target.

After a relatively long ride to the ground, the team leader got a head check and ordered the men to move out. GPS coordinates indicated approximately 6.5 kilometers south-southwest to the target location. A quick hike in, secure the camp, and extract.

The desert is a strange place; it can be unbearably hot during the day with the temperatures at night falling forty-plus degrees in a matter of hours. One of the weirdest things is how it might be one hundred and twenty degrees during the day then plunge to eighty degrees and it make you feel like you're freezing.

But the hike in would keep the core temperature up and the men would be fine.

Let's step it out gents, we have an appointment to keep with a bunch of bad guys that really need us to pay them a visit . . .

Lieutenant Commander Yeager smiled at the thought. He had been on dozens of missions with his troops but each time he still got excited. From the time he was a young kid growing up in the Midwest he had always dreamed of doing missions just like this one. It was a dream come true and sometimes he still couldn't believe he was getting to live it with some of the bravest and toughest men in the world.

He knew that there would be at least one militant guarding the camp, but the disdain that these people had for the canine species meant it was unlikely they had any guard dogs roaming the area. That would make the approach that much easier.

In the bandit's camp, the men were zoning in and out as they came off their massive khat high. Many of them were asleep and their captives lay curled up in the fetal position, trying desperately to sleep. Jessica Buchanan, miserable from the pain of her infection, wondered if she would even wake up should she finally, mercifully, fall asleep. She wasn't sure anymore if it mattered.

Hope can keep one alive, perhaps not indefinitely, but well past normal physiological limits. It has been rightly said that if you have lost hope, you have lost it all. Jessica and Poul clung to hope night after night in the desert as the remorseless bandits around them, some no more than ten years old, decided daily if they could eat, lay down, or even go to the bathroom. It was maddening and filled them with deep despair.

One thing she hadn't shared with her friend and colleague was the fact that she had picked out a star in the sky—she wasn't sure of its name, but she knew exactly where to look and on this night it shined just a little brighter. She didn't know why for sure, but it was almost as though there was a twinkle for a brief moment meant just for her.

As she thought on her star she found herself whispering a prayer, "Please Lord, I just don't know if I can go on any longer . . . please . . . we need help and if we don't get out of here now I don't think I'm going to make it."

Jessica felt another one of the thousands of sand beetles scurry over her leg as she laid there helpless to do anything about it. Too tired . . . too sick. Her captors were nearly all asleep except for one she had nicknamed "Helper" and he was zoning yet again.

Just then, she heard an inexplicable bizarre scratching noise. What could it be? It didn't make sense; she assumed maybe it was another beetle or a small wild animal. She heard it again and this time glanced over to her captor just long enough to see Helper stand up straight as a board, grasp his rifle tight, and chamber a round—and then she saw his eyes go wide.

Boom!

The sky around them erupted in a cascading river of orange light and thunderous sound like a typhoon. *Crack–Crack . . . Crack–Crack.* Perfectly synchronized rounds flew over Jessica's head as the bodies of the militants began to hit the ground.

Oh my God . . . it's another militant group . . . probably al-Shabaab . . . they are here to take me from them and ransom us off themselves . . . I can't take it . . . I can't go through it all again . . . what will they do to me?!

As Jessica contemplated what was going on, someone grabbed her shoulder, not painfully, just enough to make it clear who was in control. She prepared herself to fight even though she had no strength . . . she wasn't about to go with whoever these people were coming to get them.

"Jessica . . . Jessica!" She heard a low, kind, but stern voice.

Her mind could not process it. *The accent . . . he has an American accent . . . what would an American be doing out here in the middle of the African desert??*

"Jessica, we are with the American military. We are here to take you home."

American military? She and Poul felt a surge of excitement and jumped to their feet. Even with all her pain, the idea that she may be leaving this hellhole was enough to get her up and moving!

As she tried to stand, Senior Chief Parker slung his weapon and scooped her up, carrying her at a full run back out toward the extraction zone. After what felt like a full minute, the SEALs stopped and formed a tight perimeter. She wasn't sure what was going on, but assumed the American warriors thought there might be a threat. Senior Chief laid her on the ground as gently as a newborn child, and two of his teammates joined him in sitting practically right on top of her—acting as a human shield from any danger that might still be coming their way.

When the SEALs were certain the coast was clear, they got her to her feet as the sound of an approaching helicopter got louder and louder in the distance. Moments later, the Night Stalker pilots of the [redacted] landed their aircraft and awaited the SEALs and the no longer imperiled survivors.

Realizing this was it and they were going to escape, Jessica and Poul both made a run for the helicopters. As they ran Poul started to put it all together, "Jessica, do you know who these guys are?"

Her mind was running a hundred miles an hour, "They are some kind of American military guys!"

Poul paused for a moment, "no, not just any military guys . . . Jessica, these are the Navy SEALs."

Her eyes widened just a bit as she tried to make sense of the whole ordeal. Once everyone was onboard the aircraft, Lieutenant Commander Yeager gave the pilot the sign that they were ready to go.

As the helicopter began to lift off, Jessica looked out at the night sky and saw the star she had watched for the last ninety-two days and whispered, "Thank you Lord . . . thank you."

Mission accomplished.

Upon return to their FOB (forward operating base) [redacted], the SEALs ensured that the former captives received immediate medical attention. One major lesson you learn as a SEAL is that no mission is over until it is over. Once back on base, head checks complete, and everyone is accounted for then you can begin to let your guard down and relax your mind. Yes, there will still be debriefings, equipment cleaning, and all the mundane and routine things a combat team must do to stay ready, but you can rest your mind knowing that the mission has truly been a success.

That evening, on the other side of the world, President Obama strode into a door in the Capitol and saw his Secretary of Defense, Leon Panetta, standing just inside. As he walked in he extended his hand, "Great work tonight," he said, shaking it firmly before continuing on to give his State of the Union address. It wouldn't be until later that evening that people would begin to understand what he had thanked Mr. Panetta for in that moment, but the men of [redacted] would have known had they been there to hear it.

After the State of the Union, President Obama personally called Jessica Buchanan's father to let him know his daughter was now safe and would be home soon.

For the SEALs, there is some satisfaction in a job well done for the missions they do, but the real honor comes from within and the knowledge that they are part of something special, a brotherhood with a bond unlike any other . . . and that every successful mission gives them one more day risking all so that others may live free.

MEDAL OF HONOR—NAVY SEALs ABOVE AND BEYOND

Throughout the history of warfare there have been countless acts of heroism and bravery on the battlefield: daring rescues, dauntless courage in the face of overwhelming odds, and a dedication to duty that far exceeds the norm propelling men to continue fighting even with loss of limb or in the face of certain death. Men who have gone above and beyond the call of duty.

In this way, the Navy SEALs are no different. Time and time again, Frogmen past and present have proved their courage on the field of battle.

Included in this company of great heroes are a handful whose actions have been recognized as the premier example of bravery, fortitude, and action in the face of overwhelming odds. No one book can do justice to the stories that could be written.

Accordingly, we would like to recognize the following SEALs for their devotion to duty–six men in the history of the SEALs who have been awarded the Congressional Medal of Honor:

Joseph Robert (Bob) Kerrey

Rank and organization: Lieutenant, Junior Grade, U.S. Naval Reserve, Sea, Air, and Land Team (SEAL)

Place and date: Near Nha Trang Bay, Republic of Vietnam, March 14, 1969

Entered service at: Omaha, Nebraska

Born: August 27, 1943, Lincoln, Nebraska

Awarded: Congressional Medal of Honor on May 14, 1970 by President Richard Nixon, "For conspicuous gallantry and intrepidity at the risk of his life above and beyond the call of duty while serving as a SEAL team leader during action against enemy aggressor (Vietcong) forces."

Other Awards: Bronze Star, for action February 25, 1969, in Thanh Phong, Vietnam.

Contributions:

Bob Kerrey served with distinction as a Navy SEAL in Vietnam from January–March 1969. On March 14, 1969, Kerrey led a SEAL unit on a daring operation to capture key Viet Cong political cadre personnel. He was severely wounded in an intense firefight by an enemy grenade that cost him part of his leg. Kerrey continued to direct his men in the firefight and extraction. The captured prisoners provided critical intelligence for the United States. Kerrey was subsequently awarded the Congressional Medal of Honor for his actions.

Summary of Action:

LTjg Kerrey's SEAL unit was called upon to execute a critical mission to capture enemy Vietcong leaders on an island in the bay of Nha Trang. After thoroughly analyzing the terrain and intelligence on the enemy encampment, LTjg Kerrey made the decision to lead his SEALs up a 350-foot sheer cliff face in order to help them achieve a tactical advantage.

In the dead of night, the SEALs scaled the cliff and prepared to descend into an ambush position with which they would have the high ground. However, an unexpected twist of fate alerted the enemy to the SEALs and they immediately retaliated with heavy small arms fire and grenades. One grenade from the enemy exploded right at the feet of LTjg Kerrey, causing critical injuries and throwing him back into the rock face.

Despite his grievous wounds and with great presence of mind, LTjg Kerrey directed his SEAL unit via radio communications, and pressed them forward into a devastating counterattack on the enemy forces. He managed to do all this while still bleeding out from multiple injuries to his head, torso, and legs. During the ensuing firefight, LTjg Kerrey fought off unconsciousness and suffered great pain, demonstrating superior mental fortitude and control.

His actions and that of his team, ultimately led to the capture of key leaders in the enemy infrastructure who then provided critical intelligence to the war effort. LTjg Kerrey's leadership, devotion to duty, and personal example under fire remains yet another perfect example in history of the kind of men who serve in Naval Special Warfare unto this day.

Citation:

For conspicuous gallantry and intrepidity at the risk of his life above and beyond the call of duty while serving as a SEAL team leader during action against enemy aggressor (Vietcong) forces. Acting in response to reliable intelligence, LTjg Kerrey led his SEAL team on a mission to capture important members of the enemy's area political cadre known to be located on an island in the bay of Nha Trang. In order to surprise the enemy, he and his team scaled a 350-foot sheer cliff to place themselves above the ledge on which the enemy was located. Splitting his team in two elements and coordinating both, LTjg Kerrey led his men in the treacherous downward descent to the enemy's camp. Just as they neared the end of their descent, intense enemy fire was directed at them, and LTjg Kerrey received massive injuries from a grenade which exploded at his feet and threw him backward onto the jagged rocks. Although bleeding profusely and suffering great pain, he displayed outstanding courage and presence of mind in immediately directing his element's fire into the heart of the enemy camp. Utilizing his radio, LTjg Kerrey called in the second element's fire support, which caught the confused Vietcong in a devastating crossfire. After successfully suppressing the enemy's fire, and although immobilized by his multiple wounds, he continued to maintain calm, superlative control as he ordered his team to secure and defend an extraction site. LTjg Kerrey resolutely directed his men, despite his near unconscious state, until he was eventually evacuated by helicopter. The havoc brought to the enemy by this very successful mission cannot be over-estimated.

The enemy soldiers who were captured provided critical intelligence to the allied effort. LTjg Kerrey's courageous and inspiring leadership, valiant fighting spirit, and tenacious devotion to duty in the face of almost overwhelming opposition sustain and enhance the finest traditions of the United States Naval Service.

≈ **LTjg Bob Kerrey**

His Own Words:

"I accepted the medal for the many people who got nothing," said Bob Kerrey . . . There were a lot of very, very brave men and women whose actions weren't recognized. I received the medal on behalf of them."

Biography:

Bob Kerrey was born in Lincoln Nebraska on August 27, 1943 and graduated from the University of Nebraska in 1966. He served as a Navy SEAL from 1968–1969, and deployed to Vietnam from January to March 1969. He was awarded the Congressional Medal of Honor for his courageous actions wounded and under fire, leading a SEAL unit on a daring operation in which he lost part of his right leg to an enemy grenade.

Bob Kerrey went on to become a successful businessman, operating a chain of restaurants and fitness centers from 1972–1982. He is most known for his eighteen-year political career, which included an unsuccessful bid for the Democratic presidential nomination in 1992. Kerrey served as Governor of

Nebraska from 1983–1987, and as U. S. Senator from Nebraska from 1989–2001. Since leaving, he has been University President of The New School in New York. Kerrey was also a member of the National Commission on Terrorist Attacks upon the United States, ("9/11 Commission"), from 2003–2004.

Thomas R. Norris

Rank and organization: Lieutenant, U.S. Navy, SEAL Adviser, Strategic Technical Directorate Assistance Team, Headquarters, U.S. Military Assistance Command

Place and date: Quang Tri Province, Republic of Vietnam, April 10 to April 13, 1972

Entered service at: Silver Spring, Maryland

Born: January 14, 1944, Jacksonville, Florida

Awarded: Congressional Medal of Honor on March 6, 1976, by President Gerald Ford, "For conspicuous gallantry and intrepidity in action at the risk of his life above and beyond the call of duty while serving as a SEAL Advisor with the Strategic Technical Directorate Assistance Team, Headquarters, U.S. Military Assistance Command, Vietnam.

Contributions:

Thomas Norris served with extraordinary distinction as a Navy SEAL on two tours of duty in Vietnam. He rescued two downed Air Force officers on separate and daring night missions amid overwhelming enemy forces.

LT Norris persevered in his repeated night sorties to find and rescue the American aviators, demonstrating the greatest courage and commitment. LT Norris was medically retired due to severe head injuries sustained when he was shot in the face during a combat mission six months later. Norris was rescued by fellow SEAL Michael Thornton, who received the Medal of Honor for his actions. Each had the pleasure of attending the other's Congressional Medal of Honor ceremony at the White House.

In 1979, after years of surgeries, LT Norris achieved his life ambition of becoming an FBI agent. FBI Director William Webster wrote that, "If you can pass the same test as anybody else applying for this organization, I will waiver your disabilities." Norris gave twenty years distinguished service to the FBI and was an original member of its Hostage Rescue Team as an assault team leader.

Summary of Action:

During the period April 10 to 13, 1972, LT Norris completed an unprecedented ground rescue of two downed pilots deep within heavily controlled enemy territory in Quang Tri Province. Lieutenant Norris, on the night of April 10, led a 5-man patrol through 2,000 meters of heavily controlled enemy territory, located one of the downed pilots at daybreak, and returned to the forward operating base (FOB).

On April 11, after a devastating mortar and rocket attack on the small FOB, LT Norris led a 3-man team on two unsuccessful rescue attempts for the second pilot. On the afternoon of April 12, a forward air controller located the pilot and notified LT Norris.

Dressed in fishermen disguises and using a sampan,

Lieutenant Norris and one Vietnamese traveled throughout that night and found the injured pilot at dawn. Covering the pilot with bamboo and vegetation, they began the return journey, successfully evading a North Vietnamese patrol.

Approaching the FOB, they came under heavy machine gun fire. LT Norris called in an air strike, which provided suppression fire and a smoke screen, allowing the rescue party to reach the FOB. By his outstanding display of decisive leadership, undaunted courage, and selfless dedication in the face of extreme danger, LT Norris enhanced the finest traditions of the U.S. Naval Service.

Citation:

Lieutenant Norris completed an unprecedented ground rescue of two downed pilots deep within heavily controlled enemy territory in Quang Tri province. LT Norris, on the night of April 10, 1972, led a five-man patrol through 2,000 meters of heavily controlled enemy territory, located one of the downed pilots at daybreak, and returned to the forward operating base (FOB). On April 11, after a devastating mortar and rocket attack on the small forward operating base, LT Norris led a three-man team on two unsuccessful rescue attempts for the second pilot. On the afternoon of the 12, a forward air controller located the pilot and notified LT Norris. Dressed in fishermen disguises and using a sampan, LT Norris and one Vietnamese traveled throughout that night and found the injured pilot at dawn. Covering the pilot with bamboo and vegetation, they began the return journey, successfully evading a North Vietnamese patrol. Approaching the fob, they came under heavy machine gun fire. LT Norris called in an air strike which provided suppression fire and a smokescreen, allowing the rescue party to reach the FOB. By his outstanding display of decisive leadership, undaunted courage, and selfless dedication in the face of extreme danger, LT Norris enhanced the finest traditions of the United States Naval Service.

Biography:

≈ **LT Tom Norris**

Thomas Norris was born in Jackson-ville, Florida, then moved with his family to Wisconsin and Washington, D.C. He entered the University of Maryland in 1963, with the intent of pursuing a criminology career with the FBI. While in college, he was the Atlantic Coast Conference ACC wrestling champion in both 1965 and 1966.

Norris graduated from the University of Mary-land in 1967 with a B. S. in Sociology and a specialty in Criminology. He enlisted in the Navy when his student deferment from the draft was not extended. Norris had hoped to become a pilot, but when dis-qualified due to visual acuity and depth perception problems, volunteered for the Navy SEALs.

Norris was on his second SEAL tour in Vietnam when on April 2, 1972 an American EB-66 electronic warfare aircraft was shot down over North Vietnam. Over 30,000 North Vietnamese soldiers were in the immediate area, in the beginning of a pincer-like Easter offensive.

One crewman, Air Force LT Col Iceal "Gene" Hambleton, survived the crash. He knew intimate information about U.S. missiles and targets from a tour at Strategic Air Command, so it was critical that the enemy not capture him. On April 3, two rescuing aviators were shot down; of the two, only LT Mark Clark evaded capture.

The Air Force launched a supreme effort to recover Clark and Hambleton, which became the most intense and costliest rescue of the Vietnam War. In five days, fourteen people were killed, eight aircraft lost, two rescuers captured, and two more stranded behind enemy lines. The 7th Air Force was communicating with Clark and Hambleton, assisting them to escape and evade, but after great losses, realized that a rescue by air was not achievable.

On April 8, Marine Colonel Albert Gray (who later went on to become the Commandant of the Marine Corps), suggested a covert, land-based rescue effort, saying, "I have a boatload of guys who would love to do something like that."

On April 10, Thomas Norris led five ARVN (Vietnamese SEALs) on a two-kilometer overland insertion into dense enemy territory. He located LT Mark Clark at daybreak on April 11, then floated him down-river in the strong current. Later, the North Vietnamese conducted a devastating rocket attack on their small outpost, killing two of Norris's original team.

On April 12, LT Norris and his three remaining Vietnamese SEALs went four kilometers into enemy territory in an unsuccessful attempt to find

Hambleton by dawn. Two of the three ARVN were so daunted by the massive enemy forces that they did not accompany Norris on further missions.

On April 13, after LT Norris was given Hambleton's location by a Forward Air Controller, he attempted another night rescue with his Vietnamese SEAL comrade, Nguyen Van Kiet. They dressed as fishermen, paddled a sampan upriver, discovered the injured pilot at daybreak, and hid him in the boat under banana leaves.

On their return down river to the base, they were pursued and fired upon by an NVA patrol on the bank, and called in air support. They were fired upon again by heavy machine guns as they neared the shore, and got Hambleton to their bunker. Norris administered first aid to the wounded pilot, (who had been on escape and evasion for eleven days), and prepared him for evacuation.

Six months later, LT Norris was leading an intelligence-collection and personnel-capture mission with one other U.S. Navy SEAL and three South Vietnamese when he was shot in the face and believed killed. SEAL Petty Officer Michael Thornton ran into a hail of bullets, dragged Norris away, and swam him seaward for two hours, saving his life. It was the first time in over 100 years that one Medal of Honor recipient saved the life of another. Both are still alive and well.

In his own words:

"All in all, I've had a pretty interesting life," Norris said a few years ago. "I've always gone after the challenge."

Michael Edwin Thornton

Rank and organization: Petty Officer, U. S. Navy, Navy Advisory Group.

Place and date: Republic of Vietnam, October 31, 1972.

Entered service at: Spartanburg, South Carolina

Born: March 23, 1949, Greenville, South Carolina

Awarded: Congressional Medal of Honor on October 15, 1973 by President Richard Nixon, "for conspicuous gallantry and intrepidity at the risk of his life above and beyond the call of duty while participating in a daring operation against enemy forces in the Republic of Vietnam on October 31, 1972."

Michael Thornton was one of only fifteen U.S. Navy personnel, (three of them SEALs), who received the Medal of Honor for their heroic actions during the Vietnam War. He is also the only recipient in over a century to save the life of another Medal of Honor recipient–SEAL Lieutenant Thomas Norris–who had performed heroic, lifesaving actions of his own just months earlier. Both men are still alive and well today.

Other Awards:
Silver Star

Bronze Star Medal with Combat "V" (3)

Meritorious Service Medal

Combat Action Ribbon with Gold Star

Vietnamese Service Medal with one Silver Star and two Bronze Stars

Summary of Action:

Michael Thornton enlisted in the Navy in 1967 after graduating from high school at the age of 18. Upon successful completion of BUD/S training, Thornton was assigned to SEAL Team ONE, and served several tours in Vietnam and Thailand between October 1968 and January 1973.

On his last tour to Vietnam, at the age of 23, Thornton heroically saved the life of his senior officer on an intelligence gathering and prisoner capture operation. The small team of two Navy SEALs and three South Vietnamese commandos was discovered by a larger North Vietnamese Army force, and a fierce firefight ensued. SEAL LT Thomas Norris, who had himself earned the Medal of Honor just months earlier, was shot in the face and believed dead.

Thornton ran into a hail of enemy fire to retrieve Norris's body, and found him badly wounded and unconscious, but alive. He dragged Norris to the beach, inflated his life vest, and swam both Norris and a wounded South Vietnamese commando seaward for two hours before they were rescued by a comrade in a support craft, who had refused to give them up for dead.

Citation:

For conspicuous gallantry and intrepidity at the risk of his life above and beyond the call of duty while participating in a daring operation against enemy forces. Petty Officer Thornton, as Assistant U.S. Navy advisor, along with a U.S. Navy Lieutenant serving as senior advisor, accompanied a three-man Vietnamese Navy SEAL patrol on an intelligence gathering and prisoner capture operation against an enemy-occupied naval river base.

Launched from a Vietnamese navy junk in a rubber boat, the patrol reached land and was continuing on foot toward its objective when it suddenly came under heavy fire from a numerically superior force. The patrol called in naval gunfire support and then engaged the enemy in a fierce firefight, accounting for many enemy casualties before moving back to the waterline to prevent encirclement. Upon learning that the senior advisor had been hit by enemy fire and was believed to be dead, Petty Officer Thornton returned through a hail of fire to the Lieutenant's last position; quickly disposed of two enemy soldiers about to overrun the position, and succeeded in removing the seriously wounded and unconscious senior naval advisor to the water's edge. He then inflated the Lieutenant's lifejacket and towed him seaward for approximately two hours until picked up by support craft. By his extraordinary courage and perseverance, Petty Officer Thornton was directly responsible for saving the life of his superior officer and enabling the safe extraction of all patrol members, thereby upholding the highest traditions of the United States Naval Service.

His Own Words:

⌃ **LT Michael Thornton**

Thornton addressed a class of middle school students in April 2007. Asked if he was scared when saving his friend he replied. "Fear is a great thing, but you have to take that fear and focus it into something good."

The students were surprised when he told them that he didn't consider himself a hero. "I feel honored, but I'm not a hero," he said. "This medal belongs to every man and woman who died serving their country. I feel honored to represent them."

Naval Career:

Michael Thornton went on to serve in the following SEAL assignments:

BUD/S Instructor at Naval Special Warfare Training Command

Senior enlisted man in a SEAL Team TWO operational platoon

Exchange tour with Royal Marine British Special Boat Squadron

Assisted in establishing and operated with Naval Special Warfare Development Group

Commission:

In 1982, Michael Thornton received his commission as a U. S. Navy Ensign, after which he served ten years as an officer in the diving and salvage community. In April of 1990, he reported as Bravo Company Commander where he coordinated a rapid response deployment in support of Desert Shield/Desert Storm (the first U.S. invasion of Iraq).

Retirement:

Lieutenant Thornton retired in 1992. He was the last Congressional Medal of Honor recipient on active duty at that time.

Michael A. Monsoor
Summary of Action
Rank and Organization: Petty Officer Second Class
(SEAL)
Place and Date: September 29, 2006

Summary of Action:

PO Michael A. Monsoor, United States Navy, distinguished himself through conspicuous gallantry and intrepidity at the risk of his life above and beyond the call of duty as a Combat Advisor and Automatic Weapons Gunner for Naval Special Warfare Task Group Arabian Peninsula in support of Operation Iraqi Freedom on September 29, 2006. He displayed great personal courage and exceptional bravery while conducting operations in enemy held territory at Ar Ramadi Iraq.

During Operation Kentucky Jumper, a combined Coalition battalion clearance and isolation operation in southern Ar Ramadi, he served as automatic weapons gunner in a combined SEAL and Iraqi Army (IA) sniper overwatch element positioned on a residential rooftop in a violent sector and historical stronghold for insurgents. In the morning, his team observed four enemy fighters armed with AK–47s reconnoitering from roads in the sector to conduct follow-on attacks. SEAL snipers from his roof engaged two of them which resulted in one enemy wounded in action and one enemy killed in action. A mutually supporting SEAL/IA position also killed an enemy fighter during the morning hours. After the engagements, the local populace blocked off the roads in the area with rocks to keep civilians away and to warn insurgents of the presence of his Coalition sniper element. Additionally, a nearby mosque called insurgents to arms to fight Coalition forces.

In the early afternoon, enemy fighters attacked his position with automatic weapons fire from a moving vehicle. The SEALs fired back and stood their ground. Shortly thereafter, an enemy fighter shot a rocket-propelled grenade at his building. Though well-acquainted with enemy tactics in Ar Ramadi, and keenly aware that the enemy would continue to attack, the SEALs remained on the battlefield in order to carry out the mission of guarding the western flank of the main effort.

Because of anticipated enemy action, the officer in charge repositioned him with his automatic heavy machine gun in the direction of the enemy's most likely avenue of approach. He placed him in a small, confined sniper hide-sight between two SEAL snipers on an outcropping of the roof, which allowed the three SEALs maximum coverage of the area. He was located closest to the egress route out of the sniper hide-sight watching for enemy activity through a tactical periscope over the parapet wall. While vigilantly watching for enemy activity, an enemy fighter hurled a hand grenade onto the roof from an unseen location. The grenade hit him in the chest and bounced onto the deck. He immediately leapt to his feet and yelled "grenade" to alert his teammates of impending danger, but they could not evacuate the sniper hide-sight in time to escape harm. Without hesitation and showing no regard for his own life, he threw himself onto the grenade, smothering it to protect his teammates who were lying in close proximity. The grenade detonated as he came down on top of it, mortally wounding him.

Petty Officer Monsoor's actions could not have been more selfless or clearly intentional. Of the three SEALs on that rooftop corner, he had the only avenue of escape away from the blast, and if he had so chosen, he could have easily escaped. Instead, Monsoor chose to protect his comrades by sacrificing of his life. By his courageous and selfless actions, he saved the lives of two fellow SEALs and he is most deserving of the special recognition afforded by awarding the Medal of Honor.

Citation:

For conspicuous gallantry and intrepidity at the risk of his life above and beyond the call of duty as automatic weapons gunner for naval special warfare task group Arabian Peninsula, in support of Operation Iraqi freedom on September 29, 2006. As a member of a combined SEAL and Iraqi Army sniper overwatch element, tasked with providing early warning and stand-off protection from a rooftop in an insurgent held sector of Ar Ramadi, Iraq, Petty Officer Monsoor distinguished himself by his exceptional bravery in the face of grave danger. In the early morning, insurgents prepared to execute a coordinated attack by reconnoitering the area around the element's position. Element snipers thwarted the enemy's initial attempt by eliminating two insurgents. The enemy continued to assault the element, engaging them with a rocket-propelled grenade and small arms fire. As enemy activity increased, Petty Officer Monsoor took position with his machine gun between two teammates on an outcropping of the roof. While the seals vigilantly watched for enemy activity, an insurgent threw a hand grenade from an unseen location, which bounced off Petty Officer Monsoor's chest and landed in front of him. Although only he could have escaped the blast, Petty Officer Monsoor chose instead to protect his teammates. Instantly and without regard for his own safety, he threw himself onto the grenade to absorb the force of the explosion with his body, saving the lives of his two teammates. By his undaunted courage, fighting spirit, and unwavering devotion to duty in the face of certain death, Petty Officer Monsoor gallantly gave his life for his country, thereby reflecting great credit upon himself and upholding the highest traditions of the United States Naval Service.

Biography:

Petty Officer Second Class (SEAL)
Michael Anthony Monsoor
April 5, 1981—September 29, 2006

≈ **Petty Officer Michael Monsoor**

Petty Officer Second Class Michael Anthony Monsoor was born April 5, 1981 in Long Beach, California. Michael grew up in Garden Grove, California, as the third of four children of George and Sally Monsoor. He has an older brother James and older sister Sara, and a younger brother Joseph.

Michael attended Dr. Walter C. Ralston Intermediate School and Garden Grove High School where he played tight end on the Argonaut football team and graduated in 1999. An incredible athlete, Mike enjoyed snowboarding, body boarding, spear fishing, motorcycle riding, and driving his Corvette. His quiet demeanor and dedication to his friends was a shining example of the "Silent Warrior" SEAL mentality. He soon had found his calling in life.

Michael enlisted in the U. S. Navy March 21, 2001, and attended Basic Training at Recruit Training Command, Great Lakes, Illinois. Upon graduation from basic training, he attended Quartermaster "A" School, and then transferred to Naval Air Station, Sigonella, Italy for a short period of time.

Petty Officer Monsoor entered Basic Underwater Demolition/SEAL (BUD/S) training in Coronado, Calif., and subsequently graduated with Class 250 on September 2, 2004 as one of the top performers in his class. After BUD/S, he completed advanced SEAL training courses including parachute training at Basic Airborne School, Fort Benning, Ga., cold weather combat training in Kodiak, Alaska, and six months of SEAL Qualification Training in Coronado, graduating in March of 2005. The following month, his rating changed from Quartermaster to Master-at-Arms, and he was assigned to SEAL Team THREE, Delta platoon. He deployed with his platoon to Iraq in April of 2006 in support of Operation Iraqi Freedom, and was assigned to Task Unit Bravo in Ar Ramadi.

From April to September 29, 2006, Mike served as a heavy weapons machine gunner in Delta Platoon, SEAL Team THREE. During combat patrols he walked behind the platoon point man with his Mk 48 machinegun so that he could protect his platoon from a frontal enemy attack. Mike was also a SEAL communicator. On fifteen operations, he carried a rucksack full of communications equipment in addition to his machinegun and full ammunition load-out. Collectively it weighed more than one hundred pounds. He bore the weight without a single complaint, even in the midst of the 130-degree Western Iraqi summer.

Mike and his platoon operated in a highly contested part of Ramadi City called the Ma'laab district. During their deployment, Mike and his fellow SEALS came under enemy attack on 75 percent of their missions. On May 9, 2006, Mike rescued a SEAL who was shot in the leg. He ran out into the street with another SEAL, shot covering fire and dragged his comrade to safety while enemy bullets kicked up the concrete at their feet. For this brave action, he earned a Silver Star.

The enemy could not deter Michael and his SEAL platoon. They fought in thirty-five heated firefights; during these incidents Mike shot tens of thousands of 7.62mm rounds to cover Delta Platoon's movement through streets that seemed to be paved with fire. In the Ma'laab district, Michael perfected his skills as an urban machine gunner. Once he and his men established a sniper overwatch position, he deftly transitioned to his role as a SEAL communicator calling in tank support and transmitting enemy situation reports to the 1–506 PIR commander.

Delta Platoon executed a broad spectrum of combat operations in and around Ramadi. They patrolled bravely through the city streets engaging in firefights while on other occasions, they ambushed insurgent mortar teams near the banks of the Euphrates River. Mike and his fellow SEALs accounted for eighty-four enemy fighters killed in action and the detainment of numerous insurgents. Most notably, the U.S. Army infantry, Navy SEALs, and Iraqi Army troops working as a combined force helped to pacify the most violent city in Al Anbar province setting conditions for the Sunni Awakening and U.S. support for it.

Petty Officer Monsoor was subsequently awarded the Bronze Star as the Task Unit Ramadi, Iraq Combat Advisor from April to September 2006. His leadership, guidance and decisive actions during eleven different combat operations saved the lives of his teammates, other Coalition Forces and Iraqi Army soldiers.

Petty Officer Second Class (SEAL) Michael A. Monsoor received the Medal of Honor posthumously in a ceremony at the White House on April 8, 2008. He received the award for his actions in Ar Ramadi, Iraq on September 29, 2006. On that day, Monsoor was part of a sniper overwatch security position with three other SEALs and eight Iraqi Army soldiers. An insurgent closed in and threw a fragmentation grenade into the overwatch position. The grenade hit Monsoor in the chest before falling to the ground. Positioned next to the single exit, Monsoor was the only one who could have escaped harm. Instead, he dropped onto the grenade to shield the others from the blast. Monsoor died approximately thirty minutes later from wounds sustained from the blast. Because of Petty Officer Monsoor's actions, he saved the lives of his three teammates and the Iraqi soldiers.

Though he carried himself in a calm and composed fashion, he constantly led the charge to bring the fight to the enemy. His teammates recall his sense of loyalty to God, family, and his team. He attended Catholic Mass devotionally before operations, and often spoke lovingly of his family—his older brother, a police officer and former Marine for whom he held great respect; his sister, a nurse; and his younger brother, a college football player.

Mike was one of the bravest men on the battle-field, never allowing the enemy to discourage him. He remained fearless while facing constant danger, and through his selfless nature and aggressive actions, saved the lives of coalition soldiers and his fellow SEALs. He was a loyal friend and exceptional SEAL, and he is sorely missed by his brothers in Task Unit Bravo.

He is survived by his mother Sally, his father George, his sister Sara, and his two brothers James and Joseph.

Michael Murphy

Summary of Action:

LT (SEAL) Michael Murphy: For actions during Operation Red Wings on June 28, 2005.

On June 28, 2005, deep behind enemy lines east of Asadabad in the Hindu Kush of Afghanistan, a very committed four-man Navy SEAL team was conducting a reconnaissance mission at the unforgiving altitude of approximately 10,000 feet. The SEALs, LT Michael Murphy, Gunner's Mate 2nd Class (SEAL) Danny Dietz, Sonar Technician 2nd Class (SEAL) Matthew Axelson and Hospital Corpsman 2nd Class (SEAL) Marcus Luttrell had a vital task. The four SEALs were scouting Ahmad Shah—a terrorist in his mid-thirties who grew up in the adjacent mountains just to the south.

Under the assumed name Muhammad Ismail, Shah led a guerrilla group known to locals as the "Mountain Tigers" that had aligned with the Taliban and other militant groups close to the Pakistani border. The SEAL mission was compromised when the team was spotted by local nationals who presumably reported its presence and location to the Taliban.

A fierce firefight erupted between the four SEALs and a much larger enemy force of more than fifty anti-coalition militia. The enemy had the SEALs outnumbered. They also had terrain advantage. They launched a well-organized, three-sided attack on the SEALs. The firefight continued relentlessly as the overwhelming militia forced the team deeper into a ravine.

Trying to reach safety, the four men, now each wounded, began bounding down the mountain's steep sides, making leaps of twenty to thirty feet. Approximately forty-five minutes into the fight, pinned down by overwhelming forces, Dietz, the communications petty officer, sought open air to place a distress call back to the base. But before he could, he was shot in the hand, the blast shattering his thumb.

Despite the intensity of the firefight and suffering grave gunshot wounds himself, Murphy is credited with risking his own life to save the lives of his teammates. Murphy, intent on making contact with headquarters, but realizing this would be impossible in the extreme terrain where they were fighting, unhesitatingly and with complete disregard for his own life moved into the open, where he could gain a better position to transmit a call to get help for his men.

Moving away from the protective mountain rocks, he knowingly exposed himself to increased enemy gunfire. This deliberate and heroic act deprived him of cover and made him a target for the enemy. While continuing to be fired upon, Murphy made contact with the SOF quick reaction force at Bagram

Air Base and requested assistance. He calmly provided his unit's location and the size of the enemy force while requesting immediate support for his team. At one point he was shot in the back, causing him to drop the transmitter. Murphy picked it back up, completed the call and continued firing at the enemy who was closing in. Severely wounded, LT Murphy returned to his cover position with his men and continued the battle.

An MH-47 Chinook helicopter, with eight additional SEALs and eight Army Night Stalkers aboard, was sent is as part of an extraction mission to pull out the four embattled SEALs. The MH-47 was escorted by heavily-armored, Army attack helicopters. Entering a hot combat zone, attack helicopters are used initially to neutralize the enemy and make it safer for the lightly-armored, personnel-transport helicopter to insert.

The heavy weight of the attack helicopters slowed the formation's advance prompting the MH-47 to outrun its armored escort. The crew knew the tremendous risk going into an active enemy area in daylight, without their attack support, and without the cover of night. Risk would, of course, be minimized if they put the helicopter down in a safe zone. But knowing that their warrior brothers were shot, surrounded, and severely wounded, the rescue team opted to directly enter the oncoming battle in hopes of landing on brutally hazardous terrain.

As the Chinook raced to the battle, a rocket-propelled grenade struck the helicopter, killing all sixteen men aboard.

On the ground and nearly out of ammunition, the four SEALs, Murphy, Luttrell, Dietz and Axelson, continued the fight. By the end of the two-hour gunfight that careened through the hills and over cliffs, Murphy, Axelson and Dietz had been killed. An estimated thirty-five Taliban were also dead.

The fourth SEAL, Luttrell, was blasted over a ridge by a rocket-propelled grenade and knocked unconscious. Regaining consciousness some time later, Luttrell managed to escape, albeit badly injured, and slowly crawled away down the side of a cliff. Dehydrated, with a bullet wound to one leg, shrapnel embedded in both legs, three vertebrae cracked; Luttrell's situation was grim. Rescue helicopters were sent in, but he was too weak and injured to make contact. Traveling seven miles on foot he evaded the enemy for nearly a day. Fortunately, local nationals came to his aid, carrying him to a nearby village where they kept him for three days. The Taliban came to the village several times demanding that Luttrell be turned over to them. The villagers refused. One of the villagers made his way to a Marine outpost with a note from Luttrell, and U.S. forces launched a massive operation that rescued him from enemy territory on July 2.

By his undaunted courage, intrepid fighting spirit and inspirational devotion to his men in the face of certain death, LT Murphy was able to relay the position of his unit, an act that ultimately led to the rescue of Luttrell and the recovery of the remains of the three who were killed in the battle.

This was the worst single-day death toll for U.S. special operations forces since Operation Enduring Freedom began. In fact, the landings on D-Day, Operation Red Wings, and Extortion 17 accounted for the largest losses of life in the history of Naval Special Warfare.

The Naval Special Warfare (NSW) community will forever remember June 28, 2005 and the heroic efforts and sacrifices of our special operators. We hold with reverence the ultimate sacrifice that they made while engaged in that fierce fire fight on the front lines of the global war on terrorism (GWOT).

OPERATION RED WINGS KIAs

On June 28, 2005, three of four SEALS on the ground (Murphy, Dietz, Axelson) were killed during combat operations in support of Operation Red Wings. On the same day, a QRF (Quick Reaction Force) of eight Navy SEALs and eight Army Night Stalkers were also killed when the MH-47 helicopter that they were aboard was shot down by enemy fire in the vicinity of Asadabad, Afghanistan in Kunar Province.

Lieutenant Michael P. Murphy
United States Navy

Citation:

For conspicuous gallantry and intrepidity at the risk of his life above and beyond the call of duty as the leader of a special reconnaissance element with naval special warfare task unit Afghanistan on 27 and 28 June 2005. While leading a mission to locate a high-level anti-coalition militia leader, Lieutenant Murphy demonstrated extraordinary heroism in the face of grave danger in the vicinity of Asadabad, Kunar province, Afghanistan. On June 28, 2005, operating in an extremely rugged enemy-controlled area, Lieutenant

Murphy's team was discovered by anti-coalition militia sympathizers, who revealed their position to Taliban fighters. As a result, between thirty and forty enemy fighters besieged his four-member team. Demonstrating exceptional resolve, Lieutenant Murphy valiantly led his men in engaging the large enemy force. The ensuing fierce firefight resulted in numerous enemy casualties, as well as the wounding of all four members of the team. Ignoring his own wounds and demonstrating exceptional composure, Lieutenant Murphy continued to lead and encourage his men. When the primary communicator fell mortally wounded, Lieutenant Murphy repeatedly attempted to call for assistance for his beleaguered teammates. Realizing the impossibility of communicating in the extreme terrain, and in the face of almost certain death, he fought his way into open terrain to gain a better position to transmit a call. This deliberate, heroic act deprived him of cover, exposing him to direct enemy fire. Finally achieving contact with his headquarters, Lieutenant Murphy maintained his exposed position while he provided his location and requested immediate support for his team. In his final act of bravery, he continued to engage the enemy until he was mortally wounded, gallantly giving his life for his country and for the cause of freedom. By his selfless leadership, courageous actions, and extraordinary devotion to duty, Lieutenant Murphy reflected great credit upon himself and upheld the highest traditions of the United States Naval Service.

Signed George W. Bush

Biography:

Lieutenant (SEAL) Michael P. Murphy
May 7, 1976—June 28, 2005

LT Michael P. Murphy, fondly referred to by friends and family as "Murph," was born May 7, 1976 in Smithtown, New York, and grew up in the New York City commuter town of Patchogue, New York, on Long Island.

⌃ **LT Michael Murphy**

Murphy grew up active in sports and attended Patchogue's Saxton Middle School. In high school, Murphy took a summer lifeguard job at the Brookhaven town beach in Lake Ronkonkoma–a job he returned to each summer through his college years. Murphy graduated from Patchogue-Medford High School in 1994.

Murphy attended Penn State University, where he was an exceptional all-around athlete and student, excelling at ice hockey and graduating with honors. He was an avid reader; his reading tastes ranged from the Greek historian Herodotus to Tolstoy's *War and Peace*. Murphy's favorite book was Steven Pressfield's *Gates of Fire,* about the Spartan stand at Thermopylae. In 1998, he graduated with a pair of Bachelor of Arts degrees from Penn State in political science and psychology.

Following graduation, he was accepted to several law schools, but instead he changed course. Slightly built at five feet ten inches, Murphy decided to attend SEAL mentoring sessions at the U.S. Merchant Marine Academy at Kings Point, New York, with his sights on becoming a U.S. Navy SEAL. Murphy accepted an appointment to the Navy's Officer Candidate School at Pensacola, Florida, in September, 2000.

Murphy was commissioned as an ensign in the Navy on December 13, 2000, and began Basic Underwater Demolition/SEAL (BUD/S) training in Coronado, California, in January 2001, graduating with Class 236. BUD/S is a six-month training course and the first step to becoming a Navy SEAL.

Upon graduation from BUD/S, he attended the Army Jump School, SEAL Qualification Training, and SEAL Delivery Vehicle (SDV) school. LT Murphy earned his SEAL Trident and checked onboard SDV Team (SDVT) One in Pearl Harbor, Hawaii in July of 2002. In October of 2002, he deployed with Foxtrot Platoon to Jordan as the liaison officer for Exercise Early Victor.

Following his tour with SDVT-1, LT Murphy was assigned to Special Operations Central Command in Florida and deployed to Qatar in support of Operation Iraqi Freedom. After returning from Qatar, LT Murphy was deployed to the Horn of Africa, Djibouti, to assist in the operational planning of future SDV missions.

In early 2005, Murphy was assigned to SEAL Delivery Vehicle Team One as assistant officer in charge of Alfa Platoon and deployed to Afghanistan in support of Operation Enduring Freedom.

On June 28, 2005, LT Murphy was the officer-in-charge of a four-man SEAL element in support of Operation Red Wings tasked with finding a key anti-coalition militia commander near Asadabad, Afghanistan. Shortly after inserting into the objective area, the SEALs were spotted by three goat herders who were initially detained and then released. It is believed the goat herders immediately reported the SEALs presence to Taliban fighters.

A fierce gun battle ensued on the steep face of the mountain between the SEALs and a much larger enemy force. Despite the intensity of the firefight and suffering grave gunshot wounds himself, Murphy is credited with risking his own life to save the lives of his teammates. Murphy, intent on making contact with headquarters, but realizing this would be impossible in the extreme terrain where they were fighting, unhesitatingly and with complete disregard for his own life moved into the open, where he could gain a better position to transmit a call to get help for his men.

Moving away from the protective mountain rocks, he knowingly exposed himself to increased enemy gunfire. This deliberate and heroic act deprived him of cover and made him a target for the enemy. While continuing to be fired upon, Murphy made contact with the SOF Quick Reaction Force at Bagram Air Base and requested assistance. He calmly provided his unit's location and the size of the enemy force while requesting immediate support for his team. At one point, he was shot in the back causing him to drop the transmitter. Murphy picked it back up, completed the call and continued firing at the enemy who was closing in. Severely wounded, LT Murphy returned to his cover position with his men and continued the battle.

As a result of Murphy's call, an MH-47 Chinook helicopter, with eight additional SEALs and eight Army Night Stalkers aboard, was sent in as part of the

QRF to extract the four embattled SEALs. As the Chinook drew nearer to the fight, a rocket-propelled grenade hit the helicopter, causing it to crash and killing all sixteen men aboard.

On the ground and nearly out of ammunition, the four SEALs, continued to fight. By the end of a two-hour gunfight that careened through the hills and over cliffs, Murphy, Gunner's Mate 2nd Class (SEAL) Danny Dietz and Sonar Technician 2nd Class (SEAL) Matthew Axelson had fallen. An estimated thirty-five Taliban were also dead. The fourth SEAL, Hospital Corpsman 2nd Class (SEAL) Marcus Luttrell, was blasted over a ridge by a rocket-propelled grenade and knocked unconscious. Though severely wounded, the fourth SEAL and sole survivor, Luttrell, was able to evade the enemy for nearly a day; after which local nationals came to his aide, carrying him to a nearby village where they kept him for three more days. Luttrell was rescued by U.S. Forces on July 2, 2005.

By his undaunted courage, intrepid fighting spirit and inspirational devotion to his men in the face of certain death, LT Murphy was able to relay the position of his unit, an act that ultimately led to the rescue of Luttrell and the recovery of the remains of the three who were killed in the battle.

LT Murphy was buried at Calverton National Cemetery less than twenty miles from his childhood home. LT Murphy's other personal awards include the Purple Heart, Combat Action Ribbon, the Joint Service Commendation Medal, the Navy and Marine Corps Commendation Medal, Afghanistan Campaign Ribbon and National Defense Service Medal.

LT Murphy is survived by his mother Maureen Murphy; his father Dan Murphy; and his brother John Murphy. Dan and Maureen Murphy, who were divorced in 1999, remain close friends and continue to live in New York. Their son John serves in a law enforcement capacity in the state of New York.

Edward C. Byers
Senior Chief Special Warfare Operator (SEAL) Edward C. Byers Jr.: For actions during Operation Enduring Freedom on December 8, 2012

Senior Chief Special Warfare Operator (SEAL) Edward C. Byers Jr., United States Navy, distinguished himself by heroic gallantry as an Assault Team Member attached to a Joint Task Force in support of Operation ENDURING FREEDOM on December 8, 2012.

Summary of Action:

Dr. Dilip Joseph is an American citizen, who was abducted with his driver and Afghan interpreter on December 5, 2012. Intelligence reports indicated that Dr. Joseph might be transported to another location as early as December 9, 2012. Dr. Joseph was being held in a small, single-room building.

The target compound was located in a remote area beside a mountain in the Qarghah'i District of Laghman Province, Afghanistan. Chief Byers was part of the rescue team that planned to make entry into the room of guards where the hostage was believed to be located. Success of the rescue operation relied upon surprise, speed, and aggressive action. Trading personal security for speed of action was inherent to the success of this rescue mission. Each assaulter in the rescue force volunteered for this operation with full appreciation for the risks they were to undertake.

With the approval of the commander of all International Security Assistance Forces in Afghanistan, the rescue force launched from its forward operating base. The infiltration was an exhaustive patrol across unimproved trails and mountainous terrain. After nearly four hours of patrolling, the rescue force was positioned to make its assault on the target compound.

As the patrol closed to within twenty-five meters of the target building, a guard became aware of the rescue force. The forward-most assaulter shot at the guard and ran towards the door to make entry as the guard disappeared inside. Chief Byers was the second assaulter in a sprint towards the door. Six layers of blankets securely fastened to the ceiling and walls served as the Afghan door. While Chief Byers tried to rip down the blankets, the first assaulter pushed his way through the doorway and was immediately shot by enemy AK-47 fire. Chief Byers, fully aware of the hostile threat inside the room, boldly entered and immediately engaged a guard pointing an AK-47 towards him. As he was engaging that guard, another adult male darted towards the corner of the room. Chief Byers could not distinguish if the person may have been the hostage scrambling away or a guard attempting to arm himself with an AK-47 that lay in the corner. Chief Byers tackled the unknown male and seized control of him. While in hand-to-hand combat, Chief Byers maintained control of the unknown male with one hand, while adjusting the focus of his night-vision goggles (NVGs) with his other. Once his NVGs were focused, he recognized that the male was not the hostage and engaged the struggling armed guard.

By now other team members had entered the room and were calling to Dr. Joseph to identify himself. Chief Byers heard an unknown voice speak English from his right side. He immediately leaped across the room and selflessly flung his body on top of the American hostage, shielding him from the continued rounds being fired across the room. Almost simultaneously, Chief Byers identified an additional enemy fighter directly behind Dr. Joseph. While covering the hostage with his body, Chief Byers was able to pin the enemy combatant to the wall with his hand around the enemy's throat. Unable to fire any effective rounds into the enemy, Chief Byers was able to restrain the combatant enough to enable his teammate to fire precision shots, eliminating the final threat within the room.

Chief Byers quickly talked to Dr. Joseph, confirming that he was able to move. He and his Team Leader stood Dr. Joseph up, calmed him, and let him know he was safe with American Forces. Once Dr. Joseph was moved to the helicopter-landing zone, Chief Byers, a certified paramedic and 18D medic, assisted with the rendering of medical aid to the urgent surgical assaulter. Chief Byers and others performed CPR during the forty-minute flight to Bagram Air Base where his teammate was declared deceased.

Chief Petty Officer Byers displayed superior gallantry, extraordinary heroism at grave personal risk, dedication to his teammates, and calm tactical leadership while liberating Dr. Dilip Joseph from captivity. He is unquestionably deserving of the Medal of Honor.

Citation:

For conspicuous gallantry and intrepidity at the risk of his life above and beyond the call of duty as a hostage rescue force team member in Afghanistan in support of Operation Enduring Freedom from December 8 to 9, 2012. As the rescue force approached the target building, an enemy sentry detected them and darted inside to alert his fellow captors. The sentry quickly reemerged, and the lead assaulter attempted to neutralize him. Chief Byers with his team sprinted to the door of the target building. As the primary breacher, Chief Byers stood in the doorway fully exposed to enemy fire while ripping down six layers of heavy blankets fastened to the inside ceiling and walls to clear a path for the rescue force. The first assaulter pushed his way through the blankets, and was mortally wounded by enemy small arms fire from within. Chief Byers, completely aware of the imminent threat, fearlessly rushed into the room and engaged an enemy guard aiming an AK-47 at him. He then tackled another adult male who had darted toward the corner of the room. During the ensuing hand-to-hand struggle, Chief Byers confirmed the man was not the hostage and engaged him. As other rescue team members called out to the hostage, Chief Byers heard a voice respond in English and raced toward it. He jumped atop the American hostage and shielded him from the high volume of fire within the small room. While covering the hostage with his body, Chief Byers

。

.

immobilized another guard with his bare hands, and restrained the guard until a teammate could eliminate him. His bold and decisive actions under fire saved the lives of the hostage and several of his teammates. By his undaunted courage, intrepid fighting spirit, and unwavering devotion to duty in the face of near certain death, Chief Petty Officer Byers reflected great credit upon himself and upheld the highest traditions of the United States Naval Service.

Biography:

≈ **Senior Chief Edward Byers, Jr.**

Senior Chief Edward Byers was born in Toledo, Ohio in 1979. He grew up in Grand Rapids, Ohio. In 1997, he graduated from Otsego High School where he played varsity soccer. Byers joined the Navy in September 1998, and subsequently attended Boot Camp and Corpsman "A" School in Great Lakes, Illinois.

Byers spent four years as a Hospital Corpsman. In 1998, he was assigned to Great Lakes Naval Hospital. In 1999, he served with 2nd Battalion, 2nd Marines in Camp Lejeune, North Carolina, where he deployed with the 26th Marine Expeditionary Unit aboard USS *Austin* (LPD 4). During deployment he earned his Enlisted Surface Warfare Specialist (ESWS) and Fleet Marine Force (FMF) warfare devices.

In 2002, Byers attended Basic Underwater Demolition SEAL (BUD/S) training and graduated with Class 242. After graduation, he attended the Special

Operations Combat Medic (SOCM) course. Byers was then assigned to an East Coast SEAL Team.

Byers has eleven overseas deployments with nine combat tours. His personal decorations include the Bronze Star with Valor (five awards), the Purple Heart (two awards), the Joint Service Commendation Medal with Valor, the Navy Commendation Medal (three awards, one with Valor), the Combat Action ribbon (two awards), and the Good Conduct Medal (five awards).

Byers was awarded the Medal of Honor from President Barack Obama during a White House ceremony February 29, 2016 for his efforts during a hostage rescue while deployed in support of Operation Enduring Freedom in 2012. He is only the eleventh living service member to be awarded the Medal of Honor for bravery displayed in Afghanistan.

Byers holds a National Paramedics license and also studied Strategic Studies and Defense Analysis at Norwich University, where he will earn a Bachelor of Science degree in early 2016. Byers is married and has a daughter.

Navy Medal of Honor facts:

Senior Chief Byers is the 6th Navy SEAL in history to receive the Medal of Honor.

Senior Chief Byers is one of only eight living Navy Medal of Honor recipients. There are seventy-eight living recipients total.

There have been 745 Medals of Honor awarded to Navy personnel (308 of those were for actions during the Civil War).

Only two Navy service members have received the Medal of Honor for actions subsequent to the Vietnam War, and both of those awards were posthumous. (Lieutenant Michael Murphy and Petty Officer Michael Monsoor, both SEALs.)

The most recent Navy recipient of the Medal of Honor was Petty Officer 2nd Class Michael Monsoor, who was posthumously awarded the Medal of Honor by President George W. Bush on April 8, 2008.

The most recent living Navy recipient of the Medal of Honor was Robert Ingram, who left the Navy in 1968, and was later awarded the Medal of Honor by President Bill Clinton on July 10, 1998 for actions during the Vietnam War.

Senior Chief Byers is the first living active duty member of the U.S. Navy to receive the Medal of Honor since April 6, 1976, when the late Rear Admiral James Stockdale and Lieutenant Thomas Norris (also a SEAL) each received the decoration from President Gerald Ford.

Senior Chief Byers is the first living active duty enlisted member of the U.S. Navy to receive the Medal of Honor since Petty Officer Michael Thornton (also a SEAL) was awarded the Medal of Honor by President Richard Nixon on October 15, 1973.

This is the fourteenth Medal of Honor awarded for actions in Afghanistan. Including Senior Chief Byers, eleven of those fourteen awards were to living recipients. Four Medals of Honor were awarded posthumously for actions in Iraq.

APPENDIX A:
THE CURRENT
PROCESS OF BECOMING
A SEAL

In this section we wish to help the prospective student understand what is involved in the process of becoming a Navy SEAL. Throughout this book we have tried to convey the elements of honor, courage, and commitment that are the core values of the United States Navy and tell the stories of heroism that will hopefully inspire others to push themselves a little harder and live a life dedicated to service. However, we also realize that even the most driven potential student will need some help when it comes to learning exactly how the system works and what is required to get on the path to achieve their goal of becoming one of the best warriors in the world.

The following information is crucial to realizing your goal for one simple reason: it will be your first test of focus, inner drive, willingness to work hard, and of your attention to detail. Being a great athlete and saying you have the drive *will not* be enough–you must follow the process that has been developing for decades. You will not be the first to try nor will you be the last. But, if you truly want to become a SEAL, then you will spend the time required learning exactly what you must do—and then go do it.

Before getting accepted into Basic Underwater Demolition/SEAL training, a prospective candidate must meet a certain number of both mental and physical requirements. These tests include: Pre-enlistment medical screening, ASVAB, AFQT, C-SORT, and PST. Then, the candidate must get a SEAL contract by passing the SEAL Physical Screening Test: 500- yard swim in 12:30, fifty push-ups in two minutes, fifty sit-ups in two minutes, ten consecutive pull-ups in two minutes, and a 1.5 mile run in 10:30. If the candidate receives a passing score, he may then be admitted into training to become a Navy SEAL, but, the competition for BUD/S contracts has increased along with the popularity, and therefore, if you want to earn a contract now it is imperative you crush the Physical Screening Test.

In August 2015, it was reported that the "Navy is planning to open its elite SEAL teams to women who can pass the grueling training regimen." Admiral Jon Greenert said he and the former head of Naval Special Warfare Command, Rear Admiral Brian Losey, believed that if women can pass the legendary six-month Basic Underwater Demolition/SEAL training, they should be allowed to serve as SEALs."

On December 3, 2015, it was announced in a landmark decision that there are now "no exceptions" to all military roles in the U.S.: women can now become Navy SEALs.

PART ONE: The Current Process

Overview:
Each year approximately 1,000 men are given the opportunity to attempt U.S. Navy SEAL training.

Although numbers will vary from year to year, approximately 200–250 will succeed and join the approximately 2,500 active duty U.S. Navy SEALs. The role of a U.S. Navy SEAL is sea-duty intensive, with approximately 70 percent of their time spent in operational roles and 30 percent on shore duty, filling slots as an instructor or other staff-related jobs.

From the date a person joins the navy to first deployment, he will go through up to two and a half years of training.

The U.S. Navy SEAL training process prepares candidates for the missions they may undertake as a qualified SEAL. U.S. Navy SEALs are responsible for training and preparation for execution of special operations in a variety of environments, including maritime, urban, desert, jungle, arctic, and mountain. U.S. Navy SEALs are experts in:

- Special Operations Tactics and Technical Knowledge
- Mission Planning
- Cultural Awareness
- Small-Unit Leadership
- Operational Risk Management
- Tactical and Strategic Operations Concepts
- Tactical Communications
- Tactical Air Control/Terminal Guidance
- Combat Diving Operations
- Parachute/Military Freefall Operations
- Small Boat Operations
- Tactical Ground Vehicles
- Small Arms and Crew-Served Weapons
- Fast Roping and Rappelling

- Demolitions/Explosive Breaching
- Trauma Care
- Intelligence Gathering and Analysis
- Chemical/Biological/Radiological/Nuclear (CBRN) Defensive Measures

In times of armed conflict and war, U.S. Navy SEALs are required to operate in small teams of enemy controlled territory. Operations of this nature require individuals of courage and high morale who are self-disciplined, intelligent, reliable, determined, and physically fit, and who possess mental, moral, and physical stamina. These units will operate in support of conventional forces or independently.

Principle missions include:

- Special Reconnaissance (SR), including information reporting and target acquisition
- Direct Action (DA), including raids or assaults on enemy positions and/or personnel
- Foreign Internal Defense (FID), including training/advising foreign military personnel
- Unconventional Warfare, including missions far behind enemy lines and separated from the logistical support structure
- Combatting Terrorism (CT)

The Navy SEALs, as part of the U.S. military's SOF community, provide America's immediate response as one of the principle Counter Terrorism (CT) and Maritime Counter Terrorism (MCT) teams, taking the lead with any mission that contains a Maritime component. During peacetime, overseas deployments for training are frequent although sometimes of a slightly shorter duration than a combat deployment—the Navy has attempted to make life for families slightly easier and more manageable by minimizing the requirement to constantly move as well (the "homesteading program").

Selection and Training for the U.S. Navy SEALS

All U.S. special forces are characterized by the determination of each individual to carry through with the mission even if they are the last one standing. That said, there is a presumption that personnel volunteering for U.S. Navy SEAL training will become very good team players, and as a result Navy SEAL training is even more team-orientated than many other elite military training programs around the world.

Statistically speaking only, there does exist a few objective data points that point toward the factors which may indicate an increase in a candidate's successful completion of U.S. Navy SEAL training, which include:

- Candidates who have played in competitive sports such as water polo, rugby, lacrosse, swimming, and combat sports (boxing, martial arts, wrestling)
- Candidates who have high academic achievement
- Candidates who have the ability to learn quickly
- Candidates with two- or four-year degrees are almost twice as likely to succeed at BUD/S as compared to those without a degree

- Candidates traditionally have an Armed Forces Qualification Test score of 78 or better
- Candidates with a higher score on the C–SORT have a higher probability of success
- Candidates who have Physical Screening Test scores below 800 are three times more likely to succeed than those candidates who only meet the minimum requirements

PART TWO: ENTRY STANDARDS AND APPLICATIONS

Currently, there are four recognized pathways to becoming a U.S. Navy SEAL:

1. Enlist with a BUD/S Contract
2. Enlist and later apply for a transfer to Navy SEAL Training
3. Enlist and later request an Inter-service transfer to the Navy for SEAL Training
4. Earn a commission and compete for a SEAL Officer Trainee slot

Navy SEAL Officer Candidates

In order to become a U.S. Navy SEAL Officer, also known as a Naval Special Warfare (NSW) officer, a candidate must first be commissioned through one of three pathways:

1. The United States Naval Academy at Annapolis (USNA)
2. U.S. Navy Officer Candidate School (OCS)
3. U.S. Naval Reserve Officer Training Corps (ROTC)

The U.S. Naval Special Warfare Command also accepts a limited number of Fleet transfers and officers from other services. Competition for Fleet transfers, also known as a lateral transfer, is exceptionally fierce and will require absolute top-tier Physical Screening Test scores, Fitness Reports, and Letters of Recommendation.

To be considered for an officer slot at BUD/S, candidates must prepare an application package for submission to a board of U.S. Navy SEAL officers. The board typically consists of one U.S. Navy SEAL Captain (O-6) and at least three other U.S. Navy SEAL officers in the rank of Lieutenant (O-3) through Commander (O-5).

In selecting officer candidates, the board looks closely at each applicant in:

- Leadership
- Honor
- Physical Fitness
- Academics
- Fleet Experience
- Letters of Recommendation

Successful officer candidates will be invited to attend the two-week SEAL Officer Assessment and Selection (SOAS) course, which is held annually at the Naval Amphibious Base Coronado, San Diego, California. Officer candidates will attend one of four SOAS courses held during May through August.

USNA and ROTC officer candidates may also serve an additional week at the Naval Special Warfare Command as part of their summer cruise, although this is not part of SOAS.

The SOAS course is a high stress physical, mental, behavioral, and psychological evaluation program that is designed to identify officer candidates who embody the attributes considered requisite for successful employment as a U.S. Navy SEAL officer.

Officer candidates, like enlisted candidates, should:

- Be able to run in soft sand for long periods, often carrying significant weight
- Be prepared to do hundreds of bodyweight exercises daily (push-ups, pull-ups, etc.)
- Be comfortable in the water and be able to swim for long distances on the surface and underwater, in a pool and in the ocean, sometimes in full uniform and/or wearing boots
- Have exceptional dedication and mental resilience
- Be prepared to be cold, wet, and sandy constantly throughout training

The SOAS course includes:
- An arduous physical screening regimen
- Psychological evaluations
- Behavioral assessments
- Intellectual and cognitive challenges
- Communication and leadership challenges
- Team-orientated activities in a competitive environment
- Assessment of competency in the water

Each year, approximately seventy to ninety officer candidates are selected to attend U.S. Navy SEAL training, so competition for slots is always extremely intense. There are typically thirty slots allocated to USNA graduates at Service Selection (with an average of two hundred Midshipmen who start the selection process). Students at Annapolis also are expected to participate in SEAL PT and successfully complete a BUD/S screening weekend, which simulates Hell-week intensity for short periods of time (two to three hours per session) over a three day period.

Navy SEAL Entry Standards

In addition to meeting the basic requirements for enlistment or commissioning in the Navy, candidates for SEAL training must also meet rigorous physical and mental requirements. A potential U.S. Navy SEAL candidate is assessed through:

- Pre-enlistment medical screening
- Armed Services Vocational Aptitude Battery (ASVAB): used to assess a candidate's mental sharpness and ability to learn
- Armed Forces Qualification Test (AFQT): used to assess a candidate's mental sharpness and ability to learn
- Computerized-Special Operations Resilience Test (C-SORT): used to screen a candidate's maturity and mental resilience
- SEAL Physical Screening Test (PST)

Pre-Enlistment Medical Screening

As well as the general physical examination requirements required by the Navy, there are also additional steps to be undertaken by U.S. Navy SEAL candidates.

Armed Services Vocational Aptitude Battery

The Armed Services Vocational Aptitude Battery (ASVAB) is used to assess a candidate's mental sharpness and ability to learn, and is typically conducted at a Military Entrance Processing Station (MEPS). The standard ASVAB contains the following subtests:

- Word Knowledge (WK)
- Arithmetic Reasoning (AR)
- Mechanical Comprehension (MC)
- Shop Information (SI)
- Automotive Information (AI)
- Electronics Information (EI)
- Mathematics Knowledge (MK)
- General Science (GS)
- Paragraph Comprehension (PC)
- Assembling Objects (AO)
- Verbal Expression (VE)—a scaled combination of WK+PC

An additional line score, Coding Speed (CS), should be requested at MEPS, and the score can be included in the calculation to determine eligibility for the U.S. Navy SEAL program. If the CS line score is not taken, only one set of line scores can be used to determine eligibility.

A candidate must score one of the following on the ASVAB:

1. GS + MC + EI: a minimum score of 170; or
2. VE + MK + MC + CS: a minimum score of 220; or
3. VE + AR: a minimum score of 110; and MC: a minimum score of 50.

If a candidate does not achieve the minimum score, they will:

- If not in the U.S. Navy: complete more studying and re-take the test
- If in the U.S. Navy: The U.S. Navy College offer ASVAB preparation courses which can be taken prior to a re-test

If a candidate's score is close to the minimum and they are considered a particularly strong candidate, they may be eligible for a waiver (although not if their MC score is more than five points below the minimum). It must be noted that waivers are granted on a case-by-case basis. A candidate's PST scores and the strength of their overall application package will be assessed in order to decide on eligibility.

Armed Forces Qualification Test

Four of the ASVAB subtests are combined to form the Armed Forces Qualification Test (AFQT). It measures general cognitive ability and is composed of verbal and mathematics subtests.

AFQT results are returned as percentiles from one to ninety-nine. A score of a fifty would mean a candidate was in the fiftieth percentile, or have an average score.

Computerized-Special Operations Resilience Test

The Computerized-Special Operations Resilience Test (C-SORT) is used to screen a candidate's maturity and mental resilience (a.k.a. mental toughness), and can only be taken once.

The C-SORT includes multiple sections designed to assess a prospective candidate's abilities in three areas:

1. Performance strategies: test for capabilities such as an individual's goal-setting, self-talk, and emotional control.
2. Psychological resilience: focuses on assessing several other areas like an individual's acceptance of life situations and the ability to deal with cognitive challenges and threats.
3. Personality traits.

The scores on each section of C-SORT are combined into a band score on a scale of one to four, with four indicating highest level of mental resilience and one being the lowest level of mental resilience.

To determine eligibility for the U.S. Navy SEAL program, the C-SORT band score is combined with the candidate's PST run and swim times. Individuals who have low C-SORT and slow combined run and swim times are not offered U.S. Navy SEAL contracts.

Although candidates cannot retake C-SORT, they can retake their delayed entry program qualifying PST and demonstrate their motivation by improving their PST score (in particular the run and swim times). Individuals improving their PST score may then increase their C-SORT band, and thus qualify for a U.S. Navy SEAL contract.

U.S. Navy SEAL Physical Screening Test

To receive a U.S. Navy SEAL contract, or even be remotely considered, a candidate must achieve a minimum pass in the U.S. Navy SEAL Physical Screening Test (PST).

The qualifying PST must be administered by a Naval Special Warfare coordinator or mentor.

Prospective candidates can increase their chances of being selected for BUD/S and succeeding in training by having optimum PST scores or better.

Candidates with a PST score of 827 or less are much more likely to be selected for a U.S. Navy SEAL contract, and consequently more likely to successfully complete U.S. Navy SEAL training. Further, candidates with a PST below 800 are three times more likely to succeed than those candidates who only achieve the minimum PST score.

Other Requirements

Age:
- Candidates must be from seventeen to twenty-eight years old
- Waivers for individuals aged twenty-nine and thirty are available for highly qualified candidates
- Individuals with prior enlisted service as U.S. Navy SEALs who are seeking to become NSW Officers can request waivers to age thirty-three

Vision:
- Must be correctable to 20/25
- Uncorrected vision must be at least 20/70 in the worst eye and 20/40 in the best
- Color blindness is disqualifying

Citizenship:
- Candidates must be U.S. citizens.

Security Clearance:
- Applicants must be able to obtain a secret security clearance.

OUTLINE OF THE U.S. NAVY SEAL SELECTION AND TRAINING PROCESS

U.S. Navy SEAL Training Phases

Special Warfare Operator selection, a.k.a. U.S. Navy SEAL training pipeline, is the only selection and training process for candidates wishing to join the U.S. Navy's SEAL community. Once Recruit Training has been successfully completed, and other training for in-fleet and in-service transfers, all U.S. Navy SEAL candidates will undertake six very specific stages of training.

During this training candidates are taught the fundamentals of Naval Special Warfare through a combination of formal U.S. Navy schooling and on the job training. The six stages of training include:

- Stage 1: Special Warfare Operator Preparatory Course
- Stage 2: Basic Underwater Demolition/SEAL (BUD/S) Orientation
- Stage 3: BUD/S First Phase: Basic Conditioning
- Stage 4: BUD/S Second Phase: Combat Diving
- Stage 5: BUD/S Third Phase: Land Warfare Training
- Stage 6: SEAL Qualification Training (SQT)

Stages one to five provide a candidate with their basic SEAL skills. Advanced SEAL skills are attained and developed during SQT and even further once assigned to a Team.

Of note, the SEAL training program has undergone a number of iterations throughout the years and will always change a bit.

The Navy SEAL training program consists of:

- Indoctrination: five weeks
- Basic Conditioning: eight weeks
- Diving: eight weeks
- Land Warfare: nine weeks
- Basic Parachute Training: three weeks
- Special Operations Technician Training: two weeks at the U.S. Naval Special Warfare Centre
- 18D – the course required to become a Special Operations Medic (Hospital Corpsmen only)
- Assignment to a SEAL Team for six to twelve months of on-the-job training; then receive NSW classification, the SEAL Naval Enlisted Classification (NEC) code

Stage 1: Special Warfare Operator Preparatory Course

The Special Warfare Operator Preparatory Course (NSW Prep) is conducted by the Naval Special Warfare Preparatory School located at Naval Station Great Lakes, Illinois. This stage of training is and has also been known as BUD/S Prep, Pre-BUD/S, and Pre-Indoctrination. The course is led by the Officer in Charge (OIC), a Master Chief Petty Officer (E-9).

The NSW Prep course was officially established on February 7, 2008, having been established the previous summer, and was designed to increase the chances of candidates successfully completing the training process. Of the 250 candidates who started before the course was officially established, typically only thirty-three were left.

This course is between five and nine weeks in duration and covers the physical and psychological preparation for BUD/S training. Essentially, this phase of training acts as a link between basic training and the BUD/S course, since many individuals will suffer from under training as a consequence of the Navy Basic Training process.

NSW Prep can be divided into three distinct elements:

1. Check-in: conducted in week 1, includes administration, physical/medical assessments, and course introduction.
2. Conditioning: conducted over four to eight weeks and includes group physical training (determined by ability level), daily academic instruction, and progress tracking.
3. Testing and transfers which includes exit standards, PST, review board, and ship to BUD/S.

The Prep School ends with a modified Physical Screening Test. The test is a 1,000-yard swim, push-ups, pull-ups, sit-ups, and a four-mile run with a significantly higher minimum standard to pass.

The minimum standards for this expanded test are as follows:

1,000-yard swim—with fins (twenty minutes or under)

Push-ups: at least seventy (two-minute time limit)
Pull-ups: at least ten (two-minute time limit)
Curl-ups: at least sixty (two-minute time limit)
Four-mile run—with shoes + camo trousers
(thirty-one minutes or under)

Candidates who do not pass a longer, more intense test are removed from training and reclassified to other jobs in the U.S. Navy, or maybe rolled into the next class depending upon instructor input. Instruction involves a variety of teaching methods including group instruction, classroom-based, and practical. The school utilizes U.S. Navy Recruit Training Command pools, indoor and outdoor tracks, and other facilities in and around Naval Station Great Lakes. The Prep School's staff and curriculum are part of the command and staff of the Naval Special Warfare Center.

The curriculum reinforces the U.S. Navy's core values of Honor, Courage, and Commitment, and is divided into three parts:

1. Physical training, which includes:
   A. Swimming (basic swimming techniques).
   B. Running (principles of running and running fundamentals).
   C. Strength and conditioning (plyometrics).
   D. Basic underwater skills.
   E. Group calisthenics.
2. Academic training, which includes:
   A. SEAL ethos.
   B. Core values (military heritage (aircraft, ships, honors and courtesies) and sexual assault,

harassment, fraternization and discrimination training).

C. Exercise science (injury prevention, stretching, rest and recovery, hypothermia related injuries, and heat related injuries).

D. Nutrition (supplements).

E. Mental toughness.

3. Continued Military training, which includes:

A. Basic military training (knot tying and operational risk management).

B. Berthing (military pay system, military rights and responsibilities, and morale, welfare, and recreation).

C. Personnel inspections.

D. Phased liberty (leave and liberty policies).

E. Professional development (principles of team building, cycle of achievement, goal setting, and alcohol and its effects).

Stage 2: Basic Underwater Demolition/SEAL (BUD/S) Orientation

The Basic Underwater Demolition/SEAL (BUD/S) Orientation, also known NSW Orientation, is delivered by the U.S. Naval Special Warfare Centre located at Coronado, California. This stage of training is also known as BUD/S Indoctrination or just Indoctrination.

This course is three weeks in duration and covers the physical and psychological preparation for BUD/S training. This training involves becoming "familiar" with the obstacle course, swimming practice, and teamwork.

Instruction involves a variety of teaching methods including group instruction, classroom-based, and practical. NSW Orientation is delivered in three elements:

- Week one: This week involves administration and check-in, including equipment issue and administrative indoctrination. Candidates will undertake two initial runs and two initial obstacle courses run-throughs.
- Week two: This is known as orientation week and involves learning the routine, skills and standards required, practicing the skills required for BUD/S entry, and also "safe student" learning and practical of high-risk evolutions.
- Week three: Known as test week, it involves:
  - BUD/S Entry Standards: standard PST; four-mile timed run (thirty-three minutes); 1.5-nautical mile Bay swim (sixty-five minutes); and obstacle course (fifteen minutes).
  - Additional skills for Student "Self-gauging": survival swim; knot tying; drown-proofing; and twenty-five meter underwater swim.

Although the length of the course has varied over the years, the subjects covered have essentially remained the same including:

- Extreme Physical Conditioning
- Small Boat Operations
- Dive Physics
- Basic Diving Techniques for Open- and Closed-Circuit Scuba
- Basic Land Warfare
- Marksmanship and Weapons
- Demolitions

- Communications
- Reconnaissance

Since the overall attrition rate during BUD/S is approximately 75 percent to 80 percent, the Orientation Course hopes to continue building on the capabilities of the best students and afford them their best chance of success.

Stage 3: BUD/S First Phase—Basic Conditioning

BUD/S First Phase of training, the basic conditioning phase, is seven weeks in duration and develops candidates in physical training, water competency, and mental tenacity while continuing to develop teamwork.

The first day of First Phase is known as Phase Up/ Class Up. During these next seven weeks, candidates are expected to do more running, swimming, and calisthenics than the week before, and each candidate's performance is measured by a four-mile timed run, a timed obstacle course, and a two-mile timed swim each week. Many students have a bit of shock during the first couple weeks of Phase One due to the sheer volume of physical conditioning performed. Even most top athletes have never trained at this intensity level for prolonged periods. However, the students who are physically prepared often now face the daunting challenge of the day-to-day mental struggle— simply being cold, wet, and sandy day in and day out twelve or more hours a day takes a toll on a student and tests his resolve to become a SEAL. For most, it will prove to be too much to handle mentally.

Students will endure various team-focused physical training and are constantly competing against each other and against other teams ("it pays to be a winner"). In addition to physical training, candidates also learn how to conduct hydrographic survey operations, perform small boat seamanship, and begin learning the basics of combat patrolling.

The fourth week of BUD/S First Phase is known as Hellweek. It is intended to be the ultimate test of a student's resolve and mental strength. In this grueling five-and-a-half day stretch, each student sleeps only about four total hours but runs more than 200 miles and does physical training for more than twenty hours per day. Because of the brutally challenging requirements of this part of the training, a significant number of candidates will quit by ringing the bell. Only those who have an absolute dedication to becoming a SEAL will successfully finish the week. Although there have been notable exceptions, it is not uncommon for over 70 percent of the class to quit. A well-known fact, however, is that if a student survives until Thursday (with the Hellweek training typically starting on Sunday evening) it is exceptionally likely they will finish the week.

Ringing the Bell

If a candidate wishes to quit (known as Drop on Request or DOR) they must "Ring Out." The tradition of DOR consists of candidates dropping their helmet liner next to a pole with a brass ship's bell attached to it and ringing the bell three times. It is in many ways the ultimate dishonor for the student as he essentially is stating that he cannot take anymore or simply doesn't want to be a SEAL bad enough to continue enduring the day-to-day punishment of the training.

Students who do not complete BUD/S training will be reclassified to another U.S. Navy specialty (i.e. job) and given orders to an assignment within that rating. Candidates may reapply to BUD/S after a two-year fleet assignment.

Stage 4: BUD/S Second Phase—Combat Diving

The BUD/S Second Phase of training, the combat diving phase, is seven weeks in duration and introduces underwater skills that are unique to the U.S. Navy SEALs.

Training focuses on becoming basic combat swimmers, with an emphasis on long-distance underwater dives simulating movement from the launch point to objective.

- Conduct SCUBA (self-contained underwater breathing apparatus) training, initially delivered in the training pool, which consists of:

⌃ BUD/S Second Phase Trainees practice basic SCUBA

- Open circuit: compressed air
- Closed circuit: 100 percent oxygen
- Receive "drown proofing" training: trainees will have their arms and feet tied.
- Receive "combative drowning victim" training: A BUD/S instructor will "attack" a trainee in the pool to simulate a combative drowning victim.
- Must complete:
  - A 3.5-nautical mile swim (pass/fail)
  - A five-nautical mile swim (pass/fail)
  - Four-mile timed run in thirty-one minutes
  - Two-mile ocean swim in eighty minutes
  - Obstacle course in eleven minutes and then 10.30 minutes

A student who successfully completes Second Phase demonstrates a high level of comfort in the water and the ability to perform in stressful and often uncomfortable environments—an absolute requirement for success in the Teams.

Stage 5: BUD/S Third Phase—Land Warfare Training

The Third Phase of training, the Land Warfare Training phase, is seven weeks in duration and involves basic weapons, tactics, basic field craft, demolitions, land navigation (individual and group), patrolling (group), rappelling, and marksmanship and small-unit tactics.

The second half of this phase of training is on San Clemente Island, about sixty miles from Coronado. On the island, candidates practice the skills they learned in Third Phase. This includes over-the-beach exercises and patrolling exercises.

⌃ **A SEAL student takes part in Land Warfare training**

Candidates will also need to complete

- Four-mile timed run in thirty minutes;
- Two-mile ocean swim in seventy-five minutes
- Obstacle course in ten minutes

Students who successfully complete BUD/S Third Phase graduate BUD/S as Special Warfare Operators. At this point successful candidates will be awarded the SEAL Navy Enlisted Classification (NEC) 5320, but still have further training to undertake before pinning on a Trident become a fully-qualified U.S. Navy SEAL.

Stage six: SEAL Qualification Training

SEAL Qualification Training (SQT) is designed to provide candidates with the core tactical knowledge and skills they will need to join a SEAL platoon, and is delivered at a variety of U.S. locations. SQT is twenty-six weeks in duration and includes advanced training in:

- Weapons
- Small–unit tactics
- Land navigation
- Demolitions
- Combat engineering
- Cold–weather training, conducted in Kodiak, Alaska
- Advanced Tactical Combat Casualty Care (TCCC) and medical skills
- Maritime operations

During SQT candidates will also undertake parachute training which covers the basic skills required for military parachuting. The Navy Parachute Course is four weeks in duration and includes:

- Static-line parachute operations
- Free-fall parachute operations:
    - High Altitude–Low Opening (HALO)
    - High Altitude–High Opening (HAHO)

⌃ **Cold Weather training in Kodiak, Alaska**

To complete the course, candidates must pass through a series of jump progressions, from basic static line to accelerated free fall to combat equipment—ultimately completing night descents with combat equipment from a minimum altitude of approximately 9,500 feet.

Finally, before graduation candidates will also attend SERE (survival, evasion, resistance and escape) training. It is the intermediate skills course that prepares candidates for the advanced training they will receive once they arrive at a SEAL team. The course is ten days in duration and covers the full spectrum of SERE training.

⌃ **An SQT Student rappels from a hovering helicopter**

Graduation

Just prior to graduation, candidates will sit on what is known as a Trident Board. The board is an oral interview that has no set length of time, to challenge a student's basic knowledge before being awarded the Trident.

Upon completing these requirements, trainees receive their SEAL Trident, designating them as qualified U.S. Navy SEALs. They are subsequently assigned to a SEAL team to begin preparing for their first deployment.

Obligated Service, is fifty-two months from class graduation date and awarding of the 5326 NEC or until completion of previous obligated service, whichever is greater.

SEAL Navy Enlisted Classifications (NEC)

Enlisted SEAL personnel are designated by Navy Enlisted Classification (NEC) codes per their qualifications:

- NEC 5320: Basic Special Warfare Operator (Student)
- NEC 5323: Seal Delivery Vehicle (SDV) Pilot/ Navigator/Dry Deck Shelter (DDS) Operator (SEAL)
- NEC 5326: Special Warfare Operator/SEAL
- NEC 5392: Naval Special Warfare Medic

Post-Graduation and Continued Training

Following graduation, candidates are assigned to a SEAL Platoon, within a SEAL Team, to conduct advanced or work-up training, which can be divided into three distinct elements:

- Individual Specialty Training
- Unit-Level Training
- Task-Group-Level Training

Individual Specialty Training can last up to six months and is based upon the individual operator, in partnership with the needs of the platoon. Individuals, with others, will attend a number of U.S. military formal/informal schools and courses, courses which lead to qualifications that collectively enable a SEAL platoon to perform as an operational combat team. Examples of qualifications/courses include:

- Sniper or Scout/Sniper
- Advanced Close Quarter Combat/Breacher (Barrier Penetration/Methods of Entry)

≈ **A SEAL student conducting "Over the Beach" (OTB) training**

- Surreptitious Entry (Mechanical and Electronic Bypass)
- Naval Special Warfare Combat Fighting Course
- Advanced Special Operations
- Technical Surveillance Operations
- Advanced Driving Skills (Defensive, Rally and Protective Security)
- Climbing/Rope Skills
- Advanced Air Operations: Jumpmaster or Parachute Rigger
- Diving Supervisor or Diving Maintenance-Repair
- Range Safety Officer
- Advanced Demolition
- High-Threat Protective Security: U.S./Foreign Heads of State or High-Value Persons
- Instructor School and Master Training Specialist

- Unmanned Aerial Vehicle (UAV) Operator
- Language School
- Joint SOF and Service Professional Military Education

Unit-Level Training

Unit-Level Training (ULT) can last up to six months and is based upon the SEAL troop/platoon. Training is run by the respective group (NSWG1/NSWG2) training detachments and is based on the core mission area skills: small-unit tactics, land warfare, close quarters combat, urban warfare, hostile maritime interdiction (VBSS/GOPLATS), combat swimming, long-range target interdiction, rotary and fixed-wing air operations, and special reconnaissance.

≈ **Man down! SEAL Students drag a buddy during an exercise**

Task-Group-Level Training

Task-Group-Level Training can last up to six months and is based upon the SEAL Team/Squadron needs and requirements. This is advanced training conducted with the supporting elements of a SEAL Squadron, including Special Boat Teams (SWCC), intelligence, communications, medical, and EOD.

A final Certification Exercise (CERTEX) is conducted with the entire SEAL Squadron to synchronize troop operations under the Joint Special Operations Task Force (JSOTF) umbrella. Following CERTEX, a SEAL Team becomes a SEAL Squadron and is certified for deployment.

Once certified, a SEAL Team/Squadron will deploy to a Joint Special Operations Task Force or Area of Responsibility (AO or AOR) to become a Special Operations Task Force (SOTF), and combine with a Joint Task Force (JTF) or Task Force (TF) in support of other national objectives.

Once assigned, the troops will be given an AOR where they will either work as a centralized/intact Troop or task organize into decentralized elements to conduct operations, ranging in size from sixty to over two hundred personnel.

APPENDIX B:
THE NAVY SEAL
WARRIOR'S CODE
AND CREED

Warrior creeds, such as the Rangers' famous creed, have been around for over a century to guide the actions of operators on and off the battlefield. The creed is a code of conduct and inspirational daily reminder of the "reason we train and fight" for the men and women of these units. Many outside observers point to the mission of the units and preparation of the Teams when describing who these people are. Warriors know better. It is the Warrior Ethos that best describes who they are, an ethos that has been shared, albeit with different words, with the Samurai, the Spartans, the Marines, and other special operations forces around the world.

The SEAL Code is relatively new. Prior to this, the SEALs had an unspoken code defined by the culture, historical experience and training. "Leave no man behind" and "Failure is not an option" are examples of cultural mantras that evolved as the unwritten "SEAL code" from the Teams battlefield experiences in World War II, Korea, Vietnam, and elsewhere. We have held to this code, never leaving a teammate in the field, dead or alive. Recent experience in Afghanistan with Medal of Honor winner Lieutenant Murphy and his teammates exemplifies this code of conduct.

The SEAL code, however, was not recorded or "written in stone" and, as the community grew, it needed some grounding. Would it be more powerful if it were more than a few mantras like "leave no man behind" and "Failure is not an option?" It became clear to the SEALs that they needed a more comprehensive creed that was not subject to interpretation and erosion over time. In 2005 a cross-functional team from all ranks was brought together to ponder the issue and come up with a durable, written code. The team took input from all quarters, and did some serious community soul-searching to penetrate the essence of what it meant to be a SEAL. The results are nothing short of extraordinary.

The SEAL Code
- Loyalty to Country, Team, and Teammate
- Serve with Honor and Integrity On and Off the Battlefield
- Ready to Lead, Ready to Follow, Never Quit
- Take Responsibility for Your Actions and the Actions of Your Teammates
- Excel as Warriors through Discipline and Innovation
- Train for War, Fight to Win, Defeat our Nation's Enemies
- Earn your Trident Every Day

United States Navy SEAL Ethos/Creed:

In times of war or uncertainty there is a special breed of warrior ready to answer our nation's call—a common man with an uncommon desire to succeed.

Forged by adversity, he stands alongside America's finest special operations forces to serve his country, the American people, and protect their way of life.

I am that man.

My Trident is a symbol of honor and heritage. Bestowed upon me by the heroes that have gone before, it embodies the trust of those I have sworn to protect. By wearing the Trident I accept the responsibility of my chosen profession and way of life. It is a privilege that I must earn every day.

My loyalty to Country and Team is beyond reproach. I humbly serve as a guardian to my fellow Americans, always ready to defend those who are unable to defend themselves. I do not advertise the nature of my work, nor seek recognition for my actions. I voluntarily accept the inherent hazards of my profession, placing the welfare and security of others before my own.

I serve with honor on and off the battlefield. The ability to control my emotions and my actions, regardless of circumstances, sets me apart from other men.

Uncompromising integrity is my standard. My character and honor are steadfast. My word is my bond.

We expect to lead and be led. In the absence of orders I will take charge, lead my teammates, and accomplish the mission. I lead by example in all situations.

I will never quit. I persevere and thrive on adversity. My nation expects me to be physically harder and mentally stronger than my enemies. If knocked down, I will get back up, every time. I will draw on every remaining ounce of strength to protect my teammates and to accomplish our mission. I am never out of the fight.

We demand discipline. We expect innovation. The lives of my teammates and the success of our mission depend on me—my technical skill, tactical proficiency, and attention to detail. My training is never complete.

We train for war and fight to win. I stand ready to bring the full spectrum of combat power to bear in order to achieve my mission and the goals established by my country. The execution of my duties will be swift and violent when required yet guided by the very principles that I serve to defend.

Brave men have fought and died building the proud tradition and feared reputation that I am bound to uphold. In the worst of conditions, the legacy of my teammates steadies my resolve and silently guides my every deed. I will not fail.

AFTERWORD

In this book we have attempted to honor the men of Naval Special Warfare by telling their stories in a way that hopefully has been both engaging and informative. Writing the book required many months of hard work and research. But, in many ways it has been much more than that—it is the result of decades of service and experience that we have tried to express through our writing. In this way, every story has in some sense a personal touch to it rather than merely a retelling of the facts. Some of the accounts in this book have been re-created and built on what happened to people we knew, met, or read about in previous works. In most cases, we chose to tell their story without invading their privacy or making them easily identifiable.

During the process of writing we discovered many little known details of the evolution of the SEALs which were both fascinating and vital to a complete understanding of how we got to where we are today. Those who have lived through the last few decades have literally witnessed the history of warfare in the making. A series of many unique factors have contributed to how the SEALs have transformed from the original combat swimmers into the high-tech and multifaceted force they are today. The explosion of science and technology since the early 1900s allowed for a unique period in all of human history as to how warfare could change and develop. In previous eras, it could literally take centuries to see only minor adaptations of a combat unit thanks to small advances in metallurgy or horsemanship or archery. However, in less than a century we have now seen the complete transformation of the battlefield. Think of it: as recent a time as World War I, there existed units like the cavalry which still used horses on the front lines of battle. Although they were ultimately replaced by tanks as the primary means of shock tactics, hundreds of thousands of horses were killed during the war. And now, we have fighter jets with stealth technology, submarines with nuclear missiles, and SEALs jumping out of planes at 36,000 feet with ultra-sophisticated night-vision and laser sights.

It is truly incredible when you think of it.

The challenges ahead are many; adapting the SEALs to the ever-changing battlespace of the future will continue to be a difficult task for the future leadership of Naval Special Warfare. It will require innovation, flexibility, and the ability to anticipate the threats we will face as a nation during the coming years. Even so, one thing will remain the same: the discipline, tenacity, skill, and courage of each member of the SEALs will remain the core of who we are as America's premier special operations force. No amount of technology can ever replace those intangible qualities that are the result of thousands of hours of training and cultivation of the warrior spirit.

For those considering following the path to join the ranks of the SEAL Teams: It is never too early to begin preparing for the trials ahead. You are seeking to join a brotherhood of warriors that has etched a unique place of honor in military history; never forget those who have labored and sacrificed long before you ever began considering this way of life. Push yourself hard and be relentless in your pursuit. Only those souls who fully commit to becoming a Navy SEAL will have a chance of making it and you owe it to those who have gone before you to put the utmost energy and focus into your preparation. Never forget you are preparing yourself to join an elite combat team—not an athletic squad.

We would be remiss if we did not acknowledge the incredible sacrifices of the families that support the SEALs. Standing by them month after month and year after year as they travel around the globe training and executing the most dangerous missions of the U.S. military is an arduous task. Without your support at home, it would be a much more difficult task to accomplish what the men must do in order to stay ready. We salute you!

Finally, to the men of the SEAL Teams: we freely acknowledge that so much more could be written! As we have stated previously, the number of missions and the work that is done each and every day by the men who make up Naval Special Warfare, if fully told, could ultimately fill volumes. In the end, it is imperative to remember that our work here is essentially a grand synopsis of the history of the SEAL Teams and we especially hope that the men of whose service is reflected within these pages will understand that we intend to honor every SEAL and every sacrifice they have made whether or not their specific accomplishments or missions were profiled in our work.

It has been our honor to tell these stories and hope in some way you will have benefited from reading our book. Thank you, and always remember those who have paid the ultimate price for the freedoms we enjoy as part of the heritage of our great nation!

Fair winds and following seas,

—Don and Lance

BIBLIOGRAPHY

This book is based on hundreds of hours of research and study including a large variety of open-source materials, books, official websites, and interviews with key personnel from the Naval Special Warfare community. Additionally, the information and stories within are also drawn from the experiences of the authors, which includes Don Mann's extensive career as a Navy SEAL for over twenty years and former member of SEAL Team SIX, as well as inside knowledge gleaned from a multitude of personal friendships and professional relationships with various members of every branch of military service. This work contains both documented and first-hand historical accounts as well as scenarios based on true events. In essence, the scenarios are a way of incorporating details about how a given mission or operation could have played out and is a mixture of real people and characters based on real people. Some true names and details have been changed for security reasons. Excessive listing of source material could lead, by collation and analysis, to identifying the real names of those involved. This book has been submitted to and cleared by a U.S. government publications review board, which would not have cleared the book for publication unless due attention had been paid to matters of security and privacy. No classified detailed information of tactics, techniques, intelligence sources and methods, or procedures have been revealed in this book.

Books

Captain Robert A. Gormly, USN (Ret). *Combat Swimmer: Memoirs of a Navy SEAL.* New York, New York, New American Library (A division of Penguin Group), 1999.

Howard E. Wasdin and Stephen Templin. *SEAL Team SIX: Memoirs of an Elite Navy SEAL Sniper,* New York, New York, Saint Martin's Press, 2011.

Mark Bowden, *Black Hawk Down: A Story of Modern War.* New York, New York, Signet, 2001.

Dennis Chalker and Kevin Dockery. *One Perfect Op: An Insider's Account of the Navy SEAL Special Warfare Teams.* New York, New York, Harper Collins, 2002.

Marcus Luttrell and Patrick Robinson. *Lone Survivor: The Eyewitness Account of Operation Redwing and the Lost Heroes of SEAL Team 10.* New York, New York, Little, Brown and Company, 2007.

Dick Couch and William Doyle. *Navy SEALs: Their Untold Story.* New York, New York, Harper Collins, 2014.

Oliver North. *American Heroes in Special Operations.* Nashville, TN, Fidelis Books (a division of B&H Publishing Group), 2010.

Bruce Hoffman. *Inside Terrorism.* New York, New York, Columbia University Press, 2006.

Dave Grossman and Loren W. Christensen. *On Combat: The Psychology and Physiology of Deadly Conflict in War and Peace.* USA, Warrior Science Publications, 3rd Edition, 2008.

Don Mann and Ralph Pezzullo. *Inside SEAL Team Six: My Life and Missions with America's Elite Warriors.* New York, New York, Hachette Book Group, Little, Brown and Company, 2011.

Orr Kelly. *Brave Men, Dark Waters*. New York, Presidio Press, 1992.

Bill Fawcett. *Hunters and Shooters: An Oral History of the U.S. Navy SEALs in Vietnam*. New York, William Morrow and Company, 1995.

Francis D. Fane and Don Moore. *The Naked Warriors: The Story of the U.S. Navy's Frogmen*. New York, Appleton-Century-Crofts, 1956.

Frank Antenori and Hans Halberstadt. *Roughneck Nine-One: The Extraordinary Story of a Special Forces A-Team at War*. New York, New York, Saint Martin's Paperbacks, 2006.

The National Commission on Terrorist Attacks. *The 9/11 Commission Report: Final Report of the National Commission on Terrorist Attacks Upon the United States, Authorized Edition*. New York, New York, W.W. Norton and Company, Ltd., 2004.

Stephen E. Ambrose. *D-Day, June 6th, 1944: The Climactic Battle of World War II*. New York, New York, Touchstone (a division of Simon and Schuster Inc.), 1995.

Linda Kush. *The Rice Paddy Navy: U.S. Sailors Undercover in China*. New York, New York, Osprey Publishing, 2012.

Websites and Publications

https://www.britannica.com/Encyclopedia Britannica Online (various articles as cited)

https://www.navysealmuseum.org/National Navy SEAL Museum

http://www.navy.mil/local/navhist/Naval History and Heritage Command

http://www.navyfrogmen.com/Naval Special Warfare Archive

https://navyseals.com/Navy SEALs Official Website

https://www.navysealfoundation.org/Navy SEAL Foundation Official Website

http://www.historynet.com/Companion Website to Historical Articles from Periodicals

http://www.sealswcc.com/Naval Special Warfare Official Website

NOTES

Chapter 1

Pg. 4 "The original idea was conceived by Master Chief Boatswain's Mate Rick Knepper . . ."

Information on the formation of the Forth Phase program was drawn from personal conversations with Master Chief Knepper.

Pg. 17–18 BUD/S training narrative is based on direct recollection of LT Lance W. Burton, USN (Ret), Class Leader of BUD/S Class 239.

Chapter 2

Pg. 30 "One of the original Scouts and Raiders, Petty Officer Matthew Kormorowski-Kaye . . ."

The quote here is taken from his personal journal: http://www .northofseveycorners.com/write/kaye.htm

Chapter 3

Pg. 56 "in the words of UDT Lieutenant Ted Fielding . . ."

LT Fielding is quoted as saying the work of the UDT was "work no one else could do, and no one else wanted to do" and was taken from an article on the Navy SEALs: https://en.wikipedia.org/wiki/United _States_Navy_SEALs

Pg. 59 "If the best possible minds had set out to find the worst possible place to fight this damnable war . . . the unanimous choice would have been Korea." A quote from then Secretary of State Dean Acheson: http://www.history.com/topics /korean-war

Pg. 61–72 The narrative of the UDT mission in Korea was based on extensive research showing that these early Frogmen had suggested "taking the fight inland" and asserting their ability to be successful beyond the beachhead.

Chapter 4

Pg. 78 "President Kennedy's stance on the matter had also been heavily influenced by Admiral Arleigh Burke . . . ,"

After the Korean War and the continued successes of the UDT, then Chief of Naval Operations Admiral Burke believed the president should consider a more permanent and official role for the Frogmen's skills, which expanded into land warfare operations—leading directly to the establishment of the SEALs.

Pg. 84–92 The Vietnam-era narrative was based on information from the variety of books, publications, and websites listed above, but also includes knowledge gained from personal conversations with SEALs who operated in the area during the war.

Chapter 5

Pg. 101 "based on my personal observations, discussion and analysis of the new international airport under construction in Grenada . . ."

Congressman Ronald Dellums (D—California) made the statement after a fact-finding trip to Grenada to ascertain the situation personally.

Pg. 105–117 The Grenada narrative is a mixture of official reports and personal knowledge of the events gained from conversations with SEALs who were part of the operations as well as some "dramatizing" of the storyline.

Chapter 6

Pg. 118 James "Cowboy" Smith is a fictitious CIA operative based on a real individual.

Pg. 119 "General Noriega's reckless threats and attacks upon Americans in Panama created an imminent danger to the 35,000 American citizens in Panama. As president, I have no higher obligation than to safeguard the lives of American citizens. . ."

This is a direct quote from President George H. W. Bush as he addressed the nation concerning the situation in Panama: http://millercenter.org /president/bush/speeches/speech-3422

Pg. 122 The account of LT Curtis and the death of the Marine officer is based on multiple sources including personal conversations with Adam Curtis as well as various archived materials such as: http://www.history.com/this-day-in-history/the -u-s-invades-panama

Pg. 123 "You died a million deaths—horrible people doing horrible things to their own people" is a direct quote from Kurt Muse, an American citizen imprisoned in Panama, after his rescue by members of Delta Force: http://www.shadowspear .com/2009/04/operation-acid-gambit/

Pg. 126–132 The Operation Just Cause narrative was based on direct experience as well as various official accounts of the invasion. In the case of conflicting stories or details we have defaulted to official publications or websites of Naval Special Warfare.

Chapter 7

Pg. 139 "In the story of David and Goliath there are many lessons . . . ".

An Old Testament reference from the Book of I Samuel, King James Version of the Bible.

Pg. 140 "Gentlemen, this will be a standard snatch-and-grab style op . . ."

A direct quote from then Commander Eric Olson (who later retired as a four-star admiral).

Pg. 141–168 The Battle of Mogadishu is exceptionally well-documented with multiple books, periodicals, and website articles telling the story. However, the role of the few Navy SEALs who participated in the fight has primarily only been told by Howard Wasdin in his book *SEAL Team Six: Memoirs of a Navy SEAL Sniper*. Our account is essentially a retelling of that story using details as seen from his perspective.

Chapter 8

Pg. 169 "Commander Tom Hanson, SEAL Team FIVE Commanding Officer, strode out into the inner courtyard of the SEAL Team FIVE headquarters and motioned for the men to circle in close. With a look of determination and intensity he began his speech . . ."

This quote is taken from direct experience of the co-author, LT Lance Burton, who was present for this speech by the SEAL Team FIVE Commanding Officer (the name of whom has been changed for security reasons).

Pg. 188–216 The Global War on Terror narrative and the various missions represented was a combination of real-world experience and storytelling using elements of public record accounts and other unclassified materials such as the official Medal of Honor citation for Senior Chief Byers. All are based on true events, but slight additions or modifications were included to make the events more vivid and understandable for the general reader, not just those interested in military history. Certain alterations were also incorporated to maintain operational security and protect the identities of the men and women involved.

Chapter 9

Pg. 229–231 "In October 2011, aid workers named Jessica Buchanan from America and her colleague . . ."

The background information and story for the narrative concerning the hostage rescue depicted was taken from multiple sources, including an interview with Jessica Buchanan, which aired on the TV show *60-Minutes*:

http://www.cbsnews.com/news/the-rescue-of-jessica-buchanan/.

Chapter 10

Pg. 239–277 The Medal of Honor citations, summary of action accounts, and official biographies are taken from sources such as official Naval Special Warfare archives or U.S. Navy websites: http://www.navy.mil/ah_online/moh/byers.html.

Appendix A

Pg. 278–307 Current information concerning the process to become a Navy SEAL is taken from official and unclassified Naval Special Warfare materials and websites as well as personal knowledge of the authors.

Appendix B

Pg. 308–311 The SEAL Ethos/Creed was the combined work of many men from the community who wished to create an official code of honor for the Teams. The final version was written by retired SEAL Commander Mark Divine.